# Power Through Bureaucracy

## Urban Political Analysis in Brazil

RICHARD BATLEY

## St. Martin's Press    New York

Printed in Great Britain
First published in the United States of America in 1983

Library of Congress Cataloging in Publication Data

Batley, Richard
    Power through bureaucracy.

    Bibliography: p.
    1. Urban policy—Brazil.  2. Bureaucracy—
Brazil.  3. Housing policy—Brazil—São Paulo.
4. Social classes—Brazil.  5. Social problems—
Brazil.  I. Title.
HT129.B7B38 1982      354.810081'8      82-16872
ISBN 0-312-63437-4

# Contents

# Maps and Figures

# Tables

# Acknowledgements

The research for this book was undertaken while I was employed by the Institute of Development Studies at the University of Sussex. The Institute and the Centre for Environmental Studies, London, financed the empirical work in Brazil as part of a programme of research into the problem of access to administratively distributed services. My colleagues in that programme were Bernard Schaffer, Geoff Lamb and Alan Rew. During the field work, I benefited greatly from the help of Gabriel Bolaffi and Zilton Macedo and from the institutional support of the Faculty of Architecture and Urban Planning at the University of Sao Paulo. I was able to complete the long business of analysis and writing in the encouraging and stimulating environment of the Institute of Local Government Studies at the University of Birmingham.

I would like to thank my wife and daughter, Juliacelia and Daniella, not only for tolerating these dislocations in employment and geography but also for easing my entry into Brazilian life. Among the various aspects of that life, the bureaucracy is one which in Brazil itself is frequently criticised. In which other country is there a Minister for Debureaucratisation? This book may be seen as offering a little more ammunition to that criticism. However, I would like to record that as a researcher I experienced only helpfulness from the many people in official positions whom I met and interviewed. This book is in no way meant as a criticism of them personally; it is a study of the pressures and constraints to which they are subject.

The following chapters of this book have previously been published in earlier versions and I am grateful to the publishers for giving permission to reproduce them in an integrated way: chapter one appeared in 'Urban Political Economy and Social Theory' edited by Forrest, Henderson and Williams (eds), Gower Publishing Company Ltd., 1982; parts of chapter two appeared in the International Journal of Urban and Regional Research Vol.2 No.1 1978; chapter six was published in 'Urbanisation in contemporary Latin America' edited by Gilbert, Hardoy and Ramirez, John Wiley and Sons Ltd, 1982; chapter seven appeared in the Public Administration Bulletin No.37 1981.

Robin Luckham, Ronaldo Ramirez and Peter Saunders offered useful criticisms of an earlier script but of course bear no responsibility for the final product. Joan Jones typed the text helpfully and efficiently.

# Introduction

There is a long tradition of studies of the interaction between officials and the public in the administration of urban policy in Britain and the USA. At one level, this book extends that tradition to another country, Brazil, where conditions of rapid urbanisation and of 'bureaucratic authoritarian' regimes make the relationship between administration and the administered especially crucial and politically significant. At another level, the approach adopted recognises the incapacity of the localised case study alone to discover that political significance. Such studies on their own leave us with a description of a particular case which can say little about the influence underlying official definitions of problems, solutions and means, and little about whether the experience of the administered is purely local, individual and specific or more systematic and general. The book is therefore illustrative of an approach to the analysis of urban politics as well as being about a particular case.

Urban political analysis generally has moved, under the influence of French marxist studies, towards a consideration of wider issues of urban politics. This implies a recognition of the need for a theoretical understanding of the place of state administration in the social structure and considers the forces beyond the locality which influence policy formation. While subscribing to this view, I also argue that the analysis of administrative practice and, in particular, of the interaction between officials and the public in policy implementation should not be demoted to a matter of purely local and trivial significance. It can itself be given a wider interpretation.

This book combines detailed analysis at the local level with a broader consideration of the development of the Brazilian state and the pressures which have implicated state administration in the 'urban problem'. This dual approach has been adopted not simply because there are factors at both local and non-local level which have to be considered as influences on the formation of policy. It is rather that all these multifarious pressures are condensed in the practice of policy implementation. Conversely, therefore, policy as it emerges in practice is a point from which to trace its origins in social processes and pressures at other levels. It is also, of course, the point at which state interventions affect people both distributionally and ideologically. On the one hand, therefore, the study moves from the general towards the specific by drawing on certain Latin American writers (especially Fernando Cardoso and Guillermo O'Donnell) to synthesise a history of the development of class relations in Brazil and of their effect on the formation of the state. Subsequently, this analysis is extended to an examination of

1

the urban problems and demands which gave rise to Brazilian housing policy and of the way in which that policy was structured to incorporate pressures for continuous modification. On the other hand, it moves from the specific towards the general by looking at the formative effect of organisational procedures on some particular cases of urban policy in the city of Sao Paulo. It attempts to show both how these procedures influence social relations and how they are derived from interests expressed as limits within which the organisation must operate.

There are some particular reasons why Brazil should be chosen to explore these themes. One is that urban policy is particularly crucial in situations of rapid urbanisation, of which Sao Paulo, with a population in 1982 of over thirteen million and growing at about half a million per year, is clearly a prime example. The administrative relationship carries a particular political significance in a country such as Brazil where representative politics is weak. Indeed, the debate in Brazil and other Latin American countries on the nature of the bureaucratic authoritarian regime provides a broad framework within which to locate more specific studies. A further argument in favour of studying urban policy in Brazil is that the scale and vigour of Brazilian state intervention in the housing question and in urban development gives this area of policy some importance as an instrument of governmental management, linking local agencies to national institutions. The particular areas and aspects of administrative practice studied are: the development of national housing policy; the influence of public policy on the operation of the housing and land markets of the city of Sao Paulo; the distributive practice of the Sao Paulo metropolitan housing company; and the social effects of plans for the demolition and urban renewal of a part of the city through which a mass transit railway was to be constructed.

In chapter one, the book makes the connection with the 'managerialist' debate about the structural situation of public officials. A considerable body of analysis has already been carried out in Britain and the USA on relations between officials and the people affected by programmes of service distribution and by physical planning. Such research has moved away from the attribution to local administrators of causal responsibility for their action and has become more concerned with 'structural limits' on policy implementation. This chapter argues for a concern with the structural constraints on administrative action but against the view that these constraints operate from outside upon organisations and in favour of the view that they are internalised in organisational practice. It suggests therefore that organisational analysis may be concerned not only with the effects of administrative distribution on social relations, but may also be taken as a starting point for the identification of influences on policy formation. However, this must be in combination with a wider analysis of the place of state administrators in the social structure and of the forces and organisational arrangements which develop policy at higher administrative levels

Chapter two surveys the historical background to the ensuing studies of policy implementation in Brazil. By reference to several Latin America writers, it examines the economic and political development which has been seen as providing the formative context for the emergence of a 'bureaucratic-authoritarian' state. This is more than historical background to the later work; it also puts forward a particular argument about managerial ('technocratic') responsibility for the nature of the authoritarian state. It thus makes some connection between broad class analysis and the study of particular political forms and practices. I argue that a next step in that body of thought might be to move beyond general statements about the 'technocratic' interest in authoritarian bureaucracy and instead through concrete cases, to examine how bureaucratic action is constrained by a complex interweaving of interests and perceptions. This is what is attempted in later chapters.

Chapter three acts as a bridge between the more global analysis and the particular case studies of the distribution of urban public services in Sao Paulo. It shows how, soon after the establishment of the military government in 1964, the national housing bank (BNH) was set up as one of the first acts of institutionalisation of the new regime. I examine the demands to which the bank was a response, the interests and perceptions which its structure incorporated and the logic of movement which it then contained. The BNH was conceived both as part of the new economic model and as a demonstration of the regime's concern for groups excluded by the model. This paradox was expressed in the conflicting demands on local subordinate agencies, but the BNH itself tended to resolve the paradox by shifting its programmes towards the demands more powerfully represented in the economic model.

Chapter four examines the market alternatives available to those who confront administrative agencies as applicants for publicly provided housing. It also demonstrates that the distinction between market and administered alternatives is unclear: no part of the housing market is free of governmental influence. Public agencies, including BNH, contribute at least as much to enhancing market differentiation and exclusion as they do to relieving these features of the market. There are thus two aspects of administrative intervention - that associated with the support of market pressures and that associated with their alleviation. Chapter five examines how these contradictory requirements affect the operation of the Sao Paulo metropolitan housing company. It begins by identifying the rules and procedures which are effective in deciding the distribution of housing to applicants and the conditions of occupancy which face successful purchasers. It then seeks to trace these rules, procedures and conditions to the major constraints or requirements experienced by the housing company and shows how they serve the effects of selecting applicants, disguising the basis of selection and allowing the realisation of organised interests.

Chapter six also looks at a case of direct contact between official agencies and the public, this time in the demolition and removal associated with the construction of an underground railway. This was one example of the continuous process of redefinition of the housing situation of the mass of the population which results from the joint and overlapping effects of market and administrative action. The chapter examines the influence of procedures of demolition, compensation and removal on different groups of the population directly affected. It shows how the differential treatment results from the application of administrative categories which are themselves derived from constraints on public organisations.

Chapter seven concludes by briefly restating the case for the research approach and then by retracing the findings emerging from earlier chap-

ters. I then attempt a general statement about the dominant constraints
affecting the organisations that were studied. These are the factors
(essentially the conditions of urban property and finance capital) which
set the terms of operation of agencies. I distinguish between the
'corporate' interests which are represented in the structure of the
organisation and hence in the formation of policy, and the 'incorporated'
applicant who is required to demonstrate individually that he can conform
with established distributive procedures. Lastly, I consider the nature
of routine organisational practice arguing that officials like applicants are bound into a chain of constraints; they operate in a context
which is itself organised, constrained and rule-bound; there is no cut
off point from which free choice and causal responsibility begin.
Administrative routines are the product of and biased towards certain
interests, but they also appear as anonymous requirements on actors at
all levels.

# 1 The political significance of organisational analysis

There is an allocative dimension to most if not all governmental policies. This is not only a matter of those programmes which set out overtly to distribute benefits in the shape of goods and services; policies which selectively penalise, regulate, give permission or with-draw resources also have a distributive or redistributive effect. More specifically, in the case of urban policy, the question of allocation is important not only in programmes for the distribution of housing or public services but also in development control, zoning, property taxa-tion, urban renewal and compensation. These are the aspects of urban policy which to a greater or lesser extent will be referred to in this book.

The politics of allocation is least of all to be got at by an analysis of policy intent. It is policy as implemented which is important. What therefore needs to be understood is the way in which policy emerges in practice as administrations respond accretively to the requirements upon them and as different sections of the public manipulate their access to or evasion of policy effects. The book is concerned with the politics which surround the administration of allocation and access. We have to consider the relationship between state bureaucracies and the social interests which determine policy, the procedures through which admin-istrative decisions emerge and their effect on the administered popu-lation.

Such issues of bureaucratic power, like many other issues in the social sciences, have been treated from quite different perspectives in the 'Latin' and 'Anglo-Saxon' traditions. The first has tended towards abstraction and generality and the second towards the examination of concrete problems and specific cases. However, this and the following chapter identify some convergence in the two traditions and the book as a whole seeks to locate organisational analysis at this point of convergence between global theory and specific case studies.

In Latin American political analysis, there is a growing literature on the 'new authoritarianism' (Collier 1979). This is not the authorit-arianism of the old individual or family dictatorships (such as that of Vargas, Peron or Somoza) where the military played a simple supporting role. The matter of interest has been the spread of more sophisticated 'bureaucratic authoritarian' regimes in which the military and the civil bureaucracy take a leading role not to maintain a dictator in power but to implement a 'modernising' programme. It is a model which has been applied particularly to Brazil and the Southern Cone nations of

Argentina, Uruguay and Chile where the military have intervened to displace radical regimes in the name of an ideology of 'national security', to suppress the labour force and to open the way to rapid economic growth. The model is bureaucratic in the sense that, in its structure, it operates through a strengthened executive and a strong central administration of technicians while, in its functioning, it has the effects of depoliticising the expression of social interests and of extending bureaucratic control over everyday life. Much analysis of this sort has remained at a rather general level, identifying the relation between patterns of dependent economic development and the emergence of such regimes, indicating their characteristics, and questioning the level of autonomy which the state bureaucracy can itself acquire. Chapter two draws on these analyses for an understanding of the development of the Brazilian state, but the book as a whole moves on from this general level into a more detailed examination of the day to day practice of bureaucratic control.

Such a concern with bureaucratic practice, especially in relation to the interaction between officials and sections of the public, has been the focus of much British and North American urban research over the last twenty years. This chapter addresses the problem of linking this sort of detailed analysis to an understanding of the wider context. The task is eased by the fact that the Anglo-Saxon empiricist tradition has already made adjustments in that direction under the influence of French marxist sociology. Indeed, the task sometimes seems to be one of rescuing the study of local bureaucratic action from an ever widening concern with the social and economic processes which generate local problems and political responses. As the discussion has moved away from any assumption that managers of public policy are independent in the formulation of their responses, there is a possibility that administrative organisations also cease to be regarded as an important area of study since their action seems to be constrained or determined externally. The centre of my argument, however, will be that the constraints on their autonomy do not simply operate externally upon organisations but are contained within their structures and procedures. This is not to suggest a return to a simple concern with bureaucratic performance to the neglect of the wider context; on the contrary, the argument is that, to the extent that they are effective, 'external' constraints lose their externality and are represented in the internal routines of administrative action. The implication is that the analysis of policy implementation provides an avenue for understanding the permutations and combinations of class and group interests which are represented in state administration.

The book, therefore, draws on and complements two bodies of theory, namely, the 'managerialist' debate about the structural situation of public officials and marxist analysis of the state and class relations. By incorporating organisational analysis to the latter my concern is: (a) to explain specific forms of policy and administrative action by locating them in a set of constraints which are the product of a particular balance of class and group interests, and (b) to bridge the gap between general theoretical statements about the representation of interests in the state and the expression of those interests in the activities of state agencies. Moreover, I see this approach to the study of organisations as providing a possible point of convergence between, on the one hand, attempts in urban sociology to move 'up' from

the managerialist assumption into the consideration of structural
constraints and, on the other hand, the attempts in Latin American
political sociology to reach 'down' from general theory to examine
the practices of state agencies.

## MANAGERIALISM IN URBAN RESEARCH

The 'managerialist' discussion is related to the examination of bureaucratic decision-making as it affects the distribution of what might in
the most general terms be called 'life chances' in the urban situation.
Rex (1973, p.66) has given one account of the case for this area of
work:

> 'The original Chicago School assumed a Social Darwinist
> position and explained the mechanism which underlay urban
> growth and development to be one of unfettered competition
> for land-use. Thus urban sociology seemed to be possible
> only in conditions of laissez faire. There could be no
> urban sociology if there was planning. But the conclusion
> only followed it if was assumed that the decisions of the
> planners were arbitrary or random. In fact the decisions
> of planners and of other decision-makers in the urban pro-
> cess are far from being random. The principal focus of
> urban sociology therefore should be the study of factors
> affecting the decisions of decision-makers whether these
> decision-makers are planners, estate agents, private
> developers, builders, councillors or housing officers.'

This was written several years after Rex's own work (Rex & Moore 1967)
pioneered the examination in Britain of the influence of housing
managers' values and decision processes in determining differential
access to urban resources; 'pioneered', not of course in the examination
of administrative process in which there is a long and separate tradition
but in the study of this process in its relation to urban form and its
direct effect on social (in particular, property) relations.

  Much of the earlier work of this sort in Britain and the USA was
stimulated by specific local authority interventions in the urban
process – urban renewal, slum clearance, 'revitalisation'. In many
cases, depending on the researchers' background, the opportunity was
taken to treat these interventions as case studies for prior academic
themes: in particular the question of the significance of 'community'
in British studies,[1] and of the location of community power in American
work.[2] The major concern of the British material was with the effect
of housing and planning policies on the breakdown of community networks
rather than with citizen response and relations with decision-makers.
The American material, perhaps reflecting the more fragmented nature
of American local government, was concerned with the coalitions
(including the residents) which were necessary for planners to achieve
their ends and with the isolation of the characteristics of neighbourhoods which were able to enter and influence these coalitions. To the
extent that the American writing of the early 1960s had already considered the whole range of city interests which participated in the
formulation of planning policy, it could be argued that it was free
of the narrow 'managerialism' for which British studies were later
criticised. However, the range of interests considered in the American
studies rarely went beyond the city boundaries.

The next wave of British urban research[3] arrived on the crest of
governmental interest in the questions of popular participation in
planning[4] and of local government reorganisation.[5] This research
was innovative in the British context because it began to question
how the implementation of planning and housing policy was influenced
by organisational requirements and by the personal and professional
values of officials. Essentially it was concerned with the imposition
of official perceptions of need on the public who were shown neither
to possess the same perceptions nor in several cases to have access
to channels of information and influence.

Pahl (1970) introduced into the course of this research the notion -
already well developed in the less policy related studies of bureaucracy - of 'gatekeepers' acting through rules and procedures of allocation 'as social constraints on access to scarce urban facilities...
(reflecting) the distribution of power in society' (1970, p.215).
Pahl explicitly or implicitly suggested several reorientations for
research towards a concern with a) questions related to controlled
access, b) the process by which control was regulated, c) private as
well as public 'managers', and d) the 'distribution of power'. As
Rex had identified class struggle over differential access to housing
as a separate phenomenon from class formation and conflict deriving
from productive relations, so Pahl was at this stage suggesting that
urban managers had power which was derived and used separately from
that relating to the sphere of production.

The research which followed from this general position, whether or
not it derived from Pahl's call for studies of the goals of urban
managers, has been most concerned with the question of the control
of access to housing in the public and the private sector. To the
planner's belief in the unassailability of his technical competence
is added the role of the housing manager as a transformer of the
preferences of tenants into a demand which is manageable within the
existing housing stock.[6] The channelling of demand through apparently
standard rules for the assessment of eligibility and of position in
the waiting list is seen as having the effect of imposing professional
values about merit and of depoliticising distribution by disguising
scarcity and individualising demand.[7] In the private sector, there
is work on the role of estate agents (Hatch 1973) and building societies
(Williams 1976) as gatekeepers operating informal and discriminatory
rules of allocation. Elliott and McCrone (1975) present an account
of the networks linking private companies of landlords, agents and house
factors which have the effect of controlling the composition of neighbourhoods.

A parallel but more or less separate body of work exists in the field
of the operation of social welfare and social security departments in
Britain and the USA. Many of the same conclusions have been suggested,
relating for example to demand management through restricted access
and the application of standard but confusing rules, but researchers
in this field even more than those in urban research have been primarily
concerned with the internal dynamic of bureaucracies and its relevance
for policy implementation. They have indicated for example, that the
area of administrative discretion, operated through informal as well
as formal eligibility rules, has tended to distort social welfare and
social security programmes away from stated intentions about the service

provided and from the 'target' population.[8] Hall (1974) focuses attention on the gatekeeper role of receptionists which comes before all the other channelling and rationing processes: eligibility clauses, charges, stigma, ignorance, complexity of procedures, the intervention through discretionary decision-making of the personal and professional values of service providers, and deflection of applicants.

The reorganisation of the social services into integrated service delivery packages has been one official response (Seebohm 1968).[9] Another has been attempts (in the US and UK poverty programmes)[9] by 'positive discrimination' to redress the balance of previous service inputs (social welfare, education, employment creation) by focusing them on deprived areas, and to remove the physical and social distance between applicants and administrators by exposing the latter to the organised demands of the poor through community action. The product of the research, if not of the action on these projects, went well beyond the official propositions. It was not just that there were found to be failures in the implementation of services (lack of coordination, discontinuities, confusion, etc.) and that the 'target' population even of these selective programmes were often not being reached; much of this research also suggested that these programmes were no remedy for 'deprivation' which it concluded was a systemic rather than a local and pathological phenomenon.[10]

Thus, a series of central government interventions, themselves based on the supposition of local responsibility for deprivation, gave rise to research which rejected the thesis that local managers were an 'independent variable' (Pahl 1970, p.215) in the urban system. Researchers and social activists associated with these interventions found that the focus on small areas and on issues of local government responsibility ignored the subjection of localities and local managers to wider economic forces and to central government definitions of problems and policies (e.g. Community Development Project 1974). A theoretical framework which put local decision-making into this wider context was needed.

## OFFICIAL ACTION AS A RESPONSE TO EXTERNAL PRESSURES

The 'managerialist' position was already a move beyond a simple pluralist assumption of the polity as an interest free body acting in response to the free expression of the interests of affected groups.[11] Research had shown that policy outcomes were at least as much affected by professional ideologies, the limits of the interests contained in the policy process, central government requirements and the 'failure' of certain groups to express their interests. To invert Almond and Verba (1963), neither the managers nor the affected public acted as if they accepted the 'democratic myth' of the influential citizen.

The idea of 'managerial autonomy'[12] can be seen as a sort of half-way house between a pluralist (free market) position and a dominant current view which sees bureaucratic decision-makers as having some variably defined role as part of a state which either reflects or represents the interests of dominant classes. The nature of the articulation between class interests and administrative action remains a matter of debate – are decision-makers agents of a state which embodies dominant class interests or are they a part of the state as a mediatory (though biased) apparatus which maintains a moving cohesion between classes?

Among the possible responses, Pahl's reformulation of his own thesis rejects the idea that local public managers are in any sense autonomous and argues that they 'play a crucial mediating role between the state and the private sector and between the central state authority and the local population' (Pahl 1974). Although the implication is that 'central state' and the private sector's interests will be dominant, the ways in which these interests are articulated through management is left unclear and local managers seem to retain some degree of autonomy as mediators. Nevertheless, the new formulation (and according to some readings, the original one[13]) put local managers into a broader context of constraints and pressures than those of their own professional predilections. The outcome is then seen to be not merely dependent on the relationship between the planners (or managers) and the subjects (or applicants). An example of such a broad consideration of the context of local authority management is the study by Harloe et al (1974) of the organisation of London housing. An important distinction of this work from the American community power studies is that it considers the influence of pressures and constraints not in a series of one-off decisions but as a component of sustained processes, that is it is more systemic in its understanding of the general processes underlying particular cases.

In the course of this debate, the growing influence of the French marxist approach to the analysis of urban politics offered a framework within which the structural limitations on policy could be understood. In this work, the role of state organisations in planning and allocation is defined in a way which really ends the debate about managerial autonomy from the state and opens up a new debate about the state's autonomy from dominant classes. However, organisational process has been given almost no weight as a sphere of analysis. If a case were to be made for such research within this highly systematic school of thinking, it would be in one or both of two clearly defined fields. According to Castells: 'The study of urban politics breaks down, therefore, into two analytical fields indissolubly linked in social reality: urban planning and policy in its various forms and urban social movements' (Castells 1977, p.261).

The urban system is seen essentially as a locational expression of the concentrative processes and effects of the social structure as a whole. Under capitalism, for Castells (1977, p.237) the basis of urban concentration is in the spatially focused reproduction of labour power; for Lojkine the capitalist city is defined also as a form of concentration of production and capital circulation:

> 'Locus of both the reproduction of labour power through means of consumption, and of capital through urban systems of meta-morphosis of commodity capital' (Lojkine 1976, p.133)

Urban planning is then seen as an adjunct to this concentrative process. In Lamarche it is an adjunct in direct support of property capital; the real planner is then property capital itself which 'plans and equips space, profiting from public investment, and feeding off other private investment' (Pickvance 1976, p.15):

> 'The development plans drawn up by municipal planning departments can only be realised if they are subordinated to the interests of developers'.(Lamarche 1976, p.103)

10

In Castells, urban planning is an adjunct to the concentrative process in a less directly supportive sense. His argument is that concentration of labour power in cities has dislocative effects given 'the inability of capitals to provide an adequate supply of housing and facilities due to the lack of profitability, itself an effect of the income stratification resulting from the system' (1976, p.166). In this case, planning is seen as part of the regulatory apparatus of the political system within a society. Part of this regulation will involve the organisation of space (e.g.zoning), part will involve the organisation of collective consumption (schools, subsidised housing, hospitals etc.) in areas which are unprofitable but which are required for the reproduction of labour, and part will involve the mystificatory element of urban planning:

> 'It is town planning through which the state apparatus claims
> to resolve insurmountable difficulties, to get round the
> conflicts, and to put an end to the disputes in the name of
> a technical rationality by means of which divergent social
> interests can be reconciled'. (Castells 1973,p.3)

Urban planning is thus not a source of social change but a means of containing contradictory demands. It does this not by direct suppression nor, as Castells points out in his later work (Castells 1978a, p.64), by any technical effectiveness in overcoming urban problems, but by negotiating between interests on a basis which is apparently neutral though actually structurally linked to dominant interests. Planning cannot be an agent of social change since it is part of the 'central administration's mechanism' and consequently bound by 'the limits defined by the structural laws of the dominant mode of production' (Castells 1978a, p.85).

For Castells, it is 'urban social movements and not planning institutions which are the true sources of change and innovation in the city' (Castells 1973, p.10). Indeed this is necessarily true since urban social movements are defined not by their organisation but in terms of their tendency to lead towards the effect of substantial social change.[14] Whereas urban planning tends to incorporate opposing interests within the political system, urban social movements are the expression of unincorporated opposition 'the logic of whose developments contradicts the institutionally dominant social logic' (Castells 1978a, p.93).

An interpretation of this view might be that urban planning is faced with a series of constraints of varying profundity - there are the structural interests of dominant classes which are never called into question, there are those particular interests of factions of dominant classes and of dominated classes which are accommodated because they are reconcilable with structural interests, and there are the interests of dominated classes which are not reconcilable and which are expressed through opposition movements, if they are expressed at all. However, even though the planner may in this way see himself as being subject to external constraints, Castells makes the point that certain of these interests are internalised in the organisation of the planning process. The organisational 'dice are loaded' to favour dominant interests and to accommodate others. In this view, planning institutions are not 'passive vessels for various pressure groups' as in the pluralist thesis, nor are they autonomous and influential in their own right as

11

in the managerialist thesis, rather they are a biased' context for conditioned and institutionalised social negotiation' (Castells 1978a, p.87).

Castells suggests some of the ways in which the 'loading of the dice' keeps the negotiation between interests within limits which are tolerable to the social structure:

> 'This effect is achieved through a number of mechanisms which vary from direct political control to administrative hierarchy and criteria for budgetary allocation' (Castells 1978a, p.87)

It is this concern with the organisational process of policy formation and implementation and with the interests which they are structured to represent that we will go on to explore.

## THE POLITICAL SIGNIFICANCE OF ADMINISTRATIVE ALLOCATION

My objective is to develop an approach to the analysis of a) the factors (the pressures, constraints, requirements and demands which are the expression of interests) which generate and affect the implementation of policy, b) the way in which these factors are represented through organisational structures and procedures of implementation, and c) the effect of this organisational framework and policy on the members of the public who are brought into contact with it.

The approach will be influenced by a particular understanding of the nature of the state and of the relation between state administration and the social structure. Why and how these connections can be made will be elaborated in later sections. The purpose of this section is briefly to make the point that state administration has an increasing importance both in the allocation of resources and in managing relations between the state and society. Furthermore, administrative regulation has a particular political significance in situations of underdevelopment, rapid urbanisation and authoritarianism.

Castells (1978a, pp.168-170) argues that the state is drawn into a contradictory situation in the urban context as capitalism develops – it is required increasingly to intervene in urban problems so as to regulate demands but in intervening it becomes the focus of conflict and provokes political crisis. The intervention is the product of a series of interrelated requirements and demands. Items of collective consumption ('housing, schools, creches and nurseries, health services, cultural activities, transport...') become important as a condition of the reproduction of a technologically sophisticated labour force con- centrated in large cities. The planned organisation of space and items of collective consumption are also required to support aspects of private commodity consumption and production – for example, the car industry depends on the development of a road network, while public investment in suburban shopping centres and urban renewal stimulates consumption in a more general sense. Moreover, Castells argues that growing state intervention in the provision of collective goods and services is the result not only of the requirements of production and consumption but also of the demands of an increasingly influential working class.

The effect of this intervention is not, however, purely regulatory.

12

While urban planning and the organisation of collective consumption represent the state's claim to technical rationality and political neutrality in its resolution of conflicting demands, they also bring the state into a position of direct exposure to demands and of responsibility for the inability to meet them all. At the same time, social groups affected by planning and the organisation of collective services are drawn into a direct relationship with the state:

> 'It is in this way that specified problems become globalised, the urban question increasingly relates the state to daily life, and provokes political crisis'. (Castells 1978a, p.3)

State intervention in urban problems thus creates the possibility of direct confrontation between the 'dominant social logic' represented by state institutions and the oppositional logic of urban social movements. In this way, the extension of administrative intervention in advanced capitalism has the effect of opening up a new structural contradiction (in addition to that between labour and capital) which can unite all 'popular classes' affected by collective consumption in a 'common opposition to the logic of the system' (Castells 1978a, p.172).

Although Castells attributes this tendency towards the politicisation of urban problems to the growth of state intervention under advanced capitalism, his own accounts (as opposed to forecasts) of urban movements in France on the whole show a fragile level of defensive organisation and little effectiveness:

> '.... these great numbers of struggles and organisations have only a weak social impact and rarely lead to mass movements. Until recently, they have kept a low profile in political struggles and have not developed new social relations – *they are not social movements*' (Castells 1978a, p.148)

Ironically, it is from less advanced capitalist countries, Spain and Chile, that examples of more mobilised and politically effective opposition come (Castells 1977, p.360; Castells 1978b).

The studies in Brazil to which this book refers relate to cases of effective control through administrative regulation. The experience of the social groups affected by urban renewal, housing programmes and service distribution has been of acquiescence, division and competition in the face of the administratively established logic. These cases can hardly be claimed therefore to have the political significance of creating the conditions for the transformation of power through the arousal of opposition movements. Instead they have the opposite significance – rather than incidents of conflict, they represent the typical, continuous and normal, the routine experience of those who are subject to state administrative action. For citizens or subjects, this is essentially a matter of incorporation into administrative procedures. This incorporation in turn has political significance because it draws subjects into a structure of relations with the state and with other interests. Politics then operate through the administrative relationship in at least three senses:

> (i) it is through state administration that access to considerable resources is decided whether this is through the creation, regulation and control of rights, or in the award or refusal of collective

services and benefits, or in the imposition of penalties
and controls;

(ii) the management of these rights, services and penalties
is not a matter of simple technical considerations but
is also in response to the interests of social groups
and classes.  Subjection to administrative action therefore implies a mediated relationship with those influential
interests;

(iii) it is in their routine contacts with public agencies that
most people have their experience of the state, where the
state gains meaning in everyday life.

While the means of collective consumption have, as Castells points out,
a particular development and sophistication in advanced capitalist
countries, there are other ways in which administrative regulation has
a peculiar importance in under-developed countries.

Firstly, rapid urbanisation is associated not only with the emergence
of new social classes and demands but also with an urgent need for the
extension of public services to permit this abrupt expansion of city
limits.  At the same time, while extreme inequalities in wealth make it
difficult to transfer the costs of these services to consumers, the
urban situation makes inequalities both in wealth and the distribution
of collective services more evident.

Secondly, administrative allocation, access and control are particularly crucial in situations of extreme poverty where markets may be
inaccessible or lacking altogether (Schaffer and Huang 1975, p.15).
The decline in subsistence, peasant and craft production and the non-
integration of large proportions of the population into new productive
activities implies both an enhanced role for the state and a peculiar
dependence of the population.  This goes well beyond questions of
physical planning and the distribution of items of collective
consumption.  As Lamb (1975, p.132) writes

'The State provides economic, social and political services
for capitalist penetration, orchestrates the de- and restructuring of elements of the pre-capitalist mode (the
family is a good example) and 'copes', so to speak, at the
level of cohesion of the whole formation, with the dislocative consequences of the expansion of the capitalist mode'.

At one level, people excluded from market provision may become dependent on the state even for basic items of individual consumption, such as
food rations.  At another, in the absence of an established market
economy, governmental administration frequently also comes to play a
developmental role in the organisation of production as well as
distribution.  State administrative control becomes crucial not only
in collective services and the organisation of space but also in the
allocation of a wide range of assets and productive resources (e.g.
land, technology, state wages or credit) and of opportunities for
distribution and production (e.g. through licensing, industrial permits
and public contracting).  As Schaffer and O'Keeffe(1978, p.3) suggest:

'In situations where administrative allocation is important,
even dominant, the arena of competition and conflict is
removed in some respects from the sphere of productive

relations of monetary and commodity-like exchanges into the
sphere of administrative and institutional relations'.

The conceptual separation of production and distribution is itself
questionable (Schaffer and Lamb 1981) - not only do relations of production have distributive consequences but also unequal distribution may
itself affect beneficiaries' productive or class position. Administrative allocation and regulation can come to be an important deter-
minant of the social structure itself. For example:

> '... it is access to the surplus product both in production
> and circulation, principally through the State, which defines
> the position of the richest Africans in Kenya, and the total
> absence of such access which defines the poorest....'
> (Kitching 1977, p.72)

Thirdly, there is the particular significance of the extension of
state activities in authoritarian political systems. The point to be
made here is that, in the absence of openly expressed popular demands
and where the state has a highly directive role, there is likely to be
greater unity in the interests served by varied state interventions
than in more open political systems. A summary comparison of Britain
with Brazil illustrates the point.

Researchers in the British context have noted the same extension of
administrative control into areas previously governed by market relations.
Pahl (1977) argues that the state has acquired not only an intermediary
role in the allocation of surplus from private production but also
increasingly an independent role in the direction of capital for
production. Saunders (1979, pp.169-180), by reference to Winkler (1977),
Offe (1976) and Cawson (1978), proposes the differentiation of these
two roles as two separate fields of state action governed by different
interests. On the one hand, there is the 'corporate sector' where the
state adopts a directive role over capital in 'close consultation' with
big business and organised labour; on the other hand, there is the
'pluralist sector' where it allocates surplus for consumption under
pressure from class and group interests. In that case, research in the
two sectors would uncover different dominant interests.

However, in the analysis of the 'bureaucratic authoritarian'(Brazilian)
state these two sectors lose their distinction. It is argued that while
the state extends its role in economic direction, the effect of its
involvement is above all to further the interests of large, especially
international, capital (Cardoso 1975, p.198, O'Donnell 1978, p.15);
state officials are able to insert their sub-interests, but the interests
of labour are repressed, controlled or excluded. Moreover, popular
demands are seen as being scarcely more influential on its role as
allocator of surplus; the state's allocative (e.g. collective service)
activities are not seen as separate from, but subordinate to, its
involvement in economics and to the interests which are dominant there.
The state's role in capital accumulation (the managed transfer of
savings to investment, the direction of infrastructural investment)
comes to set the terms and conditions on which the state acts in its
allocative and redistributive role. Moreover, the elimination of the
organised expression of popular interests itself means that there are
no forceful pressures to demand that the state should operate in its

distributive activities on terms other than those emanating from the
productive sphere.

The implications are twofold:  first that, particularly in
authoritarian systems, it should be possible to trace back from the
terms operating in distributive programmes to conditions founded
in the state's involvement in  production;  second that administrative
allocation takes on a special significance where open forms of
political representation are limited or extinguished and where
therefore 'the political game concentrates on the executive' (Cardoso
1975, p.205):

> 'Involvement of bureaucracies in public policy becomes
> unavoidable and, in consequence, central to the under-
> standing of questions of national politics' (Tapia-Videla
> 1979, p.291).

## A PLACE FOR ORGANISATIONAL ANALYSIS

The nature of state interventions, their political significance
and the response which they evoke in the public are clearly matters
which vary with the particular state at particular times.  Urban
policies should therefore be explained (in terms of the forces
which give rise to them and of their social impact) by reference
to these specific circumstances.  This position is based on two
underlying points.  The first, already made earlier in this
chapter, is that the explanation (rather than mere description)
of urban policy and its impact requires that the policy be located
in the wider context of the whole structure.   The second point
is that this wider context cannot be derived for all time and all
places from an abstract and mechanistic model of a sort of universal
capitalist state.

Specification of the context requires two steps identified by
Castells (1978a, pp.45,181) in his explanation of the formation
of French urban policy.  One is to develop a 'theorised history' of
the development of the particular state in response to the emergence
of social classes.  This would take into account 'the evolution of
capital;  the evolution of production relations;  the evolution of
social struggles;  and the evolution of the state apparatus itself'.
The next step is to consider how these elements have affected the
development of urban policies and how, conversely, policies  have
affected social relations.

The need to specify the analysis goes further.  Urban policy (its
generation and effect) has to be explained not only by reference to a
global analysis of the particular state but also by reference to an
analysis of the interests represented in and affected by the particular
state intervention.  This position is based on an understanding of the
state as representative not only of dominant classes but also, unequally,
of other interests.  Castells rejects that marxist tradition which sees
the state as 'the passive and direct instrument of the dominant classes'
and which renders explanation of the particular case unnecessary except
as a matter of demonstrating how dominant class interests apply there:

> 'The state is the expression of society, and thus both the
> crystallisation of the historical process and the expression

16

of contradictory social relations which are at work in each
period and in each social formation. But while such a
formulation, which is mainly rooted in the Gramscian tradition,
is the most fruitful and flexible, it is still too general. In
order to specify it one must be much more precise about the
relations between class struggles and the state, and one must
also stress the internal differentiation within the state,
recognising its contradictions as well as its homogeneity, its
diversity as well as its unity' (Castells 1978a, pp.180-181)

In that case, the action of administrative agencies (in for example urban
planning or the allocation of public services) is not predictable as an
effect of dominant class interests (even if these were easily disting-
uishable in specific cases). Administrative organisations respond to
a variety of interests or constraints besides the 'objectives' of one
particular class. If there is no simple and single association between
dominant class interests and the state apparatus, then the interests
which underlie particular policy actions cannot be inferred or assumed
but have to be identified.

The point of interest is therefore in the practical reality which is
not simply accounted for by the determination of the economy on political
process in the ultimate or 'last instance'. To assert economic
determinism in particular cases or in a 'section of history' is both
to elevate every case to a reflection of the last instance and to reduce
to simplicity the 'complexity of interactions' which compose political
process[15]. The application of the analysis itself becomes deterministic
where general theory is taken to require that any particular administrative initiative or response be interpreted as an expression of
ruling class interests.

Having adopted a more open view of the state, the problem is how to
take account of it in analysis. How is the analysis to be specified
so as to identify the particular circumstances which shape urban
policies and their effects? How is this to be done while avoiding a
return to mere specificity in which each case is distinct because there
is no consideration of their relation to a common social structure?
Part of the answer is in Castells' call for the placing of case studies
within the context of a 'theorised history' of class relations and their
manifestation in the particular state. Part, I suggest, is in the
organisational analysis to which I have already referred, the identification through studies of administrative practice in policy implementation of the interests which are present as constraints on policy.

Without such organisational analysis, we are faced with the sort of
reporting which leaves a hiatus between a full blown theoretical statement (e.g. about planning institutions as part of the state's regulating
apparatus) and its blanket imposition on often very localised events.
One consequence of such a position is that individuals and organisations
are forced (on paper) to act under an inescapable determinism. Where
it is not placed in a field of constraints, action can only be accounted
for either by some gross reading of the class composition of the state
or by direct reference to the actor's imputed personal interests (or to
his interest-free rationality); this leads to the sort of explanation
which smacks of conspiracy theory. Without organisation, the response
of the 'authorities' to demands emerges from a vacuum; with organisations, responses are seen to be not those of simple interest but the

17

product of processes which are structured to include some interests and to exclude others.

I therefore adopt a 'two way' approach, linking together these routes to the specification of the analysis. On the one hand, this implies moving from the general analysis of class relations and the formation of the state towards an attempt to explain the incidence of specific problems and policies. On the other hand, it means starting with those specific policies and moving outwards to more general explanations of the interests which are lodged in them and of their effect on social relations.

It is the connection between these two levels of analysis (the history of the state and the study of particular cases of administrative action) which are considered in the next section.

AN APPROACH TO ORGANISATIONAL ANALYSIS:   STRUCTURAL LIMITS ON ACTION

This 'two way' approach does not suggest that there are two independently operating sets of interests - on the one hand, the wider class interests which are to be discovered by analysis of the social structure as a whole;  on the other hand, the group interests (of officials, financiers etc.) which are identifiable through the analysis of particular policies. On the contrary, I mean to suggest that these are united at the level of state administrative action. If general, societal interests are to be effective they have somehow to be operative at the particular and concrete level;  they cannot remain general and abstract. I have suggested that one way in which they become effective is through their internalisation in the organisational structure and processes of policy implementation. For their part, the particular groups which implement and are affected by particular policies have to find a place and to interpret their objectives within the limits permitted by this selective representation of structural interests.

What is required is both an exploratory (rather than deterministic) analysis of the influences on and effects of administrative action and also a capacity to interpret the particular case in the light of a wider analysis of class relations and the formation of the state. The connection between these levels of analysis is in the conception of state administration as incorporating structural limits, that is as being organised so as to guarantee its operation within limits which are tolerable to the social structure. In this sense, planning and the administration of policy do not encounter politics only as external phenomena (whether in the shape of class interests or of political 'obstacles' to efficient management);  rather they contain politics both because they are a means through which people are drawn into a relationship with the state and also because this relationship while appearing neutral disguises a bias.

Castells (1976, p.81) indicates the area which needs elaboration:

'To study the question of housing is not to contrast popular 'needs' with the 'wickedness' of capitalists, but to reveal the structural limits of the solutions to the problem of shelter, and the complex set of correspondences between the practices of agents and their place in the social structure'.

The scope for policy analysis which this position opens up is greater than Castells himself allows. He suggests that the analysis should be concerned with the effects of urban planning on social relations at two levels. There is its ideological effect in rationalising and legitimising social interests particularly through planning documents. Then there is its political effect 'as a privileged instrument of negotiation and mediation' between interests (Castells 1978a, p.86). The interests served are to be identified by examining the actual outcomes of policy, that is

> '.... the transformations which it provokes in the areas affected by it. Based on the social content thus established, the study of the institutional processes whereby the programme is carried out becomes intelligible, for, beyond the description of the actors' activities, we perceive the social determination of the interests being catered to by the various agencies'. (Castells 1978a, p.95)

But Castells' concern with what policies actually do as well as with what they claim to do needs further elaboration. Organisational (or institutional) processes have a much greater significance than he suggests and this cannot be read off simply by references to their production of concrete outcomes. Castells' 'politics of urban planning' is almost wholly concerned with the more overt aspects of administrative action - policy statements, open exchanges between citizens' groups and agencies, and the social effects of the physical outcomes (new towns, breaking up ghettos, urban renewal) of interventions - and hardly at all with the social effects of the more routine and often informal processes of policy formation and implementation. His interest in 'analyses of the social content of interventions' (Castells 1977, p.323) only rarely extends[16] to examination of the social content of the procedures of intervention. And yet, if the structural limits to change are internalised in administrative practice, what seems to be implied is precisely an analysis of the organisational structures and procedures through which class and group interests are included or excluded and outcomes arrived at. Moreover, besides their ultimate distributive effects, the procedures of bureaucratic intervention are themselves producers of social outcomes. The effect of administrative action as an instrument of control, regulation, legitimation or incorporation, cannot be deduced simply from the nature and distribution of concrete outcomes. At least as important as what is distributed are the procedures of administration and the relationships which these establish between social groups and state agencies.

An analysis of the nature of the state (and of Brazilian development) which is compatible with the above approach, that is with the combination of the analysis of organisational processes and the global analysis of the political economy, can be found in the work of Fernando Cardoso (1973, 1975, 1977, 1979) and Guillermo O'Donnell (1973, 1978, 1979). They focus precisely on the relation between the development of economic forces, the form of the state and the content of state action. Their concern is to explain the emergence of 'bureaucratic authoritarian' regimes in the context of dependent economic development. This is the analysis which will be pursued in chapter two. The point to make now is that their approach to the understanding of the state locates the 'structural limits to solutions' in the structure of the state itself and therefore makes them amenable to organisational analysis. Their approach invites and even requires to be met by a form of analysis which begins with the specific practice of state agencies. It does so, first because it is non-deterministic about the class interests which may be represented in the state and about the particular form which the state may take, and second because it therefore adopts an 'explanatory methodology' to reach an understanding of which interests are served by the particular political arrangements. The concern is with the explanation of concrete situations rather than with the application of pre-established generalised explanations on specific events which are then seen as inevitable:

> 'What was significant was the 'movement', the class struggle, the redefinition of interest, the political alliances which maintained the structure while at the same time opening the possibility of their transformation' (Cardoso 1976, p.10)

In this view, the historical development of a mode of production has a determining effect only in the sense that it defines the structural situation and interests of classes, and not in the sense that the future is predictable in terms of the specific class 'alliances' or the political struggles which may arise. While relations of production structure the interests of classes, the way in which these interests combine and the political forms in which these combinations are achieved are indeterminate. The focus of attention is therefore on the exploratory understanding of the forms and practices of the state.

The limitations to change, the way in which the existing order is reproduced and its possibilities for transformation are to be established by examination of the organisation and ideology of the state itself. Which interests are represented in the state and how they maintain the 'norms of exclusion' and inclusion are matters for explanation and therefore research. In this interpretation, the state is not the creature, the product, of a balance between classes worked out elsewhere; it is itself an 'arena' within which class and group interests are worked out. The particular case therefore requires particular study of its organisational and ideological arrangements:

> 'Understanding the Brazilian 'political model' consists, before anything else, in explaining the form, organisation, ideology and policies of the state. In so doing it becomes clear who direct, who are benefited, who are excluded and who participate'. (Cardoso 1975, p.196) [17]

Cardoso therefore firstly directs attention to the identification of the interests which are represented in the practices of the state; secondly, he argues that the ideologies which maintain and justify that representation (and which implicitly justify the exclusion of other interests) are themselves projected through the procedures, practices and policies of state organisation (Cardoso 1975, pp.194-195).

The 'structural limits to change' are not then external to the state organisation but internal to it. They are contained within the routine activities of organisations which implement policies. The organisational framework defines the included interests and how they are related and thus sets limits on the action and perceptions of participants. Organisations are thus conceived, on the one hand, as products of a definition of a reality, and on the other hand 'as principal agents in the social construction of reality, providing an inventory of legitimate logics and axioms, and a repository of acceptable vocabularies, legitimate motives and laudable ambitions' (Dillon 1976, p.58). In other words, organisations are both the product of interests and understandings and help to reproduce them; they are both the creature of ideology and are the context within which ideologies are modified and emerge; they are part of what Berger and Luckman (1971, p.135) call the 'reality-defining and reality-producing process'.

The 'structural limits', in this view, are the definitions of reality which organisations incorporate and purvey, setting the limits on what is and is not possible in the formation and operation of policies, rationalising the organisational procedures in which administrators and the administered find themselves involved, and justifying the outcome or making it seem inevitable[18]. The problem is then not that administrators are malevolent or incompetent, nor that they are simply the direct agents of class interests. The point is to understand the structural limits on organisational performance and who benefits from them.

Structural constraints conceived in this way (as the interests incorporated in organisations) bridge two broad areas of concern:

i) the relation of organisational structure and process[19] to societal interests;

ii) the relation of organisational structure and process to the outcomes of policy (in terms both of the distribution and of the effect of the distributive relationship).

In either case, whether the concern is with organisational effects on outcomes (e.g. the distribution of housing) or with the organisation as an expression of social interests, the field of study is the same – organisational performance or action. As structural constraints limit organisational performance, so organisational performance is one avenue to the identification of those structural constraints.

POINTS OF ENTRY FOR ORGANISATIONAL RESEARCH

The analysis of the administrative distribution of services, resources, permissions and penalties, outlined above, implies several levels of research including examination of the following main points: the effect of the distribution in terms of who does and does not receive the facility, service or imposition; the way in which organisational procedures themselves influence these distributional outcomes; the effect of the access relationship on those who are the object of the administered programme and their response; and the complex relationship between the constraints and interests which condition the establishment of a policy and the structures, processes and perceptions which then incorporate these constraints and interests in decision-making.

There is continuity in these relations between effects and responses and between interests, organisational structures and the reflection of interests in outcomes which make it difficult to find a point of entry for research. There are, however, two key points where these multifarious pressures and responses are crystallised, allowing a toe-hold for research which seeks to understand how they relate to each other.

One of these tangible points where processes emerge as decisions is at the stage of the establishment of programmes and organisations to implement them. The questions to be asked are the following. In response to what interests and demands in a particular polity are policies and programmes of intervention generated? What are the operational conditions and the organisational framework imposed at the outset? Once choices have been made about the organisations which are to implement programmes and the way they are related, these choices will themselves act to influence the nature of the service offered and the direction of change. The policy acquires its own momentum as a product of the demands which can be effectively expressed through it and of the limited range of interests and perceptions available within the organisational structure.

The second point of entry for research is the point at which administrative interpretations are crystallised and become operative as allocative procedures or, in the view of the applicant or subject, rules of access or avoidance. As suggested earlier, interests and constraints are only real (in the sense that they are effective) if they have an impact on the eventual decision about the allocation of resources and the treatment of groups of the population. This is, therefore, a useful beginning because it is one from which the experience of the applicant (or beneficiary or subject of a policy) can be traced back to its origin in logics established at other levels - in other actors' definitions of reality[20]. The questions asked at other levels of the administrative structure are therefore those which would explain processes which ultimately impinge on the subject.

It is at the point of access or allocation that it is possible to observe the effect of a policy in discriminating between groups with different resources and in establishing a relationship between state agencies and subjects. Policies or programmes of collective consumption may correspond to collective demands and will almost always be expressed in terms of the satisfaction of needs on an equitable basis, but the subject's experience is usually as an individual applicant having to make his particular connection with the distributing organisation through a barrage of excluding rules and different channels of access (Schaffer and Huang 1975).

The idea that it is allocation by rules and categories based on criteria of selection which distinguishes administrative allocation from price-based market mechanisms, has been implicit to much of the work already mentioned and it is explicit for example in some recent work in Britain such as that of English et al (1976), Lambert et al (1975 and 1978), Gray (1976), Hatch (1973), Hall (1974) and Saunders (1976 and 1979), and in Brazil by Valladares (1974 and 1978). The organisation of rules into stages of application which involve applicants queuing for consideration has been used in particular by Lambert et al and Gray who have seen the queue as a mechanism for disguising scarcity, promoting a myth of availability and rationality, and depoliticising demands by a process of individuation. It is also, however, the bureaucratic solution to the problem of competition for service - it structures the process of organisational connection, apparently making this process orderly and equal (Schaffer 1973, p.289).

Principles of social justice, of more equal access, commonly underlie

the formal case for the establishment and operation of programmes of
public service distribution.  In practice, however, such programmes
find themselves continuously operating in a situation of scarcity,
having to limit access in the face of mass eligibility in principle.
The problem for the bureaucracy is partly resolved through the
establishment of formal selective procedures which apparently reflect
policy objectives (e.g. the British council house points system as a
reflection of the policy concern with 'need').  Formal procedures,
though exclusive in intent, may also serve a function as symbols of
the principles of openness and fairness:

> 'Queues are a bureaucratic structure, but they are also
> sometimes a symbol for the avoidance of its pejorative
> or ideological connotation'. (Schaffer 1973, p.289)

On the one hand, there is the organisational necessity for selecting
between competing claims through a system of rules establishing
eligibility, priority rating and eventual service allocation.  On the
other hand, beyond the formal intention, there is a series of constraints which work within and on the organisation to produce their
own requirements about what is to be distributed and about the basis
of distribution:  costs, technical standards, professional interests,
the requirements of organisational control and survival, the different
capacity of applicants to express their demand, the nature of the
service itself become important (usually concentrative rather than
re-distributive) determinants of the rules of access.

Any organisational arrangement for distribution, control or production has, on the basis of the interests, perceptions and understandings
it contains or represents, to evolve routines for deciding between
competing claims for inclusion in or exclusion from a policy.  Some
system of rules of inclusion and exclusion is inescapable, the point
is to understand why any particular set of rules exists, whose interests
are served by them and what their effects are for different groups.
Understanding gained at this level of the analysis can be compared with
and added to the understanding gained from the analysis of the circumstances which led to the establishment of the policy and organisation
in the first place.

CONCLUSION

The 'structural limits' on policy cannot by this view be deduced by a
direct leap from an analysis of dominant class interests, just as they
cannot be assumed away by the belief that there are no limits to
technical or managerial rationality in the 'best interests of all'.
The limits, the constraints on administrative action and perceptions,
are a matter for study;  the effects of administrative action are no
more self-evident.

The concern with state administration arises from the view that the
nature and effects of administrative action cannot be predicted from
universal laws nor even from a global reading of the class composition
of the particular state.  The combination of interests and the understandings which are vested in urban planning and administration will
vary from place to place and time to time and will also depend on the
content of the policy and the groups it affects.  Research has to be
sufficiently specific and exploratory to discover rather than rule out
these variations.  At the same time, the specific policy intervention,

its formulation and effect cannot be explained simply in terms of local circumstances and actors. These have a place in the wider social structure - whether through the forces which generate urban problems, the social relations, interests and perceptions of actors, or the constraints on organisational responses. The following study of urban policy in Brazil attempts to combine these two levels of analysis.

One way towards an interpretation of administrative or bureaucratic action emerges from an analysis of the class basis of different forms of state. The state is considered as the expression of the particular and shifting conflicts and alliances of interests which arise in the course of economic development; the form of the state represents the interests of the included and ideologically accommodates those classes whose interests are excluded; it is in that sense, 'a structural variant of the civil society' (Perez-Diaz 1978, p.93), that is, selective in the degree to which it represents the interest of social classes. The limiting factor on 'substantial change' is then the included classes' mutual interest in the survival of the state which incorporates them and of the economic system on which they depend. Among the participant interests in the state is the civil bureaucracy itself which, in Marx's terms, is not only a 'parasitic body' dependent on capitalist production but also a body containing its own particular interests (Marx 1973, p.237). This 'independent power' (Engels 1948, p.45) is taken to have a life of its own though within the constraint of the survival of the economic system which sustains it.

This last paragraph broaches the issues and the form of analysis which have concerned Latin American writers such as Cardoso and O'Donnell in their attempt to explain the emergence of 'bureaucratic authoritarian' regimes. Essentially, they examine the effect of economic development on class formation and interests, thence its conditioning effect on class relations and on the emergence of particular forms of political institutionality. The operative word is 'conditioning' not determining; the form and practices of the state can be explained but not predicted in terms of the interests they serve.

Beginning at this level of generality may lead to hypotheses about, but does not easily reach down to explanations of, particular cases of administrative action or, in Castell's terms, planning 'interventions'. While the general analysis, particularly of Cardoso, raises the question of the role of organisational process in managing relations between social groups and classes (for example, in selectively canalising interests through the bureaucracy) it does not really go beyond general statements on the question.

The other route, from the particular to the general, towards the explanation of state administrative action is distinguished by its concern, firstly, with the experience of those who are affected by the routine operation of organisations (rather than especially with the exceptional incidents of mobilisation and conflict) and, secondly, with the interpretation of institutional operations, outputs and rules of procedure as an objectified product of the interplay of interests incorporated in organisations. On this second point, it is crucial that we do not only mean the particular interests of the bureaucracy but all the social interests which eventually affect and are affected by the operation of bureaucracies.

Governmental administrative organisations are not autonomous of nor merely exposed to politics; their procedures contain politics. Perez-Dias (1978, p.95) makes the point:

> '... that while these political institutions do incorporate conflicts and are, therefore, the battlegrounds for class struggles, they are not neutral battlegrounds. They are not a homogeneous space, but a structured space, with limits and rules that provide different groups with a repertoire of obstacles and advantages'.

The risk in this form of analysis, working from the 'bottom up', is that it might be unable to escape from the level of the particular. It is best pursued complementarily to the historical analysis of the emergence of class relations and the formation of the state in response to economic development. The link between the two approaches is the location of organisational performance in a set of social, economic and political constraints which are the product of a particular balance of class and group interests.

The focus of this chapter is clearly on the analysis of the practice of state organisations in relation to their publics. This is not to suggest that organisational analysis alone offers access to an understanding of relations between the state and class interests. Such studies will tend to discover and explain demobilisation. There is also overt political action (in popular mobilisation or social movements) which is not mediated by administrative agencies. However, it is the political significance of the routine practices of official organisations which is relatively the more neglected.

NOTES

1. e.g. Vereker and Mays (1961), Willmott and Young (1957), Anderson (1960), Jennings (1962).

2. e.g. Kaplan (1963), Rossi and Dentler (1961), Clarence-Davies (1966), Polsby (1963).

3. see for example, Bull (1967), Dennis (1970)(1972), Davies (1972), Batley (1972).

4. The eventual governmental views of participation crystallised around the Report of the Skeffington Committee, HMSO, 1969.

5. see the Royal Commission on Local Government in England, Cmnd 4040, 1969.

6. see for example English et al (1976), Ungerson (1971), Batley (1972), Niner (1975).

7. see Lambert et al (1975), Gray (1976) and for much earlier American work Deutscher (1968). Lambert et al (1978) elaborates their work.

8. see in particular Blau (1955), Parker (1967), Rees (1972), Hill (1969), Lynes (1967), Allen (1968), Cloward and Piven (1974).

9. in the USA, the Ford Foundation Gray Areas Project, Headstart, the Community Action Program, the Model Cities Program. In the UK, Educational Priority Areas, the Urban Aid Programme, the Community Development Project, the Neighbourhood Schemes, the Comprehensive Community Programme, the Inner Area Studies and the Inner City Partnerships.

10. see for example, on the US Programmes: Marris & Rein (1971), Warren (1973), Kramer (1969) and, for the 'systemic' conclusion, in particular Rose (1972); on the UK programmes, Community Development Project (1974), Lees & Smith (1975), Edwards and Batley (1978).

11. see for example Dahl (1961) and Almond & Verba (1963).

12. the rejection of the notion that managers were an independent social category had been effectively performed much earlier by Gerth and Mills (1941-42) in their reply to Burnham's (1941) managerialist thesis.

13. see Norman (1975) for a discussion of Pahl's formulations.

14. an urban social movement is defined as: 'a system of practices resulting from the articulation of a conjuncture of the system of urban agents with other social practices in such a way that its development tends objectively towards the structural trans-formation of the urban system or towards a substantial modifi-cation of the power relations in the class struggle, that is to say, in the last resort, in the power of the state' (Castells 1977, p.263).

15. The quotes and the general point made in the sentence come from Engels (1948).

16. As for example, in his account of the effect of house allocation procedures on residents' choice in an urban renewal area of Paris (Castells 1978a, p.112).

17. translations from Portuguese and Spanish texts are by the author.

18. The concern is close to that of Selznick (1949, p.252): 'Attention is being focused on the structural conditions which influence behaviour, we are directed to emphasize constraints, the limitation of alternatives imposed by the system upon its participants'. As he goes on to write 'We are speaking of the logic of action, not of contractual obligations freely assumed'.

19. The terms 'structure' and 'process' are difficult to define precisely and whatever definition is adopted difficulties emerge: processes may be regarded as structured (e.g. queuing for allocation) and in turn structures only exist in as much as they interact through processes. 'Structure' has been taken by some to describe the formally set up 'rules and procedures, the prescribed framework of the organisation' and by others to signify the informally evolved ways of doing things, the 'patterned regularities and processes of interaction....

describing how actors actually transact their work, formulate
policy and allocate resources' (Ranson, Hinings and Greenwood
1980). The term 'structure' has also been used to distinguish
'the organisational framework set up to carry out the management
task' from 'process', 'the way that the management task is
carried out' (Stewart 1971, p.22). Two main distinctions are
being made in these definitions, first between formal-intended
and informal-emergent procedures and second between bodies and
the procedures adopted to do things. My use of the term is
closest to the second (structures are bodies, processes are
the procedures through which they interact), but my concern is
with the structure and processes (often not formally recognised)
which are operative in fact.

20. Williams (1978) present a very similar case for this point of
entry as '... a way of penetrating into the complex of
relationships that structure urban areas. It penetrates this
web at the point of contact between individual consumers and
the allocation of scarce resources. Not only can the allocation
process be exposed but also the reasons for it can be pursued'.

Map 2.1 Brazil: States and Capital cities

Boa Vista
RORAIMA
AMAPA
Macapá
Belém
Sao Luis
Manaus
AMAZONAS
PARA
MARANHAO
Fortaleza
Teresina
CEARA
RIO GRANDE DO NORTE
Natal
Rio Branco
Porto Velho
PIAUI
PARAIBA
João Pessôa
PERNAMBUCO
Recife
Maceió
ALAGOAS
SERGIPE
Aracajú
MATO GROSSO
Cuiabá
GOIAS
FEDERAL DISTRICT
Brasilia
BAHIA
Salvador
Goiania
MINAS GERAIS
Belo Horizonte
ESPIRITO SANTO
Vitoria
SÃO PAULO
RIO DE JANEIRO
PARANA
São Paulo
Rio de Janeiro
Curitiba
SANTA CATARNA
Florianópolis
RIO GRANDE DO SUL
Portoalegre

BRAZIL
SOUTH AMERICA

28

# 2 Incorporation and exclusion in Brazilian development

## INTRODUCTION

An understanding of the processes which have contributed to the
emergence of political authoritarianism as an accompaniment to
(dependent) economic development has been one of the main practical
concerns of the South American literature to which I will refer. The
essence of this material is that it seeks to offer explanations for
particular phenomena and not to establish prescriptive or predictive
laws of political change for economically dependent countries.
However, while the relationship of 'dependence' between the economic,
political and social structures of a country and the international
capitalist system is not regarded as one which in itself determines
political relations and change in a country, it is regarded as defining
the structural situation of that country's dominant classes.  This
external relationship therefore provides part of the framework within
which internal class and group relations are formed but it conditions
rather than determines them;  it does not explain exactly what form
these relations will take.

It is from this perspective that some South American writers
(particularly Cardoso and O'Donnell) have approached the question of
the role of the state and of state bureaucracies.  The state requires
explanation because it is neither a neutrality open to prescriptive
(modernising) recommendations nor purely the subject of universal laws
of capitalist development.  Cardoso adopts the classical marxist thesis
that the state is the means for maintaining dominant class interests
while, unequally, attending the interests of dominated classes;  but
the particular structure adopted by the state 'as a form of articulation
between classes and as the source of values rationalising this articulation' (Cardoso 1975 p.194) will vary in time and place as the balance
between classes and groups can vary.  The particular form which Cardoso
and O'Donnell seek to explain is 'bureaucratic authoritarianism'.  This
chapter will be concerned with retracing, through these and other
authors, the main steps towards this development.  The argument hinges
on the emergence, with changes in the organisation of production, of
two rapidly expanded groups:  the 'urban popular sector' (the working
class and segments of the middle class) and 'the incumbents of technical roles'.

THE DEVELOPMENT OF THE URBAN INDUSTRIAL POPULATION

Before the turn of the century, and for most of them well beyond it, the major Brazilian cities such as Rio de Janeiro, Recife, Salvador and Belem could be characterised as centres of government administration and of relatively confined hinterlands of agricultural production. The urban growth which occurred up to and during the first twenty or thirty years of the twentieth century was more a feature of the expansion of trade in primary products and the consequent development of cities as warehousing and exchange centres than of the expansion of urban-based production. The initial phenomenal growth of Sao Paulo was precisely an expression of the sudden acceleration of this process, as the development of the railways financed by British commercial interests opened up new areas for coffee production. The city's annual growth rate reached fourteen per cent in the 1890's before falling back in the second decade of the twentieth century to a rate of between four and five and a half per cent, which it has maintained up until the present.

These large ratios around the turn of the century were, then, not only on the basis of small absolute figures but also represented an expansion of rural more than of urban industrial production.

'... the city at this time is basically anti-industrial. It is the bastion of oligarchic interests which support the growing integration of the country into the international division of labour, as a specialised producer of primary products'. (Singer 1975 p.109)

Most writers[1] attribute the growth of industry and of an urban working class to the phases of import substitution which began from about the end of the 1920's. From this point, the Brazilian urban population has grown faster than that of the rural areas, the difference being due to a process of migration to the cities.[2] (tables 2.1 and 2.2).

The stimulus to substitution of foreign imports was initially the European and North American depression which reduced Brazil's export earnings from raw materials and therefore its capacity to import. The fact that this had the effect of stimulating production, rather than depression, in Brazil is attributed by writers such as Furtado (1965) and Tavares (1972) to the policy of the government (dominated historically by agricultural export interests) in purchasing surplus coffee to maintain its price above a minimum. Besides protecting coffee growers, this had the secondary effect of maintaining internal purchasing power which expressed itself in a demand for consumer goods which could not now be so easily imported. Domestic production was in this way stimulated:

'Between 1929 and 1937, while imports declined by 23 per cent, industrial output increased by 50 per cent'. (Furtado 1965 p.10).

There were two further effects of this protection of the export agricultural sector. One was, ironically, that, by contributing to the development of the urban industrial sector, it promoted class interests opposed to the political dominance of agrarian landowners. The second was that it set in train an inflationary pressure that itself contributed to the process of import substitution and

Table 2.1

Growth of the Brazilian urban population

| Year | Total Brazil | | All rural areas | | All urban areas | | All cities over 20,000 popn. | | |
|---|---|---|---|---|---|---|---|---|---|
| | Popn. Millions | Annual Average Growth Rate % | Popn. Millions | Propn. of Total | Popn. Millions | Propn. of Total | Popn. Millions | Propn. of Total | Annual Average Growth Rate % |
| 1872 | 10.1 | – | | | | | | | |
| 1890 | 14.3 | 1.9 | | | | | | | |
| 1900 | 17.4 | 2.0 | | | | | 1.3 | 7.0% | |
| 1920 | 30.6 | 2.8 | | | | | – | – | |
| 1940 | 41.2 | 1.5 | 28.4 | 69% | 12.9 | 31% | 6.3 | 15.3% | 3.3 |
| 1950 | 51.9 | 2.3 | 33.1 | 64% | 18.8 | 36% | 10.5 | 20.2% | 5.0 |
| 1960 | 71.0 | 3.1 | 39.0 | 55% | 32.0 | 45% | 19.9 | 28.1% | 6.2 |
| 1970 | 94.5 | 2.9 | 41.6 | 44% | 52.6 | 56% | 37.4 | 39.6% | 6.1 |
| 1980 | 120.3 | 2.6 | 39.0 | 32% | 81.3 | 68% | 56.5 | 47.0% | 4.1 |

Sources:  Fundacao IBGE (1971)
Fundacao IBGE (1973a)
Yap (1972) in Berlinck (1975)
Costa (1975)
World Bank (1982) and Inter American Development Bank (1982)

Table 2.2

Population of the largest cities (in millions)

| Cities | Area of municipalities | | | | | | | | Metropolitan areas | | |
|---|---|---|---|---|---|---|---|---|---|---|---|
| | 1872 | 1890 | 1900 | 1920 | 1940 | 1950 | 1960 | 1970 | 1960 | 1970 | 1980 |
| Sao Paulo | .03 | .06 | .24 | .58 | 1.33 | 2.20 | 3.83 | 5.98 | 4.79 | 7.88 | 12.71 |
| Rio de Janeiro | .27 | .52 | .81 | 1.16 | 1.76 | 2.38 | 3.31 | 4.32 | 4.86 | 6.72 | 9.15 |
| Belo Horizonte | – | – | .01 | .06 | .21 | .35 | .69 | 1.26 | 0.89 | 1.52 | 2.59 |
| Recife | .12 | .11 | .11 | .24 | .35 | .52 | .80 | 1.08 | 1.24 | 1.62 | 2.40 |
| Salvador | .13 | .17 | .21 | .28 | .29 | .42 | .66 | 1.03 | 0.73 | 1.04 | 1.80 |
| Porto Alegre | .04 | .05 | .07 | .18 | .27 | .39 | .62 | .89 | 1.03 | 1.42 | 2.29 |
| Fortaleza | .04 | .04 | .05 | .08 | .18 | .27 | .51 | .87 | 0.66 | 0.89 | 1.62 |
| Belem | .06 | .05 | .10 | .24 | .21 | .25 | .40 | .64 | 0.41 | 0.56 | 1.02 |
| Curitiba | .01 | .02 | .05 | .08 | .14 | .18 | .36 | .62 | 0.51 | 0.67 | 1.47 |
| Brasilia | – | – | – | – | – | – | .14 | .55 | 0.23 | 0.44 | 1.20 |

Source: Fundacao IBGE (1971) and Hogan (1972) and Barat (1982)

Note: The lower rates of growth of the major municipalities (especially Sao Paulo and Rio) in more recent years can be partly attributed to the squeezing out of population to surrounding municipalities of the metropolises.

industrialisation.  It created the possibility of industrial capital
accumulation in the initial phase of substitution simply by maintaining
purchasing power which had previously been satisfied from abroad.
Later, with protection for home producers effectively sustained by the
1939-45 war, the government's control of the foreign exchange rate at
a stable level, as domestic inflation continued, had the effect of
increasing the value of business and government reserves.  There was
an effective transfer of real income from foreign producers, home
agricultural producers and home consumers to industrial producers and
government.  The post-war effect was of a massive capacity to import
materials and equipment for a new round of industrial expansion.

Government monetary policy is seen by Furtado (1965) as acting during
this period in harmony, though quite by chance, with domestic business
interests.  In the first wave of import substitution, until 1945, all
that was needed was a market with purchasing power;  extra demands on
production could be met from idle capacity and the level of technological sophistication (and amounts of capital) required to produce the
consumer goods was low.  As the consumer goods market, at a fixed
technological level, became saturated the post-war increase in coffee
prices and the government's foreign exchange control combined with
inflation to produce the capital concentrations which were required
for investment in production of consumer durables.

Besides the effects of general inflation and government protection,
the import substitution process had its own circular momentum:-
'A policy of industrialisation in itself created the need for imports'
(Furtado 1965 p.86) of intermediary equipment and materials;  the
demand for imports stimulated high prices which themselves justified
new waves of substitution in more sophisticated products which had
hitherto been imported.  This dynamic process continued into the post-
war period as production moved into consumer durable and capital goods,
defended by government protection policies, paid for by high coffee
prices and permitted by the investment which resulted from the income
transferring effect of inflation.[3]

Inflation and the concomitant import substitution had been effective
in transferring income a) from the agricultural to the urban-industrial
sector and b) from the population in general to producers in particular.
Throughout the period until the mid 1950s, the process had been able to
continue apparently without anybody in a very broad 'alliance' losing.
A large number of small firms (see table 2.3) were able to spring up
and survive in the protected market as inflation carried internal
prices and salaries up while the price of imported materials and
infrastructural equipment all remained stable.  An effective transfer
of income from abroad and from export agriculture supported the growth
not only of industrial investment but also of the population of urban
workers.

The other side of the coin was that consumers and export agriculture
were paying the price for this growth, through, in the first case,
inflation and, in the second, discriminatory rates of exchange.  But
at the same time, their losses were disguised, at least temporarily.
Export agriculture earnings were at first sustained by government
purchases and then by the post-war boom in commodity prices;  while

Table 2.3
Number of industrial establishments
and employed workers, 1920 - 1960

| Year | No. of establishments | Employed workers |
|------|----------------------|------------------|
| 1920 | 13,569 | 293,673 |
| 1940 | 49,418 | 781,155 |
| 1950 | 89,086 | 1,256,807 |
| 1960 | 110,339 | 1,422,986 |

Source:  IBGE Comissao Censitaria Nacional, 'Sinopse do Censo
Industrial e do Censo de Servicos' 1948 and 'Anuarios
Estatisticos' of 1958, 1960 and 1963, in Guimaraes de
Souza (1975)

domestic agricultural producers benefited directly from the expansion
of urban markets.  If the urban middle class and industrial working
class were constantly losing from inflation as consumers, they gained
as employees, a) as participants in the growth of employment
opportunities, and b) from the pre and post war labour legislation
delivered by President Getulio Vargas.

POPULISM AND LIMITED INCORPORATION

Vargas's accession to the presidency by coup in 1930 marked the
beginning of a slow transference of power from the traditional ruling
elite, the big landowners associated with coffee culture in the south
eastern States of Sao Paulo (especially), Minas Gerais and Rio de
Janeiro (see map 2.1).  The change is commonly seen as an abrupt one:

'the big coffee cultivators, having lost their great economic
power, helplessly watched the displacement of their
representatives from central and state governments' (Rodrigues
1968)

The transference was however neither sudden nor complete;  no more was
it clear which groups other than the President himself had become the
new elite.  Skidmore shows that Vargas's first coup was supported by a
wide range of 'revolutionary and non-revolutionary supporters of the
change of power' (Skidmore 1969 p.9) who included organised groups as
diverse as the liberal, constitutionalist Democratic Party, the
*tenentes* (a group of military 'semi-authoritarian nationalists whose
main concern was 'national regeneration' and modernisation',  Skidmore
1969 p.9), the higher military, opposition leaders in the States and
even the coffee growers themselves.  The first continuous period of
government by Vargas up until 1945 (and especially the events leading
up to the coup of 1937) can be characterised as one in which all
elements of this initial alliance saw themselves being pulled in and
out of favour and influence, as the President shifted his power base,
weakening the position of organised groups who came too near to
establishing themselves in power.

Removing the focus from the manipulations of the President, the
period can be seen as one of confused conflict between organised groups
expressing different class interests (the rural landowners, urban
industrialists and merchants, and the labour movement) following the
collapse of the old regime's economic basis (in primary production

resting on high export coffee prices) which had sustained the dominance of the rural landowners: 'with the collapse of external relations, this hegemony ended in vacuum' (Oliveira 1976 p.31). For Oliveira (1976), this collapse was the necessary but not the sufficient condition for industrialisation and the dominance of the 'new entrepreneurial, industrial bourgeois classes'. The 'sufficient' condition would be to find a new form of accumulation which would depend on a new relationship between capital and labour. Corporatism and populism would be the political expression of and the condition for establishing this relationship; the urban population (subsuming industrial workers) is associated as a direct, but dependent and disorganised, mass beneficiary of a personalised state.[4]

It can be argued that corporatism/populism and industrialisation/ urbanisation were themselves the outcome of the conjuncture between the country's external relations and internal class conflicts. Thus, industrialisation was partly a consequence of the satisfaction of coffee growers' interests, the collapse of import capacity, and the availability of capital for new forms of investment. On the other hand, the suppression of regionally based oligarchies (including the coffee growers) contributed to the intervention of the federal government into fields of previously local responsibility - education, labour, credit, inter State tax and coffee marketing - and eventually into industrial production. Moreover, the incorporation of the growing urban working class into the emerging structure of the state through the passage of the labour laws was itself a part of the attempt to suppress the 'subversive' Left, through pre-emption of its potential base. The effect of this sort of interpretation is to argue neither that the outcome was intended by a manipulating Vargas or even by the 'nascent industrial bourgeoisie', nor that the outcome was inevitable, but to see the corporate industrialising political economy which emerged as the product of a shifting balance of class interests. The effect, if not the intention, was 'a class pact in which a nascent industrial bourgeoisie will use the support of the urban working class to politically liquidate the old rural propertied classes' (Oliveira 1976).

The labour legislation, which had the effect of including the industrial working class as direct beneficiaries or clients of the state, organised workers into unions registered and regulated through the Ministry of Labour, established minimum wages set by government, and channelled pension and medical benefits through the unions and social welfare institutes. From 1937, the newly organised unions were given a role in the formal (and nominal) political institutional structure with the establishment of a National Constituent Assembly representing professional groups including union members. In the war years, intervention became more direct with the appointment by government of certain union leaders and the imposition of a tax on members and its redistribution by government to unions. The unions were in effect tied into an allegiant relationship with the presidency; the price for the right to organise and for the income and welfare rights which were channelled through them was that (if it ever had had it) 'the trade union lost its character as an instrument of working class defence and struggle and increasingly participated in the sphere of social domination --- And the syndicalised mass became a politico-electoral support for Vargas and his political successors'

(Rodrigues 1968 p.78). The growth of union organisation and at the same time its vulnerability to government regulation is illustrated in table 2.4.

Table 2.4
Numbers of unions and union members 1930-1961

| Year | No. of unions (a) | No. of members approx.(b) | Percent of active industrial population(c) |
|------|------|------|------|
| 1930 | 372 | 179,330 | - |
| 1931* | 21 | - | - |
| 1932 | 115 | - | - |
| 1933 | 256 | - | - |
| 1934* | 367 | - | - |
| 1935 | 440 | - | - |
| 1936 | 682 | 308,387 | - |
| 1937 | 916 | - | - |
| 1938 | 955 | - | - |
| 1939* | 1208 | 351,514 | 23% |
| 1940 | 8 | - | - |
| 1942 | 644 | - | - |
| 1945 | 873 | 474,943 | - |
| 1952 | 1096 | 747,309 | 32% |
| 1961 | 1669 | 1,023,517 | 35% |

Notes: All figures are approximate
       * Years in which government imposes regulatory decrees

Sources: Boletim do Ministerio de Trabalho, Industria e Comercio
         and Servico de Estatistica da Previdencia e Trabalho (in
         Rodrigues 1968).

         From 1955, Anuario Estatistico do IBGE (in Rodrigues 1968).
         Pre 1955, estimates collated by Rodrigues.

         Calculation based on figures from Fundacao IBGE (1973) for
         years where there is a data overlap (within 1 year's
         difference).

The degree to which the industrial labour force actually benefited from their 'rights' is at least questionable: the application of the labour laws was (and is) scarcely supervised and periodic.[5] Singer shows that post-war industrial salaries increased against the cost of living though not consistently as a proportion of industrial value added (table 2.5).

The benefits of all classes participating in this 'alliance' were, then, periodic and set against each other. In that sense it can perhaps be described less as an alliance than as a system which included them all as political actors. The mass of the population, rural workers, were excluded from this participation, although they were in various ways affected by the processes which had brought other classes into a relationship articulated through the state. They were affected whether it was by the permeation of capitalist relations of production into sectors of agriculture[6] or by the subordination of

Table 2.5
Industrial salaries and cost of living

| | Sao Paulo | | | Rio de Janeiro | | |
|------|-----------|---------|-------------|---------|---------|-------------|
| Year | Average Salary | Cost of living | % of value added | Average Salary | Cost of Living | % of value added |
| 1945 | 100 | 100 | 22.5 | 100 | 100 | 21.6 |
| 1948 | 172 | 159 | 23.0 | 174 | 145 | 26.0 |
| 1949 | 193 | 157 | 25.5 | 203 | 152 | 28.4 |
| 1950 | 189 | 167 | 23.3 | 227 | 167 | 27.2 |
| 1951 | 213 | 181 | 22.5 | 228 | 187 | 26.7 |

Source:  Singer (1976 p.32)

export agriculture to industrial accumulation.[7]  For many, the direct
effect was expulsion from the land either with the destruction of the
subsistence economy, or with the freeing of tied labour, or with
competitive land acquisition, or as the result of under-investment
in agriculture.  Vargas's labour laws in no way protected agricultural
labour and the only way out was by migration to the urban centres and
to the agricultural frontiers of Goias and Mato Grosso (table 2.6).

Table 2.6
Rates of emigration and immigration by state 1940 and 1950

| State | Rate of emigration(E) | | Rate of immigration(I) | | Difference (I-E) | |
|-------|------|------|------|------|--------|--------|
| | 1940 | 1950 | 1940 | 1950 | 1940 | 1950 |
| Immigration States | | | | | | |
| Parana | 6.2 | 4.9 | 17.5 | 31.4 | + 11.3 | + 26.5 |
| Goias | 5.1 | 3.8 | 18.8 | 23.2 | + 13.7 | + 19.4 |
| Rio de Janeiro | 5.9 | 4.9 | 14.6 | 18.2 | + 8.7 | + 13.3 |
| Sao Paulo | 4.0 | 6.4 | 10.4 | 11.8 | + 6.4 | + 5.4 |
| Acre | 15.0 | 13.7 | 28.7 | 25.6 | + 13.7 | + 11.9 |
| Mato Grosso | 4.6 | 7.8 | 16.5 | 19.3 | + 11.9 | + 11.5 |
| Maranhao | 6.5 | 6.6 | 10.6 | 10.2 | + 3.7 | + 3.6 |
| Intermediate States | | | | | | |
| Santo Catarina | 5.6 | 7.9 | 9.2 | 9.8 | + 3.6 | + 1.9 |
| Para | 4.6 | 7.2 | 8.2 | 8.8 | + 3.6 | + 1.6 |
| Amazonas | 6.1 | 10.4 | 12.3 | 12.0 | + 6.2 | + 1.6 |
| Rio Grande do Norte | 9.5 | 10.4 | 8.3 | 8.0 | − 1.2 | − 2.4 |
| Pernambuco | 8.8 | 8.9 | 4.9 | 6.2 | − 3.9 | − 2.7 |
| Emigration States | | | | | | |
| Rio Grande do Sul | 4.0 | 4.8 | 1.3 | 1.1 | − 2.7 | − 3.7 |
| Piaui | 13.2 | 13.1 | 8.2 | 8.3 | − 5.0 | − 4.8 |
| Ceara | 9.3 | 9.4 | 4.3 | 4.1 | − 5.0 | − 5.3 |
| Bahia | 8.2 | 8.4 | 2.7 | 3.0 | − 5.5 | − 5.4 |
| Espirito Santo | 9.6 | 16.3 | 14.2 | 10.8 | + 4.6 | − 5.5 |
| Paraiba | 10.8 | 13.3 | 7.4 | 5.9 | − 3.4 | − 7.4 |
| Sergipe | 13.0 | 15.1 | 6.2 | 5.7 | − 6.8 | − 9.4 |
| Alagoas | 13.1 | 16.8 | 6.3 | 6.1 | − 6.8 | − 10.7 |
| Minas Gerais | 11.3 | 15.5 | 2.9 | 2.8 | − 8.4 | − 12.7 |

Source:  Lopes (1968)

The participation of the new urban population sector both in the expansion of the economy and as a force which could express itself politically leads O'Donnell (1973 p.55) to characterise Brazil through this period until 1964 as an 'incorporating political system --- that purposely seeks to activate the popular sector and to allow it some voice in national politics'. Cardoso is clear about the dependent and transitory nature of this participation: where the state is 'a form of articulation between classes and --- the source of the rationalising values of this articulation' (Cardoso 1975 p.194), populism is just one expression of a continuously and essentially 'patrimonial' state in which the masses are always disorganised and dependent on political elites for the satisfaction of their interests: 'In Latin America it is not the state which has to present its credentials, but the individual' (Cardoso 1975 p.156).

## THE COLLAPSE OF THE POPULIST ALLIANCE

The interlinking of effects - market protection, import substitution, inflation, export prices and exchange rates - which sustained this shifting balance of classes was, however, vulnerable to (a) the increasing capital requirements of import substitution and (b) the fall in coffee prices which occurred after 1954. Some of the momentum of industrialisation was sustained by the investment undertaken by industrialists in the early 1950's (Tavares 1972 p.61) which allowed a further growth in production, employment and industrial salaries. But industrialisation had reached a stage requiring more sophisticated and capitalised investments at a time when the terms of trade began to deteriorate.

The effect of these strains was to bring the state further into the operation of the economy in an increasingly conscious attempt to maintain industrial development against growing contradictions. The extension, in the pre-war period, of central government intervention into local administration, labour relations and coffee marketing can be seen as the response to group pressures which had the effect but not the intention of promoting industrialisation. From 1938, and especially in the post-war Vargas period (1951-1954) and under Kubitschek (1956-1961), it becomes possible to see state intervention in economic management as a much more direct and planned response to national and international business pressure and increasingly in the state bureaucracy's own interests.

State involvement grew specifically in the organisation of the capital market and in the ownership of highly capitalised production. The Bank of Brazil was used to channel loans at sub-inflation rates to entrepreneurs, and, as a much more directive instrument, the National Bank for Economic Development (BNDE) was set up in 1952 to 'eliminate or reduce the infrastructural deficiencies which impede the regular development of the Brazilian economy'. Whereas, the Bank of Brazil effectively contributed to inflation by subsidising easy credit, the BNDE acted as an instrument of capital accumulation by financing investment (much of it public) in future productive capacity out of income tax. It represented a significant step towards more planned and technically sophisticated intervention in economic management:

> 'The realisation of the necessity of thinking before investing
> began to develop in Brazil in the 1940's. The foundation of

BNDE coincided with the beginning of the more ordered Brazil of today...' 8

The BNDE was one result of a Joint Brazil - United States Economic Development Commission whose intention and effect was to create conditions not only for domestic but also for foreign investment. The Commission's plans for infrastructural development, especially in transport and power, were designed to be 'technically adapted to the requirements of foreign financing institutions, such as the Export-Import Bank, and the Bank for International Reconstruction and Development'.[9] Direct investment of foreign capital was also officially promoted and protected, at times by Vargas and consistently by Kubitscheck, as a supplement to Brazil's reduced capacity to borrow and earn capital from abroad. This programme of sustained investment at a time of decline in the terms of trade was in the end deeply inflationary. Private and public, domestic and foreign investment rested on incentives, credit, guarantees about the maintenance of domestic and publicly stimulated investment opportunities (among which the building of Brasilia can be counted). At the same time, as the exporting underpin to the programme, the coffee growers received continuous government price support.

By the end of the 1950's, the government found itself caught in a series of contradictions. Foreign investment and loans were more than ever necessary to sustain development, but demanded (most notably through the International Monetary Fund) anti-inflationary, stabilisation policies as guarantees of their return. But sudden deflation would lead to the collapse of the whole rapid development strategy and the costs would be borne by no group willingly. The income transferring effects of inflation, differential exchange rates and direct taxation became unsustainable as the groups suffering the withdrawals attempted to maintain their incomes and capital. The hitherto key to industrial growth - the effective taxation of coffee exports and subsidisation of equipment imports - had to be abandoned and gave way to attempts to 'cover the lack of reserve funds by further emissions of paper money':

> '... inflation ceased to be an effective mechanism for the redistribution of income and more and more, became simply a sterile game of passing the buck'. (Furtado 1965 p.107)

The populist 'alliance', 'pact' or 'coalition' was shown to be vulnerable to the fortunes of the agrarian exporters and ultimately to be internally divided. The common interest between urban workers and unions, middle class employees and technicians (*tecnicos*) of private industry and government, and industrial and agricultural producers supplying the urban market broke down when rapid inflation[10] and consequent foreign exchange shortage exposed their different capacity for self defence. The last pre-military government under Joao Goulart saw the populist alliance collapse under it as it oscillated between the unacceptability to investors and lenders (including the IMF) of sustained inflation, to producers of policies to control prices and credit, and to consumers/workers of leaving inflation uncompensated by pay increases. Essentially, Goulart's identification by investors and producers with the syndicalised labour movement, as the result of his posts as Labour Minister under Vargas and Kubitschek, and his unwillingness to undertake deflation as a whole and wage suppression

in particular, forced him back on the mobilisation of the unions as a
last bastion of support.  The only other alternative, the development
plan launched by his Finance and Planning Ministers (Dantas and
Furtado), depended on foreign debt refinancing and high taxes as a
basis for investment in manufactured exports.  It required but failed
to get the support of the groups it would penalise.

Goulart's annual presidential message to Congress on March 15
signalled his resort to the radical mobilisation which was crushed by
the Army on 31 March 1964:

> 'I have chosen to fight the privileged and to assume the
> initiative for basic reforms, which will make possible the
> replacement of the structures and institutions that are
> inadequate for the peaceful continuation of our progress
> and for the establishment of a complete and effective
> democratic community'. 11

TOWARDS EXCLUSION

O'Donnell (1973) argues that the conditions for a new class alliance
to exclude the demands of the 'popular sector' had been created during
the period of industrial expansion.  The 1964 military coup had the
support of all propertied classes and of the new 'technocratic sector'
which had grown with government intervention and the development of
larger scale public and private, domestic and foreign production. What
essentially united them was that the political and economic demands of
the urban 'popular sector' (the working and non-professional middle
classes) were now dysfunctional to all other classes.  Where previously
the development of urban demand had promoted the ascendancy of
industrialists and commercial businessmen over agrarian landowners,
now, with import substitution exhausted partly for lack of capital,
continued wage and consumer demand implied political and economic
redistribution away also from owners, investors and the managing
'technocrats'.  The reality of this threat was apparently confirmed
by the recent example of the Cuban revolution and by the evident
vulnerability of the Brazilian Government.

If the exclusion[12] of the urban popular sector was, in this view,
desirable it was also eminently possible, both in the sense that working
class political incorporation had historically been as a dependent
adjunct to a 'patrimonial' state and in the sense that the fragility of
the incorporating political system had itself been demonstrated.
Ultimately it was not only the urban working class which was to find
itself excluded but also all those petty producers who had grown up
in the period of protected import substitution and who depended now
on the expansion of their traditional markets.  If one interpretation
of the crisis was lack of demand to sustain the horizontal development
of the Brazilian economy, the dominant post-revolutionary understanding
was that the crisis was in over demand of this sort, under demand for
sophisticated products, inefficient production, an insufficient foreign
earnings capacity and in lack of access to capital for a new wave of
investment.

> '... the years 1967 and 1968 represented a watershed in Brazilian
> economic history.  By then it was evident that import
> substitution as a motor force for development had practically
> run its course and that a new emphasis on export growth was

40

essential'. (Baer in Roett 1976 p.64).

The interests which underlay this sort of interpretation of development needs had grown up within but were no longer satisfied by the economic and political structure which had preceded. We have seen that the stages of import substitution increasingly depended on state management of capital access and infrastructural development and on the participation of foreign (and international) creditors, investors and producers. The very development of the Brazilian economy and its urban market both required this participation and also attracted it.

O'Donnell argues that not only had new elements been introduced into the productive base but also that these elements had themselves generated a semi-independent set of political actors:

> 'Larger organisations engaged in more complex production, the effects of industrialisation upon communications, marketing, publicity, and information-processing services, as well as the need for coordination of more diversified social units and activities - all require increasing 'inputs' of persons who have gone through prolonged training in techniques of production, planning and control. As modernisation proceeds, more techno-cratic roles are to be found in more and more social activities'. (O'Donnell 1973 p.80)[13]

It is the incumbents of these roles in civilian government, the military and larger private firms that O'Donnell places at the core of the 'coup coalition' and of the post-revolution political system. Cardoso similarly identifies the emergence and political role of the 'technobureaucrat':

> 'In the current stage of development of monopoly capitalism, the large firm, differentiated in its products and markets, extends itself globally - uniting by internationalisation markets which were previously national - and meets in the bureaucratic organisation and in the technocratic ethos its form of expression' (Cardoso 1975 p.161)

Both Cardoso and O'Donnell are cautious and speculative about the relationship of the 'technobureaucracy' or the 'incumbents of technical roles' with dominant social classes and with the state. They are a distinct social group (an 'elite sub-set' for O'Donnell) but not a social class with an independent relation to the mode of production. Cardoso (1975 p.41) comes close, though tentatively, to a class definition when he identifies his interest as being in a 'state bourgeoisie' without ownership but with control of the 'state productive apparatus'.[14] However, he extends his 'technobureaucracy' to include not only the managers of 'state capitalist companies' concerned with infrastructure, credit and communication but also the less defined and broader civil and military bureaucracies which 'control the state'.

O'Donnell is concerned with those involved in 'production, planning and control' in public and private large scale organisations. While he explains their emergence in terms of changes in the productive structure and describes them as the'core of the coup coalition' which included large scale capitalist interests, he insists that technocratic role performance cannot be simply explained as the expression of 'the objective interests of social sectors (including classes) and organisations' (O'Donnell 1973 p.87) but also in terms of the technocrat's particular experience and perceptions.

Cardoso is more specifically concerned with the social structure of the relation between the 'technobureaucracy' and dominant classes, and what he proposes is a complex and often apparently contradictory (or dialectic) relationship. The 'technobureaucracy' (and the corporate state with which it is associated) is not merely an expression of the interests of monopoly capital nor is it, on the other hand, anti-capitalist:

> '... even if it frequently contradicts private interests, it ensures the conditions for capital accumulation and for the private appropriation of the means of production' (Cardoso 1973 p.46)[15]

The state undertaking may have been set up 'as a countervailing power to the internationalisation of the market' (Cardoso 1973 p.45) but, ultimately, in a context of dependent development, state (as also private national) enterprises are drawn into an 'alliance' with multinational companies, and '... the functionary and the businessman come to share the new role of 'technobureaucrat'. (Cardoso 1975 p.161). While there will be differences of interest between state functionaries and private capital:

> '... in terms of the political relations between the bourgeoisie and the state, between the technocrat and professional middle class and the business owner, this (technobureaucratic) transformation permits the interests of these distinct groups to bury themselves in the framework of a new corporatism'. (Cardoso 1975 p.161)

Within this corporatism the 'technobureaucrat' is exposed and responsive to a narrow range of class interests expressed through 'bureaucratic rings' which seem to give the state itself the character of an independent political actor. The national and international private (and even public) undertakings which benefit from the new regime ('industrial exporters, works contractors, extractive exporters, multinational capital linked to production and finance capital') come to stand in an ambiguous, mutually manipulative relationship with the state, articulated through the technobureaucracy. Narrow bureaucratic 'rings' serve to give privileged access to dominant class interests, but the effect of bureaucratic processing, even on these, is to separate and 'de-class' them so that only 'specific and individualised political and economic interests can be present in the decision-making system' (Cardoso 1975 p.209). The relation between state and society comes to be mediated by bureaucratic organisations, and through these channels 'the interests of civil society come to exist within the state' (Cardoso 1975 p.184).

While the authoritarian bureaucratic state is thus capable of coopting and satisfying dominant class interests, Cardoso argues that there is no simple or even necessary relationship between the interests of capital and the emergence of an authoritarian state. It is here that he tentatively allows an independent place for the 'state bourgeoisie'. It supports and does not alter the mechanism of capital accumulation, but it can influence the particular political form which guarantees this activity so as

'to impose a vision of the state capable of leading to the
expansion of its spheres of economic and political influence.
Could it be that the real basis of current authoritarianism
rests on this 'state bourgeoisie' and the power axis (military
and civil) which forms around it?'. (Cardoso 1975 p.41).

Both Cardoso and O'Donnell therefore argue that public functionaries
have acted, at least in the evolution of political form, to expand
the range of influence of their own roles and perceptions.[16] The
political forms so derived even influence the expression of dominant
class interests. What is proposed is a complicated relationship
between social structure and action, where the 'technobureaucrat's'
action is affected not only by class relations but also by the
peculiar perceptions and constraints which emerge from particular
role situations. The distinction is not final: the productive base
is influential through the socio-economic structure both on the
frequency and nature of societal roles and on the configuration of
class relations and organisational arrangements which affect role
performance. Indeed, even if the connection is not simple or direct,
the case for an authoritarian, excluding political system which rests
on the fulfilment of technocratic roles was coincident with the large-
scale capitalist case for the suppression of popular economic demand
at this particular time in Brazil. As Cardoso (1975 p.40) says the
common and uniting 'principal enemies' were 'the democratising
pressures of the mass and the various revolutionary groups'.

Having derived the emergence and extension of technocratic roles in
Brazil (and Argentina) from an examination of changes in the
'productive-industrial base', O'Donnell seeks to explain their part
in the inauguration of a bureaucratic-authoritarian regime largely
from an examination of the technocrat's role expectations. His
explanation depends on the idea that role models are transferred from
industrialised societies (as a component of their technologies and
administrative apparatus as well as by direct and indirect education)
and are then placed in a social context which differs from that of the
originating society. Together with the particular technical expertise,
expectations are transferred about patterns of role performance and
the sort of support, rewards and achievement criteria through which
they can expect to relate to society as a whole. Much of the transfer
may be incidental to the penetration of foreign capital and technology,
as Sunkel (1970, 1974) has described, but it is clear that in the case
of Brazilian public administration, since Vargas's reforms, there have
been direct attempts to adopt foreign (and especially North American)
administrative models (Graham 1968).

In the encounter with the new social context the technical knowledge
and role expectations are found to be at least partially inapplicable,
or, from the 'incumbent's' point of view, his role expectations are
frustrated. Graham identified this sense of frustration in his study
of the pre-revolutionary civil service:

'Most of the interviewees took refuge in the idea that the goal
of 'modern' economic, efficient administration will become
realizable only in time, as the social and economic system
matures. But they are equally aware that there is not the time

43

to wait. Administrators in Brazil have increasingly emphasised
the necessity for more effective public administration if further
progress is to be made in the area of economic development'.
(Graham, 1968 p.92)

O'Donnell (1973 p.82) suggests that the frustration of the role model
leads to 'a drive to reshape the social context in forms that, it is
hoped, will be more congenial to the learned expertise and reward
expectations of these individuals'. Briefly, the technocrat takes
direct action to remove the 'obstacles' to 'rational', 'efficient'
government and economic growth which are expressed in the ambiguities
of open politics and in the developmental 'bottlenecks' of small-scale
business and dispersed demand. The possibility for doing so in
organised political action becomes more apparent as technocratic roles
spread (with the changes in productive structure that we have noted)
through large scale business, government and the military and as it
becomes apparent that views are shared in all the main centres of
administrative capacity.

O'Donnell's explanation hinges on a dependency theory which allows
little autonomy in role formation to the receiving society. A less
'dependent' case can be made if we argue with Cardoso that it is part
of the 'patrimonial' history of Brazil that dominant classes have
tended to appropriate and privatise the public sector, and with Graham
that the ideology surrounding Brazilian public administration
(especially under Vargas) has fused it with rather than separated it
from politics, so that the civil and military authorities attribute
to themselves a modernising mission. Bolaffi (1977) puts particular
emphasis on the self-conscious tradition of the Brazilian armed forces
as the institutional expression of national integration, and on their
peculiarly managerial and technocratic character.

From this position, if others fail to appreciate the rationality of
the technocratic view it is because they do not have access to the
techniques which give rise to the understanding, and not because
interests are fundamentally different. Civilian politics and popular
participation then appear as the expression of ignorant self-interest,
corruption and incompetence. Opposition quickly comes to be seen as
mistaken, malicious or selfish; repression can then be justified in
the broader interest, or in the interests of the 'future' or even in
the interest of the repressed.

ACTS OF EXCLUSION

The 1964 'revolution' did not bring with it a sudden and complete
programme of exclusion. Rather an excluding momentum developed from
the new government's initial institutional changes and policy
commitments and, more generally from the interests and values which
were most closely associated with it. By a definition which saw
existing political and union leaders as the representatives of
blockages and irrationality in the system rather than of legitimate
interests, there was nothing inherently illogical in the new
government's first acts to establish its authority over these groups,
in the name not only of economic development but also of

> 'the restoration of Brazilian democracy. Not only of the people
> by the people and for the people, but also to bring about a

conception of life in which there exists respect for human
dignity and social justice'.[17]

The political rights of selected politicians, union leaders,
intellectuals, officials and military officers were suspended in the
first months of the new government;  congressional powers were reduced
severely;  and the new military-appointed President was given reserve
powers to declare a state of seige and to cancel the mandates of
elected representatives.  Control over the expression of political
dissent grew as the excluding effects of the new regime's economic
policy became more apparent.  Gubernatorial electoral losses, urban
guerrilla activity and street demonstrations contributed successively
to the introduction of an indirect election system for governors and
President, the reorganisation and control of political parties, press
censorship, political imprisonment and repression.  Ultimately, there
was no room for mass support in an economic policy based, on the one
hand, on anti-inflationary wage suppression and the restriction of
credit to inefficient producers and, on the other hand, on long term
expansion through sustained public and private capital concentration.
The economic model itself came to act as an instrument of exclusion and
selected incorporation.

Brazil entered a period of rapid economic growth from 1968 (table 2.7).

Table 2.7
Yearly growth rates of real GDP and
per capita GDP for industry and agriculture

| Years | Real GDP | Per capita real GDP | Industry | Agriculture |
|---|---|---|---|---|
| | | (per cent) | | |
| 1956-62(a) | 7.8 | 4.0 | 10.3 | 5.7 |
| 1962-67(a) | 3.7 | 1.3 | 3.9 | 4.0 |
| 1968 | 9.3 | 6.3 | 15.0 | 1.5 |
| 1969 | 9.0 | 5.9 | 11.0 | 6.0 |
| 1970 | 9.5 | 6.4 | 11.1 | 5.6 |
| 1970-78(a) | 9.2 | 6.0 | 10.1 | 5.3 |
| 1979 | 6.4 | 3.9 | 6.9 | 3.2 |
| 1980 | 8.0 | 5.5 | 8.3 | 8.1 |
| 1981 | -3.0 | -5.3 | - | - |

Note (a) Yearly average

Sources: for 1956-70, calculated from data of Fundacao Getulio Vargas,
         published in 'Conjuntura Economica' (various issues);
         for 1970-81, from World Bank (1980); CEPAL (1982);  Latin
         American Regional Reports Brazil 6 February 1981.

The overall massive increase in gross domestic product was the result
of expansion in investment and output specifically in the sectors
promoted by government economic policy:- state infrastructural industries
(steel, electric power and road construction), associated manufacturing
industries (transport equipment, electrical equipment), and the manufacture of consumer durables (cars, televisions, refrigerators) and
chemicals.  In manufacturing, the growth areas were precisely those
which required large scale capital intensive production and foreign
investment, while the areas of relative or absolute decline were the

45

established industries (textiles, clothing, food products) requiring labour intensive production and an extension of low income demand (table 2.8).

Table 2.8
Average annual growth rates of individual sectors

| | 1967-70 | 1971 | (per cent) 1972 | 1973 | 1974 |
|---|---|---|---|---|---|
| Nonmetal minerals | 17.3 | 11.1 | 13.7 | 16.4 | 15.1 |
| Metal products | 14.4 | 5.6 | 12.1 | 6.3 | 4.3 |
| Machinery | 22.7 | 3.6 ) | 18.9 ) | 27.8 ) | 11.6 |
| Electrical equipment | 13.4 | 21.3 ) | | ) | |
| Transport equipment | 32.6 | 19.0 | 22.5 | 27.6 | 19.1 |
| Paper and paper products | 9.1 | 6.3 | 7.0 | 10.1 | 3.5 |
| Rubber products | 15.3 | 11.8 | 13.0 | 12.4 | 10.8 |
| Chemicals | 15.6 | 13.6 | 16.3 | 22.3 | 8.5 |
| Textiles | 7.4 | 8.8 ) | 4.1 ) | 8.4 ) | -2.8 |
| Clothing, shoes, etc. | 1.7 | -1.8 ) | | ) | |
| Food products | 8.3 | 3.6 ) | ) | ) | |
| Beverages | 8.2 | 4.8 ) | 13.3 ) | 9.6 ) | 4.4 |
| Tobacco | 9.6 | 5.7 ) | ) | ) | |
| Total Manufacturing | 14.2 | 11.6 | 13.6 | 15.8 | 7.1 |
| Construction | 14.4 | 8.4 | 13.0 | 15.4(a) | 11.2(a) |
| Public utilities | 12.2 | N.A. | 11.1 | 12.5(a) | 12.0(a) |

Note (a) Estimates based on January-November results in 1973 and 1974.
     N.A. = not available.
     Source:  Baer (in Roett 1976).

   This highly focused and directed form of economic development was based on increases in

a)   direct government involvement in production through state enterprises;[18]

b)   state enterprise participation in private enterprise through investment and asset ownership;

c)   state direction of credit through state banks, savings institutions, and tax incentives;

d)   direct multinational company involvement in production, especially of consumer durables;

e)   foreign official loans and private investment;

f)   imported capital equipment and technology.

The massive inflow of foreign official and private capital and the rising trade and service debt are indicated in table 2.9.  The pattern of production which emerged from this form of development excluded the mass of the population from its market in two essential ways:  the nature of the products and the need to pay for imported capital and equipment required (a) an export orientation and (b) a relatively rich and sophisticated home market.  The capital-intensive and highly regionally and sectorally focused pattern of production itself excluded the mass of the population as income-earning beneficiaries, while increasing the earnings of skilled workers, technicians, managers and investors.[19]  By contributing to a geographical and a social

Table 2.9
Brazil's foreign economic and balance
of payments positions
(US $ billion)

| | 1960-64[a] | 1965-69[a] | 1969 | 1972 | 1975 | 1978 | 1980 | 1981 |
|---|---|---|---|---|---|---|---|---|
| Exports | 1.3 | 1.8 | 2.3 | 3.9 | 8.5 | 12.5 | 20.1 | 23.3 |
| Imports | 1.3 | 1.5 | 2.0 | 4.2 | 12.1 | 13.6 | 23.0 | 22.1 |
| Trade balance | .91 | .33 | .32 | -.25 | -3.6 | -1.2 | -2.8 | 1.2 |
| Service balance | -.34 | -.51 | -.64 | -1.4 | -3.5 | -6.0 | -10.2 | -12.4 |
| Net foreign direct investment | .07 | .08 | .14 | .38 | .97 | 1.0 | 1.2 | 1.6 |
| Net foreign loans | .35 | .61 | 1.1 | 4.3 | 4.9 | 8.4 | 8.1 | 10.0 |
| Foreign debt | 2.9 | - | 4.4 | 12.6 | 22.0 | 43.5 | 58.5 | 61.4 |
| Reserves | - | .40 | .65 | 6.8 | 4.0 | 12.2 | 6.9 | 7.1 |

Note (a) Year average
Sources:  for 1960-69, Baer (in Roett 1976)
          for 1972-81, World Bank (1980, 1982);  Latin American
                       Regional Reports Brazil (6 February 1981);
                       Inter-American Development Bank (1982);
                       CEPAL (1982).

concentration of income, the productive structure thus helped to create
a 'demand profile' suitable to its output.[20] Table 2.10 shows that
income concentration increased over the ten years from 1960, at the
expense of the bottom 80 per cent of the population. Wells (1974) and

Table 2.10
Changes in Brazil's income distribution

| Percentile groups of households | Percentage shares of household income | | Per capita income in US dollars | |
|---|---|---|---|---|
| | 1960 | 1970 | 1960 | 1970 |
| Lower 40% | 11.2 | 9.0 | 84 | 90 |
| Next 40% | 34.3 | 27.8 | 257 | 278 |
| Next 15% | 27.0 | 27.0 | 540 | 720 |
| Top 5% | 27.4 | 36.3 | 1645 | 2940 |
| Total | 100.0 | 100.0 | Average 300 | Average 400 |

Source:  calculated from IBGE 1970 (from Baer in Roett 1976).

DIEESE (1975 pp.33,61) show, furthermore, that real wages fell in the
second half of the 1960's and then rose only at a rate substantially
below the increase in the rate of productivity (table 2.11).

Direct government action helped not only to focus investment but also
to sustain income concentration and capital accumulation by its effect
on the income and disposal of income of wage-earners.  This was partly
by direct control of wage negotiation and partly by the operation of

Table 2.11
Value of modal wage compared with index of production

| Year | Index of per capita productivity [a] | Year | Real value of modal wage [b] |
|---|---|---|---|
| 1964 | 100 | 1964/65 | 100 |
| 1965 | 100 | 1965/66 | 90 |
| 1966 | 102 | 1966/67 | 73 |
| 1967 | 104 | 1967/68 | 74 |
| 1968 | 110 | 1968/69 | 72 |
| 1969 | 117 | 1969/70 | 75 |
| 1970 | 124 | 1970/71 | 82 |
| 1971 | 135 | 1971/72 | 80 |
| 1972 | 144 | 1972/73 | 79 |
| 1973 | 156 | 1973/74 | 71 |
| 1974 | 167 | 1974/75 | 73-70 |

Source:  DIEESE (1975 pp.33,61)
Notes:  (a) an index of the increase of the real national product
per head of population, with 1963 as the base year.
(b) an index of the real value of the most commonly
occurring wage, based on the wages of 81 categories
or workers.

old and new instruments of fiscal welfare - the 'minimum wage' which,
as the government fixed basis for salary agreements, was suppressed
below 1966 real values until 1976 (table 2.12), and the state savings
and insurance schemes for regularly employed workers.  'Forced' savings
from lower income groups (among others), as well as private voluntary
and government savings, have thus been added to the resources available
for governmental infrastructure development.[21] Two ex planning
ministers (Simonsen and Campos 1974 p.10) argued the technical case
for these 'sacrifices' in 'the orthodox recognition that any type of
developmental process has to be based on savings and market considerations:  the first requirement for rapid and sustained growth is a high
rate of savings'.

    The case for 'letting the cake grow before dividing it' (Simonsen
1975) rests on the assumption that the model of economic growth is not
inherently exclusive and that it will eventually draw the mass of the
population into its circle of beneficiaries.  Baer (in Roett 1976)
suggests and Pereira (1973) argues that for the foreseeable future the
20 per cent of the population receiving 63 per cent of the income offers
a sufficient market and labour force for the 'modern' sector's expansion.
In the meantime, proponents of the present model argue that
redistribution can only be reconciled with the key objective of maximum
economic growth if it is offered indirectly through untransferable
public services so that no 'distortive' demand is created:

    '... an extension of free education, an improvement in the
    educational pyramid, credit facilities for low income housing,
    small business and small rural establishments, retirement
    benefits for rural workers and the creation of the retirement
    funds for industrial and government workers and the programme
    for social integration'. (Simonsen and Campos 1974 p.187)[22]

Table 2.12
Changes in real value of minimum salary in Rio de Janeiro
and Sao Paulo 1959 and 1963-1978 (1963=100)

| Year | Rio de Janeiro (a) | Sao Paulo (b) | (c) |
|------|------|------|------|
| 1959 | 117.5 | 127.4 | 133.2 |
| 1963 | 100.0 | 100.0 | 100.0 |
| 1964 | 100.4 | 102.7 | 108.9 |
| 1965 | 93.4 | 98.0 | 101.6 |
| 1966 | 86.2 | 86.9 | 86.1 |
| 1967 | 82.8 | 84.0 | 81.5 |
| 1968 | 83.7 | 83.9 | 80.8 |
| 1969 | 80.6 | 79.9 | 76.8 |
| 1970 | 78.9 | 80.7 | 78.1 |
| 1971 | 79.0 | 80.2 | 75.8 |
| 1972 | 81.1 | 81.2 | 74.6 |
| 1973 | 84.2 | 82.4 | 69.2 |
| 1974 | 78.8 | 78.6 | 63.2 |
| 1975 | 82.9 | 82.0 | 65.5 |
| 1976 | 83.9 | 86.8 | 66.7 |
| 1977 | 84.1 | 89.0 | 68.4 |
| 1978 | 86.0 | 91.3 | 69.8 |

Notes: (a) The figures are calculated for Rio against the cost of
living index of the Fundacao Getulio Vargas.
(b) The first Sao Paulo figure is calculated against the
cost of living index of the Sao Paulo stock exchange
with the Fundacao Instituto de Pesquisas Economicas
de Sao Paulo.
(c) The second Sao Paulo figure is calculated against the
cost of living index of the inter-union statistical
and socio-economic studies department (DIEESE).
Source: Conjuntura Economica Vol.34 No.4, April 1980 p.65.

Cardoso argues that these programmes serve another, ideological,
purpose:

'... among the many actions and plans kept in the anonymity of
technico-bureaucratic cabinets, a few were chosen... to
communicate to the population that the government (and
especially the President) had a policy and was concerned for
the national 'interest'.(Cardoso 1975 pp.203-4)

Bureaucratically channelled and specific benefits have the capacity to
operate as instruments of political incorporation for economic non-
beneficiaries. The expression of demand, as Simonsen and Campos
themselves suggest, is kept within these defined limits, and supply
becomes the product of state benificence. The state, it is argued,
thus excludes en masse and re-integrates selectively and individually.
There are two aspects to this reintegration. One is the symbolic
inclusiveness of relatively small scale redistributive 'impact projects'
which Cardoso mentions. The other is through the interaction between
state institutions and individuals which takes place in the process of
allocation of all governmentally controlled values, not only of benefits
and rights but also of controls, permissions and penalties.[23] It is to
these issues that we will return more specifically in the following

chapters.

## AN OPENING?

Can events since about 1975 be seen as part of this institutionally
ordered world?  A series of steps were taken which were represented
by the government itself as part of a programme of movement towards
its goal of democratisation or at least of achieving a political
'opening' (*abertura*).  President Ernesto Geisel (1974-1979) had held
out this possibility but the clearest manifestations came in the first
year of Joao Baptista Figueiredo's presidency.  At the beginning of
1979 institutional act number five was abolished;  since 1968 this had
given the president powers to prorogue elected assemblies, to intervene
in  State governments, and to suspend the political rights of elected
representatives and citizens and to censure the press.  Political
exiles, including representatives of the Communist Party, began to
return to Brazil in the second half of 1979, following the announcement
of an amnesty for about 5000 (non-violent) 'adversaries of the
revolution'.  The two party system was abolished and permission given
to the formation of new parties which could demonstrate that they were
not based on 'class bias'.  The government's own party (Partido
Democratico Socialista) adopted at least as radical a manifesto as
any other, with, for example, proposals for worker representation
(*co-gestao*) on company boards.  Furthermore, at the beginning of 1980,
the government promised a return to direct elections for State
governors and the abolition of governmental nomination of one third
of federal senators.

These changes were significant, if not always all that they seemed.
They were not simply the product of a programmed movement towards
political relaxation;  nor were they simply a product of shifts of
opinion and persons within the regime, although these were certainly
taking place.[24]  The changes emerged from a context of pressures and
policy failures in which the regime was at least as concerned with
limiting as responding to new demands.

First, with regard to Brazil's external orientation, the question of
dependency became more clearly an issue even within government.  Under
President Geisel, there was an apparent attempt to move from the
particular relationship with the USA towards extended trade and
technology exchanges with Europe and Japan and with other developing
countries.  However, the general dependence of the economy on foreign
capital increased markedly.  The foreign debt rose to US $ 44 billion in
1978 and the current account deficit reached US $ 7 billion (see table
2.9). 'You pay off one loan, take another loan and go on like that'
(Planning Minister Simonsen in Veja 2 August 1978) ; but in the long
term the requirement was either to reduce imports or (as Simonsen and
his successor Delfim Neto chose) to promote exports.  The further
orientation of the economy to exportation and the devaluation of the
cruzeiro which this required contributed to food shortages and to large
increases in internal inflation (reaching about 70 per cent in 1979 and
100 per cent in 1981).  By 1982 the foreign debt had reached more than
US $ 70 billion and the annual interest on it amounted to US $ 11
billion, equal to about half the total annual value of exports.

Second, there were increasing manifestations of organised dissent
within the nation, partly attributable to inflation and the continued

suppression of wages. Until the end of the 1970's, there was a
sustained pattern of high levels of economic growth (averaging more
than eight per cent per year throughout the decade) co-existing with
levels of income which remained low for the majority of workers (table
2.13). A series of strikes took place between 1978 and 1980 throughout
the nation but especially in the State of Sao Paulo. This action
effectively broke the prohibition on strikes and on direct negotiation
between workers and particular employees. The leaders of the labour
movement were employees of large firms in the better paid heavy and
durable consumer goods industries – especially metalworkers, but also
lorry drivers and construction workers, and eventually the middle class
public sector professions (teachers, doctors and state officials).

Table 2.13
Wage distribution by sector in 1977
(% of employed population)

| Monthly income in minimum salaries (sm) | agriculture | industry | construction | commerce | services | total |
|---|---|---|---|---|---|---|
| nil | 31.7 | 1.0 | 0.6 | 4.4 | 1.2 | 12.4 |
| up to 1sm | 43.9 | 23.7 | 21.0 | 27.7 | 55.2 | 35.9 |
| 1-3 sm | 19.2 | 50.4 | 60.8 | 42.5 | 29.2 | 34.7 |
| 3-5 sm | 2.6 | 12.3 | 11.1 | 11.8 | 7.0 | 8.3 |
| 5+ sm | 2.5 | 12.5 | 6.4 | 13.4 | 7.2 | 8.6 |
| undeclared | 0.1 | 0.1 | 0.1 | 0.1 | 0.3 | 0.1 |
| | 100 | 100 | 100 | 99.9 | 100 | 100 |

Source: Latin American Regional Reports Brazil 9 November 1979.
Note:   the minimum monthly salary varies by region. At its maximum
        (in major urban centres) in 1977, it reached Cr 1,106.4, then
        equivalent to about US $ 71 or £35.

The other major manifestation of dissent was the increase in the
opposition party's vote in the federal congress and State assembly
elections of 1974 and 1978. The opposition (MDB) won more votes than
the government party in the 1978 federal senate election. Votes,
however, were not reflected in seats gained, due to the concentration
of the opposition's support in urban centres and to the presidential
appointment of a proportion of federal senators. The government's
later action in abolishing the two party system, which had operated
since 1965, and in permitting multiple parties and the return of exiled
politicians helped to divide the opposition. However, in the elections
of 1982, the leading opposition party (now known as PMDB) gained several
State governorships including those of Rio de Janeiro and Sao Paulo.

In their later analyses of the course of bureaucratic-authoritarianism,
Cardoso and O'Donnell attribute these tensions to the problem of the
regime's legitimacy, that is to its isolation, in the absence of
mediating links between the state and civil society (Cardoso 1979 p.37;
O'Donnell 1979 p.296). The problem consists in the paradoxical need
to maintain the momentum of a political and economic model which is
inherently exclusive but which itself generates new demands for
inclusion – demands which emanate, if not from the population as a whole,

at least from sectors with a crucial involvement in production: the national bourgeoisie and the employees of large-scale enterprises and state administration.

Cardoso (1979 p.36) distinguishes bureaucratic-authoritarianism both 'from the democratic model of bonds between representatives and electors' and from corporatism in which classes are mobilised through structures associating them with the state. Social interests in the bureaucratic-authoritarian model are divided, declassed and selectively included. The state

> 'does not try to stimulate class organisation, to promote a doctrine of organic harmony among social groups, or to establish corporative links among them that could form a base for political domination. Rather the links between civil society and the bureaucratic authoritarian regime are achieved through the cooptation of individuals and private interests into the system'.(Cardoso 1979 p.37).

Whereas, corporatism offers the organisational structures and the ideology for the association of civil society with the state, the bureaucratic-authoritarian regime is distinguished by its selectivity and its justification of the exclusion of organised interests in the name of economic efficiency, of political order and of the future prospect of generalised participation in the benefits of growth. According to Cardoso (1975 pp.201-209), even capitalist classes have only an occasional and individualised representation in decision making circles.[25] The Brazilian regime cannot therefore claim legitimacy through any demonstration of the (representative or corporative) identity of society with the state; instead it depends more closely on the regime's capacity to create the conditions for capitalist expansion. Without this, it can neither maintain the support of national and international investors, creditors and entrepreneurs nor hold out the promise of social mobility to a wider population (Cardoso 1979 p.56; Dye and de Souza e Silva 1979 p.89).

In the pursuit of rapid economic growth based on large injections of foreign capital and the reorganisation of the national economy, the executive power of the state is strengthened in order to deal with economic management, with the organisation of capital for investment, with direct participation in infrastructural production and with the resolution of intervening social tensions. In the process, several contradictions emerge.

Firstly, within a regime 'oriented towards private interests and eager to expand relationships with foreign capital', state involvement in production nevertheless causes the development among sections of the military and civilian administration of new aspirations towards national autonomy and the expansion of state enterprise (Cardoso 1979 p.53; O'Donnell 1979 pp.320-4). Secondly, national entrepreneurs, initially in favour of the military coup, become disaffected by the growing intervention of state and foreign capital, the opening of the economy and the decline in the purchasing power of their mass markets. Eventually, O'Donnell (1978 pp.20-23) argues, this disaffection meets a response in new state action to re-emphasise the development of national enterprises as part of the 'deepening' in the process of national industrialisation; this action may be relatively unimportant compared with the major

internationalisation of the economy but it is politically useful in
promoting a national basis for support.

Thirdly, O'Donnell (1979 p.298) argues that the national bourgeoisie,
even if its support could be ensured, nevertheless 'hardly provides an
adequate legitimating referent' since it is clearly not national but
transnational capital which is dominant. 'As a consequence, the ultimate
basis of the state-coercion is starkly revealed'. The state, O'Donnell
(1979 pp.311-318) argues, stands isolated, exposed both to the trial
of its general capacity to provide the conditions for capitalist
expansion and to the special pleading of particular elements of the
bourgeoisie who have private access to the state. The state is therefore subject to often contradictory general and particular interests,
and therefore to a 'corrosion' of its 'proclaimed unity, efficiency and
technical rationality'. A reduction in special access and a strengthening of the state's management capacity requires some other more general
basis for legitimation. The implication, O'Donnell suggests, is of the
resurrection of mediating structures between the state and the hitherto
excluded population, either through corporatism or through some
controlled form of representative democracy. The problem is in finding
a form which provides the mediations and reinforces the state's
legitimacy without threatening the 'dominant alliance' of upper
bourgeoisie, armed forces and civilian technocracy.

To put an interpretation on these explanations, it appears that the
regime's own success in creating the conditions for capitalist
expansion and in increasing the executive power of the state generates
pressures for a rearrangement of the balance of classes in the state.
The interests of international capital continue to set the limits within
which adjustments can be made, but other interests become newly assertive,
especially the state 'technobureaucracy', national capitalists and the
employees of the industrial enterprises and public institutions on which
the politico-economic model rests. There are correspondences of interest
between the nationalist orientations of some public and private sector
entrepreneurs, but they are also divided on the issue of state intervention in production and by their separate links with international
capital. The regime's need for a wider legitimation of the state has
some correspondence in the demands by workers for further economic
participation and trade union reform, but the overt mobilisation of
organised workers has unknown limits and threatens to go beyond the
capacity of the state for manipulative accommodation.

CONCLUSION

The analysis of the emergence of an excluding authoritarian bureaucracy
starts at the level of economic development and the changing social
structure, and works towards the more specific explanation of the
technocratic interest. It avoids any direct and simple relationship
between particular class interests and the authoritarian state, but
in the intermediate analysis a heavy weight of explanation comes to
rest on the 'technocracy' (which remains an unclear social category).

The authoritarian and excluding effects of professional and managerial
dominance have been noted in other contexts.[26] Indeed much of the theory
of technocracy (to which Cardoso and O'Donnell do not refer) is based
on the premise that technocratic domination of policy-making will be

most thorough in post-industrial societies.[27] The Latin American writers, on the other hand, see it arising in the process of industrialisation partly as an attempt to extend technocratic rationality and to suppress antipathetic demands. Moreover, Cardoso and O'Donnell, though differently, present their analysis of the 'technobureaucracy' within a context of class conflict and not as if it marked the succession of a new basis for social structuration. In this view, the technobureaucratic role in particular, and authoritarian bureaucracy in general, are the product of, serve and are conditioned by a form of capitalist development but the technocracy also has interests which are separate from those of private capital.

What needs further consideration is less this particular role, which, isolated from the constraints surrounding it, is in danger of becoming an idealised concept, and more the logic of the organisational structures and processes within which not only managers and technocrats find themselves but also all other groups and individuals who have contact with the machinery of the state. These roles are defined by their performance in organisations and it is to the organisations before the role which we must look for explanation. Beyond that we must look to the social factors which have historically structured the organisation. A concern with organisational structure and process is not an alternative to class analysis but, as we argued in chapter one, 'an avenue for understanding the permutations and combinations of class and group interests which are represented in state administration'. Public organisations represent a point of conjuncture between state, class and role: it is through organisations that the state is made operational, that group and class interests are mediated, satisfied (or not) and regulated, and that roles are defined and perceptions formed.

In the case of Brazil, the particular practical point which is not answered by global statements of class interaction, and to which more detailed organisational analysis can contribute is the question how the arrangement of mass political and economic exclusion has been maintained. Cardoso (1979 p.47) has himself identified the lack of 'study of the control capacity of authoritarian regimes'. Whatever the longer term outcome of recent popular mobilisation and of the regime's reforms, the routine and continuous aspect of the relationship between state and society will remain important. Even in a period of greater class organisation, the experience of interaction with the state for the mass of the people most of the time is not of mobilisation, confrontation and suppression by force. Their routine experience is of the managed bureaucratic relationship between the individual and the state agency about the distribution of a wide range of resources, services, permissions and controls. Through these agencies there are continuous mediating links between the state and civil society even in the absence of representative or corporative channels.

NOTES

1. See for example Furtado, 1965; O'Donnell, 1973; Morse, 1970; Tavares, 1972; Castells, 1970.

2. Even then it is clear from several studies (for example, Singer, 1975; Castells, 1972; Aguiar, 1973) that the association between urbanisation and industrialisation is neither simple nor direct. The expansion of industrial employment has in all periods proceeded

at a slower rate than the expansion in the population of the larger urban concentrations (over 10,000 population). Indeed industrial employment increased only in the State of Sao Paulo between 1950 and 1960, while urban populations expanded everywhere (Aguiar 1973). Given the tertiary or service sector's incapacity to make up the difference except in extremely ill-rewarded employment migration has to be accounted for as much by rural expulsion as by urban attraction. The changes in the productive structure which contributed to urban growth were effective not only in the urban industrial centres but also in agriculture. The focus of this account on the development of an urban popular sector should not obscure the fact that the rural and growing urban 'marginal' populations were part of the same process although for the most part excluded from politics.

3. See for example Singer (1972) for a full account of this inter-linking.

4. See especially Cardoso and Faletto (1969, chapter 5).

5. See Dean (1971) and Singer (1976).

6. For example, the creation of a class of salaried agricultural workers (see D'Incao e Mello 1976), the 'rationalisation' of marketing and the growth of medium sized farms (Dias 1977).

7. See for example Oliveira (1976).

8. Glycon de Paiva (President BNDE 1955-1956) in interview by the journal Veja (20 July 1977) on the 25th anniversary of BNDE.

9. 'The Development of Brazil: Report of the Joint Brazil-United States Economic Development Commission' quoted in Skidmore (1969 p.94).

10. Inflation rates averaged 60 per cent between 1960 and 1965 (UN - Commission Economica para America Latina 1970) but the level reached 100 per cent (Baer in Roett 1976).

11. Quoted in Skidmore (1969 p.300) who gives a detailed account of this period.

12. O'Donnell (1973 p.53) defines 'exclusion' as 'consistent governmental refusal to meet the political demands made by the leaders of this sector. It also means denying to this sector and its leaders access to positions of political power from where they can have direct influence on national policy decisions'.

13. Indeed, after Apter (1965), O'Donnell defines 'modernisation' precisely in terms of the spread of roles and institutions operating in and around industry in the more industrialised countries.

14. The terms are similar to those of Djilas (1957) in his identification of a 'new class' with bureaucratic control of production in East Europe.

15. Cardoso speaks of a 'capitalism without capitalists' which is similar in its conception to Giddens' (1973) argument that state intervention and the bureaucratisation of capitalism represent aspects of capitalism's fulfilment not its death.

16. A very similar argument can be found in Pereira (1973) but he proposes a much more direct relationship between the techno-bureaucracy's interests and actions.

17. The then President, Castelo Branco, quoted in O Estado de Sao Paulo (16 July 1964), from Cardoso (1975).

18. These now include oil, steel, electric power, rail and sea transport, ports, banking, iron ore, telecommunications, atomic energy and roads (Pakenham in Roett 1976).

19. Kowarick (1975 pp.171-173) elaborates this point and argues further that 'marginal groups' contribute to the process of capital accumulation in the large scale capitalist sector.

20. See Furtado (1974) for an elaboration of this interlinking of effects, and Sunkel (1974).

21. We will show later that these savings schemes have operated partly through the national housing programme's link with the social security fund.

22. The argument was reasserted at the twenty fifth anniversary of BNDE by ex-minister Roberto Campos '... the improvement in man's quality compensates for the lesser accumulation of physical capital' (Veja 20 July 1977) .

23. Kowarick (1976 p.29) makes a similar point.

24. Most overtly, in the resignations of Simonsen (the Planning Minister) and Rischbieter (the Finance Minister) and in the imprisonment of Hugo Abreu, Chief of Military Staff in President Geisel's government, following publication of his book 'O Outro Lado do Poder' (the other side of power). Also in semi-private exchanges such as the manifesto signed by sixty colonels demanding a return to barracks on the grounds that 'the army as an institution was being spoiled by its participation in politics' (quoted in Bolaffi 1977).

25. Other writers (Dye and de Souza e Silva 1979 pp.89-90) have identified a more continuous and mutually dependent relation between the state and 'the most strategic segments of capital'. These segments are prioritised in the order of international capital, state capital, national private capital producing for export and national private capital producing for the internal market.

26. Relevant to the subject of this book is the technocratic dominance which has been noted in British studies of urban planning, for example Dennis (1970), Davies (1972), Fagence (1977), Saunders (1979).

27.  For example, Habermas (1968), Touraine (1969), Bell (1971),
     Marcuse (1971), Giddens (1973).

# 3 The housing finance system

'Social justice consists in the opportunity of home ownership
which is open to all Brazilians and not just to a few friends
of the powerful or to members of privileged groups as has been
the case in recent decades'. (Alfonso Albuquerque Lima, Minister
of the Interior 1967-1971 in BNH 1974 a  p.22).

The historical examination of the emergence of classes and class
relations has offered an explanation of the correspondence between the
dominant interests and the changing form of the state.  It is another
matter whether, in the explanation of the transition from an
incorporating, populist to an 'authoritarian' state, the 'technobureaucracy' is properly attributed an instrumental role.  The further
point is that the analysis referred to identified bureaucracy itself
as essential to the nature of the Brazilian state's authoritarianism
partly through its disorganising and canalising effect on popular
demands and partly through its effect in reorganising suppressed
sections of the population into administrative categories tying them
into an allegiant relationship to the state.

'Redistributive' programmes should perhaps be the last place to test
hypotheses about the excluding effects of authoritarian bureaucracy and
of a concentrative economy.  However, as part of the federal
government's proclaimed tactic of compensation for its own economic
growth strategy, the practical question is whether the tactic  can be
isolated from the strategy.  The question is particularly pertinent for
the Brazilian housing programme due to its close ties to key areas of
the government's economic strategy - the savings and credit system, and
the construction industry.  The question is also relevant because the
various limbs and arteries of the housing system have a particularly
large component of the bureaucratic roles held responsible for the
state's exclusive nature.

In the examination of the administration of the housing programme,
this chapter begins at one of the two 'points of entry' for research
identified in chapter one - that is at the formation of the organisation
which was to deal with the programme, the interests and perceptions to
which it corresponded and the logic of movement which it then
incorporated.  This involves an examination of the circumstances which
led to the establishment of the programme, the organisational structure
set up at the outset and the operational conditions imposed.  This
chapter will also offer a very general analysis of the effect of the

interaction of these factors on the evolution of the programme (and sub-programmes) on a national scale.

It would be no revelation to show that the National Housing Bank (BNH) and its various agencies have not served the poor mass of the Brazilian population. To the extent that the bank has claimed to be providing 'popular' housing, what requires explanation, as Lehmann (1974 p.15) has written about agrarian reform in Chile, is 'the sociology of the mystification which permitted anyone ever to take the policy seriously'. At one level this may imply a concern with the justifications which are made through public statements about goals and achievements. At another, much more powerful level, what is suggested is a concern with the definitions of reality which are embodied in the organisation itself. By defining the included interests and how they are related, the organisational framework sets limits on the action and perceptions of participants. These are limits not only in the sense that administrators are bound to operate within certain patterns, but also in the sense that both administrators and the administered come to accept that the organisational structures and processes which govern their action are legitimate, rational, justifiable or inevitable .

The second 'point of entry' for the research was the identification of these limits as they operated at the point that the applicant connected with the administrative apparatus of the housing system. In fact the two points of entry suggested in chapter one are complementary to each other. The questions which were asked at the higher levels of the administrative apparatus were those which would explain processes which ultimately impinged on the applicant. The formal and informal administrative rules which determined the applicant's experience were traced back through the structure of the system to identify their force and origin in logics which were often established at other levels. To begin the writing from the opposite end, that is from the establishment of BNH, is not to relegate the applicant's experience to secondary consideration but to recognise as important conditioning factors on that experience: a) the pressures and understandings which led to the establishment of BNH and its agencies; b) the structure created and evolved and the interests it incorporated.

THE ESTABLISHMENT OF BNH

BNH was established by law 4380 on the 21 August 1964 with the object of 'orienting, disciplining and controlling the housing finance system' in order to 'promote the construction and acquisition of houses, especially for low income groups'. Housing reform had been discussed well before the military coup, but the rapidity with which the new government prepared and presented its plan to the Press and then to the national congress indicated that housing (or something associated with it) had now acquired a special urgency. One month after the coup

> 'On 1 May 1964, the Press in Rio de Janeiro announced that the President of the Republic had requested the Minister for Planning and Economic Cooperation to give priority to the problem of popular housing. On the following day (2 May) it was announced that the Plan was already prepared and would be with the President by the following week. Five days later

59

(6 May) the newspapers announced that the Plan had been delivered
to the President, and the following day (7 May) the principal
points of the Plan were released'. (Serran 1966 p.99)

This was the first piece of legislation presented to Congress which
was not directly concerned with the establishment of the new regime,
and it emerged out of the initial political repression under the
government's emergency powers. It was greeted with scepticism by
Congress but approved.[1] By the government's own definition, there
was a 'crisis' in housing to account for this urgency:  'The 1964
Revolution faced a critical housing situation... The housing deficit
was increasing by 500,000 units per year' (BNH, 1974 b p.13).
Moreover, the government's analysis of this critical 'deficit' was
compatible with its more general understanding of the national problem;
not only was housing a part of the general problem, and not only were
the solutions therefore similar, but also the solution to the housing
problem could be part of the solution to the economic problem. As the
'national problem' was characterised by the incoming regime as one of
financial laxity, a distorted and protected economy, and political
paternalism, corruption and subversion, so numerous government
publications have described the situation in the housing market which
BNH was established to remedy.  The recurring themes are that

a) population growth at three per cent per annum was concentrated
   in the cities where it reached five per cent per annum.  The
   search by the rural population for higher urban wages had
   created a rate of growth 'exceeding all possibilities of housing
   accommodation'.

b) this had contributed to a condition of disorderly urban growth
   with the development of slums and shanty towns (*favelas*), an
   increasing deficiency of infrastructural services and the
   'problem of the squatter'.

c) previous governments lacked any coherent, short, medium or long-
   term policy which embraced all aspects of the problem.

d) above all inflation had upset the housing market by discouraging
   long-term investment. Construction had been brought to a stand-
   still because the basis on which loans were repaid to the
   investor took no account of inflation.  Instead capital was being
   invested in speculative holdings of land and buildings which made
   access to house purchase for the 'middle and working class'
   impossible.

e) the collapse of the housing market and the decline in construction
   were aggravated by government rent controls which led rents to fall
   behind inflation.

Past government action had not only disrupted the private housing market
and contributed to an estimated deficit of seven million housing units,
but had also failed to provide adequate publicly financed housing in
response:

f) output by the various existing housing agencies reached no more
   than 4800 units per year or a total of 120,000 between 1939 and

1964, according to BNH calculations[2].

g)  access to this housing had come to be by 'personal mediation and
    special arrangements' and government interference had brought
    discredit to the housing agencies.

   This small and reserved output was said to result from a situation
of financial confusion and impropriety, as was explained in the
'Justification' attached to the explanation of the proposed reforms
which was addressed to the President of the Republic by the Ministers
of Labour and Social Security and of Planning and Economic Coordination:

> 'The savings banks only manage to maintain this sort of operation
> because they hold the savings of people whose level of education
> is too limited or whose individual savings are too small to allow
> them to invest to cover inflation.  The pension funds by applying
> their own reserves to such loans worsen the financial instability
> which they already suffer due to the non-payment of contributions
> by the government and other employers.  The Popular Housing Fund
> can only operate because it receives funds annually out of tax.
>
> These agencies in carrying out their programmes simply take no
> account of inflation.  They concede long and medium term loans,
> on a fixed repayment basis, which are avidly sought after
> through favours and pressures and which rarely benefit the
> unprivileged.  A few people manage to solve their individual
> problem at the cost of income transfers from other people who
> in effect pay for inflation'.  (Ministro do Trabalho e
> Previdencia Social and Ministro Extraordinario para o
> Planejamento e Coordenacao Economica, 1964)

The problem was seen as 'fundamentally financial' but the financial
confusion was itself seen as the result of political pressures from
which the new regime claimed to have freed itself:

> 'The revolution takes power, producing for the first time the
> possibility of meeting the housing problem without making
> demagogic, political, regional, State or any other concessions'.
> (BNH 1974b p.13)

Part of the problem had been identified as one of rapid rural-urban
migration and a focus of urban growth in the large centres, but the
'solution' in no way reflected this.  Indeed, the criticism was not of
the fact of patterns of migration which reflected a pattern of
concentrated economic development, but rather of the failure of public
authorities to cope with the influx and in effect to sustain the
concentration.  Urban growth was not only irresistible but was also an
indicator of and support to economic development:

> 'Thus the intensive process of urbanisation instead of aggravating
> the problem represents a dynamic factor in the economy since it
> increases employment opportunities and transforms each city
> worker into a new consumer'. (Otero & Amaral 1973 p.59).

As a later president of BNH suggested, the planner's job was to take
population growth into account and allow it to be a positive factor:
'We have to have one exogenous variable in our planning' (Trindade
1971 p.16).  The solution was to be in a housing system which removed
controls on the profitable sale and renting of housing, capitalised

the construction industry and stimulated an increase in production, was self-financed and which offered a 'market' return and hedge against inflation for capital. Public intervention was to be primarily in the captation and canalising of capital, in the guarantee rather than in the suppression of its profitable application. The effect, it was suggested, would be to provide conditions for the remedy of the dysfunctional aspects of rapid urbanisation:

'by the balancing of the process of urban development, avoiding its disorderly and excessive concentration in certain areas'. (BNH 1974a p.21)

In the place of the administrative disorder which was taken to characterise the past, the coordination of the housing programme by BNH would obey the following principles:

' in planning, unity;
in implementation, rationalisation;
in criteria, depoliticisation'. (BNH 1974a p.23)

These elements of the housing solution - the capitalisation of productive capacity, and state intervention to support and order rapid development - were sectoral reflections of the new government's more general commitments. Indeed, the housing programme was in some respects from the outset, and came even more to be, a part of the government's general development policy:

'I conceive the housing problem as an integral part of the questions relating to the total development of the country, and, consequently, to the general wellbeing of the Brazilian people'. (President Costa e Silva (1967-1969) quoted in BNH 1974a p.20)

Dr. Mario Trindade, President of BNH between 1966 and 1971, specified the contribution which the housing programme could make to economic development as a means of

'generating employment
generating economic activity
generating income
generating consumption
generating savings
generating investment'. (BNH 1973 p.8)

Such statements about the association between housing and economic development were made from the beginning of BNH's operation (see annex), but it would be a mistake to conclude from the bank's later size and importance that it was always conceived as a significant element in economic planning, although this is what government spokesmen suggest. The bank had a small beginning, uncertain of the scale of its own future finance and uncertain of its structure and programmes. But even then, the housing programme can be seen as having two embryonic relationships with economic policy: one as a component of development policy and the other as a type of compensation to groups damaged by the form of the development.

As a component of economic development policy, the BNH legislation carried with it the first measures incorporating monetary correction (that is, inflationary indexation) which was to become a principle means for the government's containment of the destabilising effects of

inflation.  The early funding of BNH out of compulsory deposits by
government agencies, banks and security funds, a four per cent tax
on rents, a one per cent payroll tax and voluntary private loans
(issued as real estate bills or *letras imobiliarias*) represented the
first steps in the government's attempt to mop-up inflationary pressure
and to accumulate capital for long-term investment without generating
either further inflation or foreign indebtedness.  It was not just the
depressed construction industry which would benefit from this investment
but also the associated building materials industries. Bolaffi (1975
p.9) points out that investment in the construction sector had the
particular virtue of long maturation so that its multiplicative effects
would stimulate employment and production without giving rise to
immediate and inflationary consumer demand while the economy was still
depressed.

While acting as one channel for the instruments of deflation, the new
housing programme was also a means of selective compensation for the
consequent recessive effects of economic policy.  The immediate effect
of wage suppression, credit restriction and the restructuring of the
economy was to reduce not only the income and employment chances of
the mass of the population but also still further to reduce private
investment, in particular, in construction.  The housing programme was
compensatory in several respects:

(a) it helped to stimulate the construction industry which was already
    depressed and would be badly affected by recession but was essential
    to the government's longer term programme;

(b) it offered alternative possibilities for the 'absorption' of urban
    labour;  and

(c) it seemed to offer the possibility of the eventual satisfaction
    of the housing needs of precisely those groups worst affected by
    the government's political repression and economic reorganisation.

The economic and employment arguments did not in themselves require
a low income housing programme.  It is clear from the arguments that
have already been quoted that there was a recognised case for the
revival of the construction industry;  and it is clear from early, if
not original, documents that the absorption of idle labour was a key
element of the policy: '... our principal objective has been - and we
are all at the service of this objective - the generation of employment
...' (BNH 1973 p.7).  The commitment in this statement by a president
of BNH (Mario Trindade 1967-1971) cannot be illustrated better than by
the complex diagram evolved by BNH and printed in his book (Trindade
1971: Diagram 1) which details down to the forty second painter the
effect of a unit of BNH investment on employment creation.

The more specific case for a low income housing programme rested, by
the government's own reasoning, on the principle of selective service
compensation argued by, for example, Campos and Simonsen (see chapter
two).  In the first formal statement to President Castelo Branco
proposing the housing plan, the future first president of BNH (Sandra
Cavalcanti) based the argument on this compensatory principle:

    '... we think that the Revolution is going to need to act
    vigorously with the masses.  They are orphaned and hurt,
    and we will have to make an effort to give them some

happiness. I think that the solution of the housing problem,
at least in the big cities, will have the effect of applying
balsam to their civic wounds... last but not least, the favela
population must not be abandoned. In reality, it is much bigger
than can be·seen in the favelas themselves, because to them must
be added the tenements, basements, shacks, etc. These people
have minimal spending power, but they are people'.[3]

The solution of the 'masses' housing problem is assumed to be available
and the case for its solution is presented in terms of a paternalistic
humanism (or patrimonialism). But the case for its adoption, as an act
of urgency within the first weeks of the new regime, must rest on the
anticipated value of the promised solution as a means of generating
political support or defusing opposition.

Even if there would be eventual beneficiaries of the new economic
model, large sections of the population would in the short term suffer
from the recession and in the long term from the reorganisation of
production. In this initial period, the new regime needed to create
some basis for immediate support, even if only, as de Souza (1975 p.31)
suggests, to avoid divergences growing up within the armed forces.
The groups whose support was courted through the initial statements
about the housing programme were those who stood to lose most from the
unfolding of the new economic policies and whose political voice had
been most immediately stifled - the urban poor and the urban industrial
working class. By this view, the compensatory programme (whether or not
it was a merely cynical promise) was the response to a threat of
political vulnerability, an attempt to capture the urban population
before it was recaptured by the populists. As elements of the
'institutional crisis which culminated in the movement of April 1964',
Trindade quotes:

'... the social and ecological mobilisation of the rural masses
and the political vacuum which this migration inevitably brings
with it, whether by the breakdown of the traditional ties of
party and electoral control or by the worsening of urban living
conditions which is produced by this new social group which is
without any preparation for urban life and therefore marginalised;
the disequilibrium brought about by the great electoral weight
that these neglected and socially resentful masses, lacking any
authentic leadership, could bring to bear on electoral choice,
resulting in an inevitable widening of the field of demagogy.
For this reason, the government of the time understood that a
simple search for new political schemes without giving this
marginalised population at least a way out of the socio-economic
impasse in which the country found itself, would never constitute
a real formula for the solution of the political problem'.
(Trindade 1971 p.12)

The validity of this perception of the *favelados* (squatters) as 'marginal'
and socially 'resentful' has been adequately disputed elsewhere (e.g.
Peattie 1974, Perlman 1976, Turner 1968 and 1970, Leeds 1970); the point
here is that this group was held by senior government officials to be
both large and a potential threat (Valladares 1974, Portes 1973, Perlman
1976, Parisse 1969).

The other major category of initial recipients of the housing programme
was to be trade unionists, who were among the groups most directly

affected by the first 'acts of exclusion' of the new government:

> 'Although the conspirators took office without fully developed
> economic plans, the unions received quick attention. Forty
> labour leaders were replaced within the first month of the
> coup, including the heads of the National Confederation of
> Industrial Workers (CNTI), the General Labour Command (CGT),
> the National Confederation of Workers in Agriculture (CONTAG)
> and the National Confederation of Workers in Establishments
> of Credit (CONTEC). By the end of May, the government
> admitted intervening in 300 unions; including almost all the
> important national unions'. (Ames 1973 p.30)

Since before the second world war, the unions had operated in a strongly
integrated relationship with government, and under Goulart had begun to
pass from being mere instruments and to acquire a more powerful
manipulative relationship with government. The sudden deprivation of
this relationship could hardly be disguised, but could be blunted. A
major element of the new housing programme – the cooperative housing
project – was to be channelled through unions which were prepared to
collaborate with and were acceptable to the new government. In effect
the programme represented one way of selectively benefiting the membership of unions and at the same time of offering an instrument of
patronage to the new and often imposed union leadership.[4]

Moreover, at least in relation to the question of a housing programme
for the favelados, the practicality and the political effectiveness of
such a programme had already been demonstrated. The plans presented
to the President of the Republic were explicitly based on the experience
of a similar programme in the city of Rio de Janeiro sponsored by the
Governor of the State of Guanabara, and with which the future president
of BNH, Sandra Cavalcanti, had been associated. The idea of transforming
this local scheme into a national one was already a part of the higher
political ambitions of the Governor, Carlos Lacerda. Though Lacerda
was at this time an important supporter of the new regime (indeed he was
one of its conspirators), he was also still a strong presidential
candidate. The frustration of his ambition came only a year later with
the cancellation of the 1965 elections and the extension of Castelo
Branco's term. The adoption in 1964 of one element of his electoral
platform had the effect (if not the intention) not only of adopting a
programme whose electoral effectiveness was tested but also of preempting
a strong representative of civilian politics.

The Banco Nacional da Habitacao, conceived as an instrument of low
income housing, was then a product of a political movement in which the
new government needed 'at least to indicate some palpable and concrete
results at the end of the tunnel' (Bolaffi 1975 p.8) and to
reincorporate groups who were being excluded from previous political
arrangements. At the outset, the programme was expressly compensatory
in its objectives, but the definition of the problem it had to deal
with and the structure of the 'solutions' it offered were compatible
with (and even part of) the excluding nature of the political and
economic clean-up (*saneamento*) and reorganisation which the new regime
had launched. We will argue that the dispensable part of the housing
policy was its orientation to low income groups as the understandings
and interests built into and surrounding the structure of the programme
asserted themselves.

Figure 3.1

Outline structure of the Housing Finance System

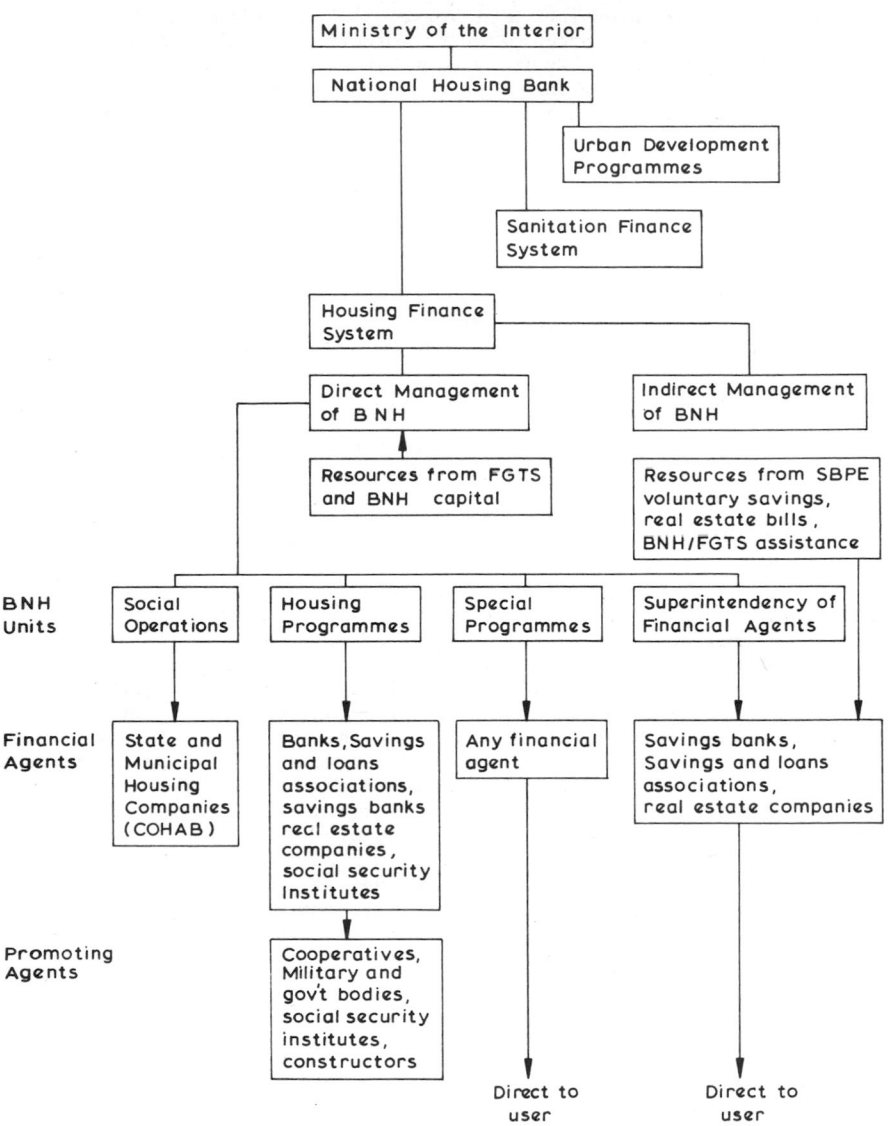

'The /Housing/ Plan and the National Housing Bank were born
at the same time, in August 1964, when the government was
concentrating all its efforts on the financial front. The
Plan's guiding principle was the monetary correction of
financial outlays, so as to preserve the value of the funds
lent and ensure an adequate return in real terms, essential
conditions if the programme were to be self-sustaining'.
(BNH 1974b p.5)

The commitment was essentially to a system in which the state would
mediate the exchange of financial capital, guaranteeing a rate of
return above the level of inflation to the lenders. The implications
of offering an 'adequate' return were that the programme would
ultimately be self-financed, that it should not be externally
subsidised, that it should be concerned with the sale, and not rental,[5]
of housing, and that it should offer long loans as a concomitant of the
high return expected. Thus 'a healthy currency' would circulate in a
housing finance system whose most suitable central organ was nominated
at the outset as a bank (see annex).

Although the bank initially received compulsory deposits from certain
state agencies, its financial function was to control and set the terms
of investment in housing construction and purchase and of the consequent
repayments. It was barred by the originating law 4380 from having any
direct part in the financing, selling, buying and building of dwellings
and was instead to operate through private and public agents for the
collection and allocation of funds and ultimately through the private
construction industry. The BNH was to be at the same time at the centre
of a controlled capital market and also at the centre of a housing
programme with the object of 'promoting construction and house purchase
especially for lower income groups' with the following priorities about
resource allocation:

'1. housing developments designed to eradicate shanty towns,
    slums and other sub-human dwellings;
 2. State or municipal projects which, through the use of
    sites provided with basic facilities, make it possible
    for work to be started immediately on the construction
    of dwellings;
 3. cooperative projects and other forms of association aimed
    at promoting home ownership among members;
 4. private projects that contribute to the solution of
    housing problems;
 5. construction of dwellings for the rural population'.[6]

The low income housing programme (comprising items one, two and three)
was to be implemented by two major types of local body - municipal or
state housing agencies (COHABs, Companhias de Habitacao) and housing
cooperatives (COOPHABs) organised through trade unions under the
guidance of private organisations (INOCOOPs).[7] The private projects were
to be credited through the financial instruments of the housing system -
at the outset, primarily the savings banks and the newly established
real estate credit companies (SCIs). In its first year of operation, as
these agencies were being established and the BNH was setting up its own
corresponding departments, three markets were identified for the housing
programme corresponding in turn to the fields of the COHABs, COOPHABs

and the private projects:

a.  the 'popular market' - for families with incomes between one
    and three minimum monthly salaries;[8]

b.  the 'economic market' - for families between three and six
    minimum monthly salaries;

c.  the 'intermediate market' - for families above six minimum
    monthly salaries.

To some extent, BNH's financial and its 'compensatory' housing
functions were represented by different sets of agencies, but there
was a considerable overlap between them:  ultimately all of these
bodies were concerned with the allocation of credit, even if the COHABs
and cooperatives were to have a directive role in the promotion of lower
income housing projects, while the financial agents of BNH (the savings
banks and real estate credit companies) had responsibility for the
implementation of the higher income part of the housing programme. The
history of the housing finance system can be represented as the working
out of two contradictory logics - that associated with the 'compensatory'
or redistributive function and that associated with the captation and
allocation of capital on something similar to market terms - and this
contradiction existed not only between the institutions of the system
but also within the COHABs and COOPHABs themselves.

A very large proportion of the population was disqualified from any
market in the housing programme since their income fell below the
official minimum salary.  De Souza (1975 p.77) shows that approximately
sixty per cent of the national population earned below this level in
1970, that is essentially below the level which could guarantee an
'adequate return' on credit.  And yet in the first two years of BNH's
life its resource base was partly in compulsory deposits (institutional
reserves and irrecoverable taxes) which could apparently require no
return at all, and only partly in voluntary personal loans (reserved
for reallocation to higher income groups).

A major change occurred in 1966 when the base of BNH's funding took
on an almost totally new form.  It ceased being a capital bank for the
reserves of state institutions and became instead a bank for compulsory
deposits made under a new scheme of social security, the unemployment
fund known as the Fundo de Garantia do Tempo de Servico (FGTS).  At the
same time the voluntary private investment element of the BNH's resources,
represented until then solely by the bills of exchange of the real
estate credit companies, was expanded to include other forms of private
saving.  The bank's resource base now rested on the compulsory and
voluntary private savings of small investors.  Both schemes bound the
BNH into a financial system whose condition of existence was that it
promised a rate of return above the level of inflation.  From this point,
the housing system was faced with the paradox of rapidly increasing
resources and growing difficulty in applying them to the housing of the
mass of the population.

FGTS substituted for a previous system of social insurance which had
guaranteed the worker his job or compensation for its loss after he had
been employed by one company for ten years.  The new scheme obliged the
employer to pay eight per cent of the employee's monthly salary into

the FGTS which was held by the BNH. The employee would be able to draw on his share of this fund for house purchase, for periods of sickness or unemployment and for his retirement. He retained his contributions and rights to benefit on promotion or change of employer. The gain for workers was therefore of transferability, freer access to benefits, and freedom from the difficult necessity of accumulating ten years employment with one employer. To the extent that the contribution was to come from employers it was apparently at no cost to the worker. Meanwhile, employers were said to have gained better labour relations and freedom from the necessity to maintain reserves for compensatory payments. Effectively capital which had been frozen could now be reinvested in the economy as risks were effectively spread between employers (Bolaffi 1975 p.10).

The voluntary savings scheme grew several new aspects which were consolidated in the Brazilian system for savings and loans (SBPE) in 1966. The BNH would operate as the central bank of the system 'stimulating and guaranteeing the operations of the system's agents'. Besides the real estate credit companies, the savings system came to include housing departments of state and federal savings banks, and newly established savings and loans associations. The real estate credit companies and the BNH itself could continue to raise credit through the issue on the stock exchange of real estate bills of exchange and, like the savings banks and savings and loans associations, could open savings accounts. The funds so accumulated would be available only to borrowers for house purchase through individual arrangements, that is not through the COHABs nor through the cooperatives which would be financed out of FGTS deposits. However, FGTS and the BNH's other own resources would be used to guarantee loans made under the voluntary system, and were until 1972 also used to buy real estate bills issued under the SBPE.

The development of the compulsory and voluntary savings schemes represented a further step in the integration of housing with economic policy. There were simple and direct mutual benefits: house construction represented a safe investment for savers and the housing programme required more funds. The BNH would have access to a fund with the potential of autonomous growth and escape from the unpopularity and uncertainty of irrecoverable taxes and deposits. More fundamentally, the promotion of the savings schemes and their channelling through the bank represented a solution for the government to the problem of the shortage of credit for investment which had partly arisen out of deflationary policy. Not only did these savings become available for investment in construction but also, through the BNH's deposit of its resources in the Bank of Brazil, for their state and private investment in other sectors of the economy. The effect was also to associate savers' (including eventually the mass of regularly employed workers) future benefits with the pattern of economic development in which their funds were invested.

The growth in the relative importance of private voluntary and compulsory savings in the sum of public financial assets is illustrated by table 3.1. As the savings policy is introduced through various new inflation indexed programmes (FGTS, real estate bills, savings accounts, profit sharing deposits), savers' holdings are switched away from monetary assets (paper money and short term bank deposits).

Table 3.1
Composition of public financial assets
(Per cent)

| Items | 1960–1963 | 1964–1967 | 1968–1971 | 1972–1974 |
|---|---|---|---|---|
| 1. Monetary assets | 56.2 | 41.5 | 24.7 | 20.5 |
| 2. Non-monetary assets | 4.7 | 9.2 | 21.8 | 33.7 |
|   – of which: | | | | |
|   Long term bank deposits | 2.0 | 2.4 | 3.8 | 4.5 |
|   Bills of Exchange | 1.0 | 3.3 | 6.1 | 7.6 |
|   Treasury bonds | – | 3.0 | 5.3 [a] | 5.0 |
|   Treasury bills | – | – | 1.1 | 3.2 |
|   Real estate bills | – | 0.3 [b] | 1.0 | 1.4 |
|   Import bills | 1.7 | – | – | – |
|   Savings accounts | – | 0.2 [a] | 1.1 | 2.6 |
|   FGTS | – | 1.3 [b] | 3.5 | 4.9 |
|   PIS/PASEP profit sharing funds | – | – | 0.5 [b] | 1.8 |
|   Fundo 157 | – | 0.1 [b] | 0.2 | 0.3 |
| 3. Shares | 39.1 | 49.3 | 53.5 | 45.8 |
| 4. Total | 100.0 | 100.0 | 100.0 | 100.0 |

Notes (a) = over two years
      (b) = over one year
Source: calculated from Ministerio de Interior (1974 p.12).

The return to the investor in these various forms of saving were themselves variable, though in each case the interest earned would be in addition to the cumulative inflationary indexation of the capital sum deposited. The real estate bills issued on the stock exchange for lump sum investors were of several types earning six or seven per cent per annum partially free of income tax; the voluntary savings accounts would offer a fixed interest rate of six per cent per annum in the case of the real estate credit companies and savings banks and a minimum of six per cent in the case of the savings and loans associations, free of income tax up to a maximum holding; the FGTS would offer six per cent also free of income tax.[9]

The period from 1966 to 1968 saw the establishment of the voluntary system for savings and loans and the beginning of the accumulation of funds through this system and the FGTS; it was a period of relatively little housing output. Thirty seven real estate credit companies and twenty six housing departments of savings banks were set up in 1967 and in 1968 they were joined by twenty seven savings and loans associations. Except for the federal savings banks, with respect to both collection and allocation these organisations were based on regions which might range from a city to a State or a grouping of States. As we will see, the attempts at regional (as well as the social) compensation would have to come out of FGTS. The bank's size and importance grew rapidly once these funds were tapped:

'By its fourth year /1968/, the BNH becomes the third largest bank in Brazil, with capital stock and reserves amounting to 333 million cruzeiros /then US $ 104m/ and assets of 2400 million cruzeiros / US $ 750m/... By its fifth year, the BNH

becomes Brazil's second largest bank with deposits totalling
3700 million cruzeiros /US $ 925m7 and assets of over
US $ 1000 million'. (BNH 1974b p.21)

There are numerous and confusingly different figures available to
indicate the development of the housing finance system. We select some
of these largely to describe the components of the system's resources
and their changing dependence on FGTS and the voluntary system (SBPE).
Table 3.2 shows the whole range of the components and the overwhelming
reliance on these savings schemes (and, incidentally, the insignificance
of foreign loans). Table 3.3 indicates the changing balance between
the most important elements of the SFH's resources. FGTS, as a compulsory fund, acquires a quick importance which declines relatively as the

Table 3.2

The housing finance system's source and level of resources 1968–1974

|  | 1968 | 1969 | 1970 | 1971 | 1972 | 1973 | 1974 | % of 1974 Total |
|---|---|---|---|---|---|---|---|---|
| Capital and Reserves | 1200 | 1823 | 2598 | 3213 | 4561 | 6957 | 10989 | 12.9 |
| FGTS deposits | 5721 | 9217 | 12930 | 17061 | 21855 | 27457 | 32897 | 38.5 |
| Other deposits | – | – | – | 30 | 409 | 310 | – | – |
| Savings accounts | 996 | 2267 | 4473 | 6645 | 11406 | 18473 | 28917 | 33.8 |
| SBPE real estate bills | 1378 | 2371 | 3579 | 4703 | 6554 | 7727 | 7954 | 9.3 |
| BNH real estate bills | 241 | 276 | 317 | 306 | 325 | 296 | 281 | 0.3 |
| Foreign resources | 120 | 217 | 272 | 349 | 340 | 365 | 449 | 0.5 |
| Others | 562 | 293 | 396 | 921 | 1178 | 1858 | 3713 | 4.3 |
| Pending | 39 | 87 | 116 | – | 486 | 596 | 267 | 0.3 |
| Total | 10257 | 16551 | 24681 | 33228 | 47114 | 63039 | 85467 | 99.9 |
| Growth rate p.a. |  | 61% | 49% | 35% | 42% | 34% | 36% |  |

Notes: Figures are (a) cumulative
                    (b) expressed in million cruzeiros
          and (c) corrected to 1974 prices
       US$ in December 1974 = Cr $7.39
Source: Adjusted from Ministerio do Interior (1974 p.55).

voluntary savings system gains a structure and the confidence of savers,
and as the beneficiaries of the new economic model began to build up
their surplus income. Nevertheless, FGTS remains the most important
element of BNH's own resources, allowing it to invest in housing through
its agents and, as the voluntary savings and loans systems central bank,
allowing it to guarantee the more independent operations of the agencies
of that system.

The priorities to which the housing finance system's funds were to be
applied had been defined in the initiating law 4380. Moreover the same
law had specified the maximum value of units which could be constructed
under the finance system so as to conform with these priorities. Thus

71

Table 3.3
Ratio of cumulative deposits of FGTS and SBPE 1967–1975
(Per cent)

| | | SBPE savings and loans system | | | |
|---|---|---|---|---|---|
| Year | FGTS gross deposits | Savings accounts | Real estate bills | Total | Overall Total |
| 1967 | 73.7 | 9.5 | 16.8 | 26.3 | 100 |
| 1968 | 69.9 | 12.6 | 17.5 | 30.1 | 100 |
| 1969 | 66.5 | 16.2 | 17.3 | 33.5 | 100 |
| 1970 | 61.8 | 21.0 | 17.3 | 38.3 | 100 |
| 1971 | 59.5 | 23.2 | 17.3 | 40.5 | 100 |
| 1972 | 54.1 | 28.5 | 17.4 | 45.9 | 100 |
| 1973 | 51.3 | 33.7 | 15.0 | 48.7 | 100 |
| 1974 | 45.8 | 42.4 | 11.8 | 54.2 | 100 |
| 1975 | 42.6 | 49.6 | 7.7 | 57.3 | 99.9 |
| Total Cruzeiros in millions | | | | | |
| 1975 | 46,128.4 | 53,710.0 | 8,385.0 | 62,095.0 | 108,223.4 |

Note: These figures are approximate and only intended to be indicative
of general trends. Marginally different proportions would emerge
from sums given in BNH (1974c) and in Trindade (1971 p.60).
Source: Derived from figures supplied by BNH, dated December 1975.

no house with a value of more than 400 times the minimum salary could
be constructed by a State or State-controlled entity; only twenty per
cent of their resources could be devoted to houses valued at between
300 and 400 times the minimum salary; and plans were to be drawn up by
region and institution for the allocation of a minimum percentage of
resources to housing units with a value of 100 minimum salaries or less,
designed to do away with slums and squatter settlements. Private
agencies of the housing finance system had to finance housing valued
between 300 and a maximum of 500 times the minimum salary, with a focus
of resources on the bottom end of the scale. Thus state entities (such
as COHABs) would focus on 'uneconomic' housing provision, leaving the
higher markets to private credit companies.

With the introduction of the FGTS and the voluntary savings and loans
system the division of the market was established on new principles
which began to reflect the BNH's new role as the guardian of savings.
The limits for operations in the 'popular', 'economic' and 'intermediate'
markets were now fixed not in terms of the maximum value of units to be
constructed but in terms of the maximum value of the finance to be
applied. Effectively, this meant that in the 'intermediate' market
(the sector for private operations), where there was no upper income
limit on clients, a house of any value could be partially financed; it
also meant that in the two lower markets there would be no impediment
to the COHABs and cooperatives (among others) moving to finance housing
primarily for the top end of their permitted income range. The abolition
of house value controls thus opened the housing finance system to the
interest of borrowers in the higher income groups, who would represent
less risk to the particular allocating credit agency and less risk
overall to the savings gathered through the FGTS and the voluntary system.

The limits of the finance (and the repayments) to be applied to each
market were expressed not in terms of minimum salaries but in terms of
a more rigorously indexed financial unit, the standard capital unit
(UPC): the minimum salary and the UPC were both adjustable for
inflation, but according to different formulae. The minimum salary
was an instrument of economic policy whose value was in fact to slip
over the period of the first ten years of the new regime; the standard
capital unit, on the other hand, expressed constant capital values.[10]
Whereas the intended beneficiaries in the three markets were defined
in terms of income groups based on minimum salaries, the level of
financing they could receive and their repayment obligations were
expressed in terms of standard capital units. Since the two systems
were adjusted differently and at different intervals they were to get
seriously out of step.

The COHABs were to operate in the 'popular' market offering credit
up to 200 UPCs; the cooperatives in the 'economic' market would offer
credit between 200-400 UPCs; and the agents of the savings and loans
system would offer the bulk of their credit in the open-ended
'intermediate' market offering between 400-900 UPCs, but would also be
expected to offer thirty per cent of their funds to clients whose
incomes matched the 'popular' and 'economic' markets. Interests rates
per annum to borrowers (over and above inflationary indexation) would
range from four to ten per cent per annum (depending on the level of
finance) for operators using FGTS funds in the 'popular' and 'economic'
markets (the COHABs, cooperatives and providential institutes). The
private agencies (credit companies, savings banks and associations)
allocating credit out of voluntary savings would be able to charge any
interest rate, except for their operations in the lower income markets
which would be limited to between ten and twelve per cent per annum.

This highly systematic arrangement for the allocation of agencies,
levels of finance and levels of interest rates to markets defined by
income groups had all the appearance of offering a technically faultless
solution to the housing problem of all sectors of the population (except
for the fifteen per cent of urban families and perhaps a half of rural
families whose earnings fall below the official minimum salary).[11] The
applicant would apparently only have to demonstrate his income to gain
access to a house he could afford:

'It was sufficient for the candidate to make his application,
fulfil the necessary requirements, and await his turn'. (Otero
and Amaral 1973 p.69)

PROGRAMMES AND PRACTICE

The operational logic of the housing finance system was to propel it
away from its initial focus on low income housing and even away from
housing itself. This movement would be accompanied by new definitions
of the problem the system existed to deal with and by new permutations
of its organisational framework.

The performance of the housing finance system in the first eight
years of its active life is illustrated in table 3.4. The trend was
towards a growing importance of housing units financed out of the
voluntary system (SBPE) as a proportion of what was, however, a more
or less stagnant (or even declining) total annual output. This

Figure 3.2
The organisation of the National Housing Bank's
main programmes in 1975

| Programmes | Agents[(a)] | Responsible BNH Unit |
|---|---|---|
| Rural Market | 1. Banks<br>2. Brazilian Rural Extension System<br>3. Other agencies | Social Operations Department |
| Urban Popular Market | 1. Housing Companies (COHAB)<br>2. Housing cooperatives )<br>3. Mortgage initiators )<br>4. Banks )<br>5. Social security institutes )<br>6. Construction or development enterprises) | Social Operations Department<br><br>Housing Programmes Department |
| Urban Economic Market | 1. Housing cooperatives<br>2. Mortgage initiators<br>3. Banks<br>4. Social security institutes<br>5. Enterprises | Housing Programmes Department |
| Urban Intermediate Market | 1. Housing cooperatives<br>2. Mortgage initiators<br>3. Banks<br>4. Social security institutes<br>5. Enterprises | Housing Programmes Department |
| Building Materials | 1. Commercial banks<br>2. National, regional,state development banks<br>3. Investment banks<br>4. State development companies | Superintendency of Financial Agents + Special Operations Department |
| Urban Development including –<br>Water & Sewerage (FINANSA)<br>Transport (FETRAN)<br>Urban renewal and expansion (including CURA) | 1. Commercial banks<br>2. National, regional and state development banks<br>3. Regional development agencies<br>4. Specialised public water, sewerage, transport, planning and urban development agencies | Superintendency of Sanitation Finance System + Urban Development Department |
| Guarantees to Brazilian Savings and Loans System (SBPE) | 1. Real Estate Credit Companies<br>2. Savings and Loans Assns.<br>3. Savings banks | Superintendency of Financial Agents |

Note: (a) 'Agents' are the executing agencies. They are guided and
supervised by BNH units but their organisation is independent.
Source: Based on BNH (1969), IBMEC (1974) and internal BNH charts.

Table 3.4
Housing units financed through the housing finance system 1967-1975
(in thousands)

| Year | SBPE Units (a) Annual output | BNH/FGTS Units (b) Annual output | Total housing Units (c) Annual | cumulative | SBPE units as proportion of Total (a÷c) % |
|------|------|------|------|------|------|
| 1967 | 28 | 115 | 143 | 143 | 19.6 |
| 1968 | 46 | 97 | 143 | 286 | 32.2 |
| 1969 | 43 | 117 | 160 | 446 | 26.9 |
| 1970 | 72 | 86 | 158 | 604 | 45.6 |
| 1971 | 50 | 78 | 128 | 732 | 39.1 |
| 1972 | 66 | 55 | 121 | 853 | 54.5 |
| 1973 | 77 | 71 | 148 | 1001 | 52.0 |
| 1974 | 60 | 44 | 104 | 1105 | 57.7 |
| 1975 | 64 | 79 | 143 | 1248 | 44.8 |
| Total units | 506 | 742 | 1248 | | 40.5 |
| Proportion of total funds applied to housing | 36% | 64% | 100% | | |

Note:  Components of the BNH/FGTS total :   COHABs - 304,000 units
Cooperative - 170,000 units
RECON materials finance
programme - 128,000 units
Mortgage finance
programme - 140,000 units

Sources:  Ministerio do Interior 1974 p.20, 53.
Ministerio do Interior 1976 p.17, 22
Figures supplied by BNH and dated December 1975

stagnation was in spite of the fact that between 1967 and 1974 the annual application of funds (in real terms) increased steadily up to a level three times higher in 1974 than it had been in 1968.  The housing financed directly from the FGTS, although it was through the media of BNH and its own agents, should not be thought to consist entirely of low income housing.  The housing sub-programmes of BNH consisted, as we shall see, not only of the activities of the metropolitan and state housing agencies (the COHABs) and of the cooperatives, but also of programmes for the finance of the private acquisition of house-building materials (RECON) and for the financing of house-builders (mortgage market programme).  Of these, only the COHABs and, until 1971, the cooperatives can be said to apply to lower income groups, that is to those defined by the 'popular' and 'economic' markets as having family incomes up to six minimum salaries.

The period 1967-1970 saw a higher annual output and also a clearer focus on lower income groups than was to be achieved later.  1971 indeed represented a turning point in institutional changes which both expressed the shifts which had already occurred in the orientation of the housing programme and helped to confirm these shifts.  Table 3.5 shows that even by 1970 the earliest emphasis on the 'popular' market had seriously waned, both in terms of the proportion of units constructed

Table 3.5

Proportion of units constructed and funds allocated per market 1967 – mid 1970

| Source of Funds | Main Agents or programmes | Markets served | 1967 % of units | 1967 % of loans | 1968 % of units | 1968 % of loans | 1969 % of units | 1969 % of loans | Mid 1970 % of units | Mid 1970 % of loans | Total % of units | Total % of loans |
|---|---|---|---|---|---|---|---|---|---|---|---|---|
| BNH/FGTS | COHABs | Popular | 67 | 51 | 45 | 38 | 37 | 25 | 26 | 15 | 46 | 34 |
| | Cooperatives | Economic | 3 | 5 | 12 | 20 | 15 | 27 | 17 | 20 | 12 | 18 |
| | Mortgage market RECON | Intermediate | 5 | 26 | 4 | 17 | 11 | 25 | 21 | 40 | 8 | 25 |
| SBPE | APEs, SCIs Savings banks | Intermediate | 25 | 18 | 40 | 26 | 37 | 23 | 36 | 25 | 34 | 23 |
| | | | 100 | 100 | 101 | 101 | 100 | 100 | 100 | 100 | 100 | 100 |
| | Total no. of units (thousands) | | 164 | | 167 | | 170 | | 56 | | 568 | |
| | Total amount of loans (million cruzeiros) | | | 1574 | | 1677 | | 1950 | | 699 | | 5900 |

Note: (a) cruzeiros corrected at 1970 prices.
(b) the figures are approximate and can be seen to differ from the annual total number of units shown in table 3.4.

Source: BNH, (no date pp.14,15).

76

and of loans made.  The switch was not only to housing financed out
of the voluntary savings scheme (SBPE) but more importantly, within
BNH, to its own higher income programmes.  Changes had thus occurred
even in the sector of the housing finance system most closely concerned
with the priority of housing 'especially for low income groups'.  The
programmes which got most quickly underway were those which were most
directly the product of the'compensatory' argument for BNH:  one was a
continuation and development of the existing favela removal programme
and the other was the programme of cooperative housing launched
nationally through trade unions.  Below we briefly describe the BNH's
experience first in the management of these programmes and later in its
attempt to set up a less directly managed operation.

## (a) Favela removal [12]

As one of its earliest acts the BNH established a federal agency,
CHISAM, to supervise the favela removal programme which was to be
executed locally with COHABs.  In cities other than Rio de Janeiro,
and including Sao Paulo, COHABs had to be established to undertake the
building programme which was to receive the favela population (the
*favelados*).  But in Rio the COHAB already existed, as the forerunner
of the new national housing programme, and was to be the main focus of
CHISAM's operation.  A programme was drawn up to expand the existing
removal campaign with the objective of replacing 200,000 shacks
containing about one million people in the Rio favelas.  The COHAB had
already constructed three estates (*vilas*) on the periphery of the city
and was now offered thirty six further peripheral sites by BNH.

In some ways the favela programme was a success for BNH.  It provided
a quick boost to the construction industry, succeeded in eliminating
central city favelas (even if they sprang up again elsewhere) and did
so with the apparent connivance of the favela population.  The underlying principle had been to build cheaply on cheap land so that almost
all the people removed from the favelas would be able to afford to
purchase a new housing unit on market terms which included inflationary
indexation and interest.  But the difficulties in applying this
principle to low income groups were quickly apparent not only to the
intended beneficiaries.  At least seventeen per cent of favela families,
those with less than the minimum monthly salary, were excluded in
principle from house purchase and were offered temporary shelter from
which they were expected to find their own exit.  To the rest, detailed
surveys were applied to assess family need, but in effect  'need'
became a disqualifying principle if it reduced the capacity to repay.
The attempt to maintain standards by fixing a maximum number of people
per room itself had the effect of excluding poorer large families whose
income would only qualify them for a small unit;at the best they would
be offered a place in a semi-collective building to await house purchase.

For favelados, although the removal was involuntary it was also
unavoidable and they were therefore, as Valladares shows, bound to
compete individually for the 'least-worst' outcome.  The competition
served the purpose of speeding the evacuation of the favelas and
breaking down any possibility of organised opposition.  However, following the competition for entrance, the authorities were faced with the
irony of large-scale refusal to make the repayments and often with
desertion or resale of the accommodation.  This itself, as Portes

(1973) shows, tended to confirm the official premises about the irresponsibility of favelados and their distance from full integration with society as a whole. Besides, the initial scale and predominance of the favela programme, and the poor quality accommodation with which it had been associated had begun to reflect badly on the impression which other sectors of the population had of BNH operations.

## (b) Cooperatives

The cooperative housing programme was free of these negative effects. The population at which it was directed was regularly employed, voluntary and better able to pay for housing, partly because much of the population would be made on cheaper land in small towns rather than in the metropolises. On the other hand, the cooperative programme was based on no precedent and had no existing structure for quick implementation. The programme was launched in 1966 with the objective of providing 100,000 housing units, but it was a year before the first cooperatives were formed.

Perhaps more important, politically, than the provision of cooperative housing was the publicity and recruitment associated with the programme. BNH officials and representatives of the new state-based but private cooperative institutes (the INOCOOPs) toured trade unions, announced the scheme, opened inscriptions and grouped applicants into cooperatives. The unions themselves were involved less as organisers and more as channels for recruitment. Indeed the intention was clearly not to let the cooperatives fall into the control of the unions or even, it might be said, of the cooperatives themselves. Partly this was to be achieved by making the cooperatives impermanent, to act only as way-stations before the transfer of the units to private owners; partly, it was that the organisation set up to guide the cooperatives, the INOCOOPs, in fact became their managers. Indeed the INOCOOPs were brought in not only to serve the explicit guiding role but also to offer some counterweight to 'communist influence' in the unions. The then director of the cooperative department in BNH, Joao Machado Fortes, made the INOCOOP leadership personally, though not operationally, responsible to the anti-communist Association of Christian Employers of which he was himself a member.

Much of the intended political effect on low income groups (and perhaps through publicity on a wider market) was achieved in the processes which led up to the provision of housing: the elimination of favelas and the dispersal of favelados, the formation of cooperatives and the aspirations which were then attached to provision by state agencies. Thereafter, with a body of demand created which had not existed before (at least as effective demand on state agencies), the problem of rapid provision at low cost in suitable locations multiplied. Meanwhile the political moment passed which had required the partial reincorporation of groups whose political voice had been suppressed; the new economic model began to benefit and enlarge a population capable of affording housing on less precarious terms.

The favela programme was socially and geographically limited, while the cooperative programme was also socially limited, nationally dispersed, organisationally complicated and therefore slow to achieve concrete results. The availability of FGTS funding from 1966 allowed BNH the possibility of escape from this slow and visually limited progress into a programme which was less encumbered by income restrictions and new administrative forms and which was less threatened by the possibility of non-return on capital invested. Indeed, the incoming funds demanded outlets for reinvestment which the COHABs and INOCOOPs could not on their own provide. The agents of the voluntary savings and loans system were already showing the way with the rapid expansion of their operation in the intermediate (that is higher income) market.

*(c) Mortgage market*

The extension in 1966 of BNH's operations into a new programme area, the 'mortgage market' acquired an operational logic as part of the housing market:

> 'We have the area of the COHABs in which housing is subsidised,
> not being sold at its market price, since the Government
> considers it to be an area of social interest; and we also
> have the area of the cooperatives which is nearer to a market
> level. But outside the areas of the COHABs and cooperatives,
> we are in the market levels financed by the Mortgage Market
> Programme or by the other programmes which are financed through
> the institutions of the SBPE'. (Costa 1972a p.14)

What passages such as these meant by the 'market level', or the regular housing market, was itself a function of the BNH's own definition of adequate standards, proper interest rates, normal building methods and materials and not of the market in which most house construction, purchase, rental and exchange actually took place. In fact the upper income market was being defined as a theatre of operation for BNH using FGTS funds. This represented a shift from the previous arrangement where the BNH would restrict itself to low income groups unable to afford housing in the markets served by SBPE agents. Ironically, however, it was in its mortgage market that BNH found itself faced with a breakdown in its house purchasers' repayments scheme which could not easily be explained as due to the purchasers' irresponsibility.

For the BNH, the mortgage market seemed to permit the possibility of quicker and less supervised operations because (a) it was to work through existing private institutions, and (b) there was to be no income limit on candidates for houses. However, the new scheme acquired its own complex structure of organisations and procedures, much of which related to BNH's own continued supervisory responsibility. There were two essential private figures in the mortgage market - the 'initiator' and the 'financier'. Initiators were bodies approved by BNH as capable of promoting house construction; usually they were building companies. The financiers were financial institutions, possibly but not necessarily agents of the housing finance system, who would manage the funds applied to house construction. The essential though complex elements of the process of funding a project were that:

(a) The initiator presents a building project for approval to BNH;
(b) BNH approves the project taking into account its financial, technical and market viability;
(c) BNH and initiator enter into an agreement whereby BNH promises to offer mortgages to purchasers of the housing units;
(d) The financier (usually the initiators' commercial bank) borrows capital (on the strength of the initiators' agreement with BNH)

from the BNH to finance the construction;

(e) After construction, the initiator issues mortgage forms to prospective purchasers whose candidacy is presented to BNH for approval;

(f) BNH concedes mortgages to purchasers who are then able to pay the initiator;

(g) The initiator pays off his credit with the financier;

(h) The financier pays off his credit with BNH.

From this point when purchasers begin to make their repayments, two further agents, which may or may not be the same body, are appointed. The BNH nominates one body (usually an agent of the housing finance system) to administer and receive payments and another to collect them from purchasers.

Much of this complexity arose from BNH's need, as the source of funds, to ensure at all stages the marketability and financial viability of the operation. The risks to all other participants (the constructors and local banks) were effectively removed. As a result the constructor's essential interests were simply to complete construction and sale as quickly as possible so as to reduce the interest on capital borrowed and to expedite the return on his investment; for all its attempts at supervision, the BNH was faced with the consequence of poor quality construction and ill-selected candidates who were often unable to maintain their repayments.

The bank attempted to limit its responsibility by introducing, in 1968, regionally variable limits on the proportion of the total house value which could be mortgaged, and, in 1969, by setting a limit on the mortgage which BNH itself could offer at fifty two per cent of the sale price. The effect of these two measures was that the purchaser who needed the fullest possible loan had to raise forty eight per cent of the finance in a second mortgage from another source (usually the real estate credit agents) and even then would have to find perhaps twenty per cent of the value of the house from his own savings. Second mortgages were often so difficult to raise that constructors had to offer credit to their own purchasers. Moreover, the terms for purchasers on second mortgages were much more severe; the result was confusion, construction delays and further failure to maintain repayments. The BNH was eventually forced to step in again to rescue the situation by taking over the second mortgages, though only where it could be shown that they had been negotiated on its terms, where there was no large backlog of uncollected repayments and where housing units were properly built and serviced.

The effects of the experience had been not only to make BNH more cautious financially and more rigorous about its terms, but also progressively to involve the financial institutions of the SBPE and commercial banks in the management of the BNH's own funds (meaning mainly FGTS). These effects emerged out of a series of oscillations (which became typical of the BNH's history) between the need to guard bank resources and the need to offer housing on terms that purchasers could afford.

REPAYMENT SCHEMES, NON-PAYMENT AND ADJUSTMENTS

The experience gained by the bank in its mortgage market operation was

applied to its management of the low income housing programmes.
Tighter selection, mortgage and repayment procedures were imposed on
the COHABs and cooperative institutes. The attempt to apply these
financially strict procedures while at the same time retaining the
low income orientation of these programmes expresses many of the
contradictory pressures and expectations to which the BNH was subject.
The resolution of the problem for the bank implied a long term trend
away from its redistributive or welfarist commitments.

Though the significance of different forms of repayment is easily
lost in technicalities, they are important as de Souza writes:

'First because in them is contained /the housing finance system's/
entire philosophy, given that the return on resources invested
and the liquidity of the system depends on them, and, secondly
but not less importantly, because it is through them that BNH
shows itself, manifests itself to the public'. (de Souza 1975
p.87)

The modifications in the repayment schemes illustrate BNH's attempt to
accommodate the major financial requirements upon it.

All the repayment schemes which have operated have been based on the
principle that the house purchaser should repay his loan at rates
which were continuously corrected for inflation. The indexation of
loans was necessary given that BNH guaranteed or indexed the return to
investors, that is to the people who were contributing their savings
via the FGTS and SBPE schemes. It is therefore essential to the
viability of the FGTS and the voluntary savings schemes that house
purchasers should have the capacity to maintain indexed repayments.
The capacity to pay was defined as existing where the monthly
repayment on the mortgage amounted to no more than twenty five per
cent of the monthly family income. The main question was whether over
time the repayments would retain this ratio to income as the two were
adjusted separately. Another complication arose from the fact that
indexation applied not only to the repayments themselves but also to
the capital debt of the purchaser. There were therefore three factors
which affected the purchaser's financial burden and which, in a highly
inflationary situation, could get out of step with each other:

  i.   the purchaser's family income
 ii.   the loan debt
iii.   the repayment rate.

Only the second and third of these, of course, were subject to any
control by the BNH.

The most convenient and logical system of correction or indexation
was the one which BNH first sought to apply. This was that the
repayment rate and the debt should be corrected in the same way as for
all BNH's operations, through the standard capital unit, the UPC. In
this way the purchaser's debt and his monthly repayment would be
adjusted at the same time (every quarter) by the same index. The
problem was that wages, or more generally family income, were not
increased every three months by the same amount or using the same index.
Moreover, for the lower income groups (covered by COHABs and
cooperatives) wage increases were periodically suppressed below
inflation rates (tables 2.11 and 2.12). The BNH experienced the problem

as periodic waves of non-repayment and accumulating deficits for some
households.

A second, alternative repayment scheme was therefore created which
linked repayments to the index used for adjusting the minimum monthly
salary. The principle of this scheme was that the level of monthly
repayments would be adjusted annually in line with the minimum salary.
The readjustment would take place sixty days after the minimum salary
was increased or sixty days after public service salaries were raised.
This new scheme raised many of its own problems. For the BNH, the
problem was now that there was one method (the UPC) used to adjust
the balance owed by the purchaser and another (the minimum salary) to
adjust the amount repaid. The two quickly got out of step (see table
3.6) periodically favouring or disadvantaging mortgagees but always

Table 3.6
Rates of increase in value of UPC and minimum salary 1966-1974

| Year | Per cent increase in UPC | Per cent increase in minimum salary (sm) |
|------|------|------|
| 1966 1967 | 40.0 | 25.0 |
| 1967 1968 | 21.1 | 23.4 |
| 1968 1969 | 25.5 | 20.4 |
| 1969 1970 | 19.3 | 20.0 |
| 1970 1971 | 17.8 | 20.5 |
| 1971 1972 | 21.2 | 19.2 |
| 1972 1973 | 14.7 | 16.1 |
| 1973 1974 | 14.4 | 20.8 |

Notes: 1) UPC or standard capital unit is reviewed quarterly and
coincides with the value fixed for Readjustable National
Treasury Bonds.
2) The minimum salary is fixed annually, nominally to take
account of inflation and increases in productivity. It
varies by region but the BNH takes into account only the
highest SM in the country.
Source: BNH in de Souza 1975 p.137.

creating more internal inconsistencies for BNH than the first scheme
had caused. For house purchasers, there were not only the consequences
of the difference between the standard capital unit and the minimum
salary (which could often mean that their debt grew rather than
diminished) but also between the increases in the minimum salary and
in their own wage. The government fixed 'minimum salary' is a notional

82

wage which is used as a guide by employers but which does not determine
employees' pay.  Rates of real salary increase could vary above or
below the minimum salary rate, and they would not necessarily take place
at the same time.  Moreover, there rapidly grew up differences between
the repayments of different mortgagees purchasing similar housing units
depending on whether they signed their contract just before or after an
annual minimum salary increase.

The gap between the rate of repayment and the growth of the purchaser's
debt was particularly significant under the first system of repayment
which the BNH adopted.  According to Prices Table the composition of
the repayment changes over time -- initially it is entirely interest
which is being paid, but ultimately it is entirely the capital which
is being paid off.  The proportion of interest paid should consistently
fall:

Figure 3.3
Prices table

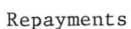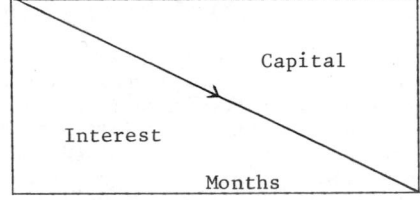

Where repayments failed to accompany the debt's growth mortgagees kept
finding themselves forced back to the first point in the diagram,
always paying interest and never paying off their debt (which in its
turn was constantly growing).

All participants in the system found themselves caught in these
confusions, but the consequences were worst for those whose family
budget was most precarious, where the housing conditions offered were
worst, and where (as in the case of the favelados) inclusion in the
system had in the first place been compulsory.  The housing finance
system was faced with refusal to pay, abandonment of property, illegal
occupation, complaints about building and service standards and location
(Valladares, 1974, 1978a, 1978b;  Bolaffi 1972).  The BNH (and
ultimately the FGTS investors) carried the onus for failure but could
not supervise effectively from a distance:  builders and private agents,
and even COHABs and State and municipal governments, had more interest
in getting something built and occupied than in maintaining standards
and in selecting purchasers who could meet the onerous repayments
schemes.  The BNH's response to this experience promoted a steady move
away from an involvement in low income housing and towards the
imposition of more rigorous controls on applicants for housing.  There
were also periodic attempts to cushion low income purchasers and to
reinvigorate the 'popular' housing programmes, but we will argue that
these actually had the more important effect of favouring the higher
income groups to whom the housing programme was progressively re-
orienting itself.  Exactly as the first president of the bank had

feared in her initial letter to President Castelo Branco: 'the resources of the Plan will be fatally diverted if they go only to those who can cope with the 'inflationary compensation' which is to be introduced' (see annex).

The BNH's first response was to systematise the selection of candidates by requiring a) that they be given much more detailed information about the terms they were taking on, and b) that their capacity to pay be submitted to much closer documentary proof and examination by the agents of BNH and of the SBPE. The terms themselves were also modified. The first inflationary correction system (based in all respects on the standard capital unit and therefore internally consistent) was retained, but the second option (based on a combination of the standard capital unit with the minimum salary) was replaced in 1969 by the 'Salary Equivalence Plan'. This had the important effect of limiting the number of repayments to be made, so that, even if there were a debt outstanding at the end of the repayment period, the mortgagee was absolved of it. Anomalies between mortgagees (which arose from the variable relation between the standard capital unit and the minimum salary depending on the time of year when the contract was signed) were removed by the use of variable readjustment formulae.

The other major change in the system took place in 1971 when a new basis for calculating the level of mortgage repayments was introduced. This, instead of requiring a flat rate (in real terms) of repayment, required higher repayments at the outset but falling with time. Under this sytem, the amount of capital paid off remained constant while the amount paid in interest fell as a component of the total repayment. Since the interest was on a falling (in real terms) debt, the interest could not accumulate as before. As the total outgoings (in real terms) were now falling, there was much less possibility that purchasers would

Figure 3.4
Constant amortization system

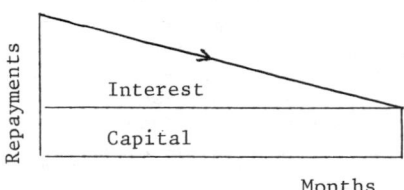

find themselves unable to maintain repayments, and none that they would be faced with the disenchantment of a rising debt. The concomitant was however that initial payments were higher which meant that lower income groups were pushed further from entry. To compensate for this effect the bank acted

a) to extend the maximum period of repayment from fifteen up to twenty five years (and even up to thirty years in special cases) and
b) to reduce the interest paid to FGTS investors and therefore by borrowers (see footnote 9).

The logic of the banking principle meant that every reduction in the

cost of money to purchasers implied a reduction in benefits to FGTS
investors. Moreover, the reduction in interest helped not only low
income but also higher income purchasers. Interest rátes were reduced
to a range from one per cent to ten per cent (instead of from five to
ten per cent), increasing with the size of the loan, but all borrowers
also benefited from a reduction in the amount of interest due (since
it was related now to a falling debt). The extension of the repayment
period was itself a two-edged sword for lower income purchasers: while
it had the effect of retaining initial repayments at their level under
the previous scheme, it also meant that the bank's circumspection about
the capacity of borrowers to take on long repayment obligations would
increase. Also, in spite of the increase in periods, for most new
purchasers the new scheme still meant higher initial repayments.

BNH - A SECOND LINE BANK

The BNH was exposed to the dilemmas of administering both a low income
housing programme and a social security fund; it had also experienced
the supervisory problems of operating a highly centralised system whose
output was all local. The case for operating through local agents and
for distancing the BNH itself from the problems of allocating and
recuperating credit was accumulating. The mortgage market had
demonstrated the possibility of working through local agents, and the
voluntary savings and loans system (SBPE) had rapidly built up an
effective network. The bank was also under pressure to 'privatise'
its operations:

> 'there was a political problem... we were under strong pressure
> not to 'nationalise' the programme... to put it into private
> hands'.[13]

Law 5762 of December 1971 transformed BNH into a public corporation
(instead of a federal agency) and at the same time into a 'second line'
bank. This meant that it would cease to have direct responsibility for
credit allocated to eventual house purchasers and would instead operate

> '... through the intermediary of hundreds of agents spread
> throughout Brazil and which are charged with the executive
> responsibility, passing on credits conceded by the bank and
> being responsible for the implementation of operations. To
> BNH fall the functions of command, coordination and
> orientation'. (BNH 1974a p.43)

By operating through financial agents the bank had access to a ready
made network of representatives, was able to satisfy demands on the
government to extend private enterprise participation in the management
of the finance capital which was accumulating through the savings
schemes, and also was able to spread the risks 'inherent' in the
operation.[14] The financial agents took over the debts of purchasers
to BNH and assumed responsibility for the collection of repayments.
In effect the units built under the mortgage market, cooperative and
housing materials programmes were passed to the agents. Since in
general, these were also agents of the SBPE, this meant that the two
systems now overlapped operationally at the level of the financial
agent who was both managing his own (SBPE) credit allocations (backed
by a BNH/FGTS guarantee) and the allocation of the bank's own funds.
The only exception was the COHAB programme where the COHABs themselves
acted as financial agents for their own ('uneconomic') operations.

The gain for the financial agents in this change were, first, the fees which went with their acquired responsibilities and, second, access to the use of credit which was channelled through them by BNH and back up through them by house purchasers. For the purchasers in the BNH programmes, the introduction of the agents meant, at least, increased rigour in the tests of their creditworthiness and additional stages in the selection process; there were also less direct effects in the implementation and nature of programmes themselves. Moreover, in order to promote the transfer, the financial agents were offered the possibility of taking legal action against purchasers already in debt and of reselling unoccupied housing units at a profit. For BNH, the change meant a reduction and simplification of its own administrative responsibilities for credit management. It was now a loan agency to other credit-worthy and regulated public and private organisations and not to thousands of individual house purchasers. Its new detachment from the front line also put it at one remove from the critics of the housing programmes. Most significantly for the future, the reduced risks to its own funds meant that it could maintain a lower level of liquidity and had greater freedom to develop alternative programmes.

Under the originating law 4380, the BNH's primary functions were clearly in the accumulation and management of savings and the promotion of primarily low income housing projects. The bye-laws of the new law (5762) broadened the overall purpose '... to promote integrated urban development, in accordance with the policy established by the federal government' within which not only dwellings construction was to be promoted but also 'planning and carrying out works and services of community and urban infrastructure.../and the/ manufacture of building materials and civil building construction'. The priority for low income families and labour absorption was retained in the legislation but now it was to be applied more broadly than to housing programmes.

NEW PROGRAMMES

The new definition of BNH's role offered recognition of a move into non-housing programmes which had already begun to take place. The originating legislation had permitted, but not promoted as a main objective, the financing of 'projects in connection with urban services and equipment...'. It was only after the FGTS had been created in 1967 that the bank acquired enough resources to satisfy the basic housing programmes at the scale to which it was already committed. From this point, BNH began to widen its field of activities.

The first new programme (FIMACO) was created in 1967 to finance the production and acquisition of building materials. A series of sub-programmes offered credit to private purchasers, to investors in the production, transport and distribution of materials, and to companies wishing to improve their technology or to 'rationalise' production methods. The new programme was justified as an essential ancillary to the attempt to maintain house construction at prices accessible to intended low income populations:

'A bank intended to finance house ownership found itself needing also to support the construction materials industry in order to ensure adequate supply. It therefore created a programme which is implemented through the private and official banking system'. (Costa 1973)

The extension of BNH's field of operation into the financing of public projects for the provision of water, sewerage and drainage was justified similarly as a necessary condition for the implementation of housing programmes:

> '... it would serve us little to finance the construction of houses without the States having resources to supply them with adequate water and sanitation. This is why the bank entered into the financing of water and sanitary drainage, and not simply because it wanted to extend its activities and because it judged that it had solved the problem of housing ownership'. (Costa 1972b p.23)

This programme, eventually formulated into a plan (PLANASA) to eliminate the 'deficit' in provision of water and sanitation, was part financed from BNH's own resources (mainly FGTS) and part from the resources of the States. It marked a move towards transference of responsibility for public utility provision from municipalities to public corporations answerable to the State governments.

A series of other programmes was created after the 1971 reorganisation of BNH had increased its liquidity and operational freedom. From this point, investment in urban infrastructural development ceased to require justification as an adjunct to low income housing programmes. Law 5762 had after all given the bank the overall purpose of promoting 'integrated urban development'. The most significant of the new programmes were: a project (CURA) which was to help municipalities promote the development of already serviced areas so as to maximise the use of infrastructure and to increase municipalities' return (through local taxes) on past investments; a programme to finance the provision of public utilities in BNH housing projects which had been built without them and to finance public services (health, education, recreation etc) and small private industries and services in the same areas; an urban transport financing programme and a sub-programme for rail passenger transport provision by municipalities and States; a series of agreements with regional banks to promote urban development in areas less urbanised than the south east of Brazil. All these programmes marked a tendency away from a single-minded concern with house construction; indeed some would add that the urban development projects actually had the effect of speeding house demolition and the expulsion of the poor from relatively well serviced urban centres (see chapter six).

Whether or not the development of BNH's wider investment interests had any other coherence, it certainly had a logic in necessity. FGTS represented a solution to the problem of resource scarcity but at the same time imposed requirements about the return BNH must earn on its investments. The clear evidence of experience was that low cost housing programmes could not guarantee an adequate (or even any) return, nor could they offer sufficient outlets for investment. The extension of the markets served, the reduction in interest on FGTS deposits, the adjustment of repayment schemes, the widening of the range of programmes, and the operation through intermediary agents can all be seen as steps towards ensuring a higher and safer return. They can also be seen as steps in the logic of BNH's role as an instrument of economic policy. We have already referred to its important part in the generation of savings for investment and to the use of the construction industry as an economic multiplier and labour absorber. These functions

were self-consciously pursued by the bank's directorship,[15] and indeed
the priority for programmes with high labour absorption was expressed
in Law 5762 establishing BNH as a second line bank. The importance
of civil construction in employment, especially in the years 1967-70
is illustrated in table 3.7.

Table 3.7
Percentage participation of economic sectors in
labour absorption 1967-1971

| Sectors | 1967 | 1968 | 1969 | 1970 | 1971 |
|---|---|---|---|---|---|
| Extractive industry | 0.9 | 2.4 | 1.2 | 1.7 | 3.6 |
| Transformation industry | 40.2 | 41.1 | 27.3 | 35.6 | 37.2 |
| Civil construction | 17.5 | 21.5 | 22.2 | 18.2 | 16.6 |
| Others | 41.4 | 35.0 | 49.3 | 44.5 | 42.6 |
| | 100.0% | 100.0% | 100.0% | 100.0% | 100.0% |

Source: Departamento Nactional de Mao de Obra, in de Souza (1975 p.112)

At least as significant for the nature of the BNH and its programmes
was its acquired role as an instrument of direct government investment
in development projects and of indirect financier for private capital
investment. The deposit of bank resources in treasury bonds at the
Bank of Brazil and the passage of credit through private and State
banks (and other financial agents) had the effect of making capital
available to borrowers from these banks for investment in quite
different sectors than directly concerned BNH itself. The important
role of BNH in the national accumulation and distribution of capital
was formalised in 1972 with the appointment of its president to the
National Monetary Council. Ultimately this role depended on the
viability of BNH's own direct investments, on the opening up of the
financial management of its operations to other banks and on the
preservation of BNH's own capital from risk.

THE FATE OF LOW INCOME HOUSING

We have already seen (table 3.4) that the annual production of housing
units declined after 1970 and only in 1973 temporarily reached 1967
levels again. This was in spite of the fact that the amount of funds
(in real terms) being applied to housing was itself more or less stable
until 1972 and then increased sharply. With the development of the new
programmes, the proportion of total BNH funds which was going into
house construction declined considerably until 1977. Using BNH figures
published in 1970, Valladares (1974 p.56) shows that of the total
available until 1970, seventy nine per cent of funds had been applied
to housing programmes, six per cent to sanitation and fifteen per cent
to the construction materials industry. Table 3.8 shows how the
proportion of total BNH resources going into housing declined to forty
nine per cent in 1976 before again rising.

Within this reduced proportion of BNH's funds going to housing
programmes, the share going to the lower income markets was itself
declining. Valladares shows that up to 1970, seventy per cent of
housing funds went to the two lower income programmes of the COHABs
and cooperatives. But by the end of 1974, these and all other BNH
programmes for the direct provision of housing units had received only

about thirty six per cent of the funds allocated to housing and complementary servicing (and the figure for 1975 was only 17 per cent). During this period from 1970 to 1976 BNH devoted the largest proportion of its housing funds to the guarantee of SBPE agents' loans and to credit for housing materials purchase by higher income groups. Indeed the only programme which really applied to the majority of the population with a family income of less than five minimum salaries, that run by the State and municipal COHABs, saw its funds cut seriously during this period. In 1975 it received only three per cent of total BNH funds and six per cent of housing funds. Between 1967 and 1970, by contrast the COHABs had received forty four per cent of all BNH's housing funds.

Table 3.8
Application of BNH funds by programme
(Per cent)

| Programme | Up to end 1974 | 1975 | 1976 | 1977 | 1978 | Mid 1979 | Total |
|---|---|---|---|---|---|---|---|
| Urban Development | 12.5 | 29.7 | 33.9 | 30.2 | 28.0 | 25.6 | 23.7 |
| – Water sanitation | 8.6 | 12.9 | 14.2 | 15.8 | 16.0 | 14.4 | 12.6 |
| – Transport, planning, infra-structure, renewal etc. | 3.8 | 16.8 | 19.7 | 14.4 | 12.0 | 11.2 | 11.1 |
| Housing and complementary servicing | 77.3 | 57.2 | 48.5 | 62.8 | 66.9 | 69.3 | 66.4 |
| – COHABs | 10.0 | 3.2 | 6.2 | 10.8 | 14.2 | 19.8 | 10.3 |
| – Cooperatives, social security institutes and official departments | 27.7 | 6.6 | 10.1 | 20.5 | 21.5 | 20.7 | 20.1 |
| – Complementary action (a) | 1.7 | 2.9 | 6.5 | 5.1 | 5.8 | 6.4 | 4.1 |
| – Construction materials financing | 14.1 | 11.3 | 11.0 | 12.1 | 11.1 | 11.0 | 12.3 |
| – applications and loans to SBPE agents (b) | 23.8 | 33.2 | 14.7 | 14.3 | 14.3 | 11.4 | 19.6 |
| Complementary operations in financial and technical support | 10.2 | 13.1 | 17.6 | 7.0 | 5.1 | 5.1 | 9.9 |
| | 100.0 | 100.0 | 100.0 | 100.0 | 100.0 | 100.0 | 100.0 |

Notes: (a) Land purchase and improvement of services for house units.
(b) This does not refer to SBPE own funds.
Source: calculated from BNH (1979).

Due to the relatively low cost of COHAB housing, it continued to account for a large proportion of loans conceded (roughly equivalent to houses built) even in the period from 1970 to 1976. But the allocation of funds and the production of houses for the low income or

'popular' market were grossly inadequate by comparison with the scale
of this market which accounted for about three quarters of the urban
population.[16] The gap between housing supply and the income
distribution of the population was expressed by an ex-president of the

Table 3.9
Number of loans made for housing - BNH and SBPE
(Per cent)

| Programme | 1967-1974 | 1975 | 1976 | 1977 | 1978 | Mid 1979 | Total |
|---|---|---|---|---|---|---|---|
| COHABs | 23.6 | 32.4 | 33.7 | 44.5 | 56.5 | 15.7 | 32.6 |
| Cooperatives etc. (a) | 26.6 | 11.9 | 16.8 | 20.9 | 21.8 | 30.9 | 23.3 |
| Construction materials | 8.5 | 9.1 | 8.0 | 7.9 | 5.6 | 12.4 | 8.1 |
| SBPE loans (b) | 41.3 | 46.6 | 41.5 | 26.7 | 16.1 | 41.0 | 36.0 |
| | 100.0 | 100.0 | 100.0 | 100.0 | 100.0 | 100.0 | 100.0 |
| Total No. of loans | (1080352) | (138471) | (245791) | (222305) | (341731) | (78582) | (2107232) |

Notes: (a) A little more than half was applied to cooperatives
(including military housing) and the rest went to the
mortgage market and social security institutes.
(b) Loans out of SBPE's own funds.
Source:     BNH (1979).

BNH.  He forecast (Costa 1972a p.16)  for the period 1972 to 1974, that
the output of the housing finance system would be unable to keep up with
the natural (demographic) growth of demand, let alone make up the past
'deficit'.  The failure would be particularly striking in the 'popular'
and 'economic' markets, where twenty four per cent and thirty nine per
cent of the natural increase would be met against eighty two per cent
and seventy five per cent in the 'intermediate' and 'superior' markets.
But even these figures were based on over-optimistic projections of
the system's output for lower income groups.

In the plans and publications of BNH, the future always does hold the
possibility of an increased output of low income housing.  Indeed even
present failure can be rationalised as a necessary step towards this
eventual outcome:

'... with progressive increases in housing construction we will
obtain progressively lower costs, so that through the financial
mechanism in which we are specialists - savings, long term
mortgages and interest - we will increasingly be able to put
the repayments within the reach of a greater number of families'.
(Trindade 1973 p.7).

Budgetary forecasts are made which express this vision of the future
but in the event the allocation to low income housing is not wholly
taken up.  The problem for the officials of the BNH department
responsible for COHABs, the social operations department (COS), is to
find enough outlets for their share of the budget.  As one official
of the COS planning section put it in interview: 'We have enough money
to approve anything and we do tend to approve anything that comes up...'

90

The most important attempt made by BNH to revive its 'popular' housing programme took shape in 1973 in a plan for popular housing (PLANHAP) for towns with more than 50,000 inhabitants.

'... to eliminate, in 10 years, the housing 'deficit' for families with an income between one and three minimum salaries and to ensure future families in this income group the guarantee of their own home'. (BNH 1973b p.7)

In the ten years it was aimed to build two million dwellings, increasing ten-fold the existing rate of construction of 'popular' housing. Long-term planning, it was anticipated, would make possible a better integration of public service provision with house-building and would encourage construction companies to make the large scale commitment which would have the effect of reducing costs. The maximum value of loans in the popular market would remain at the level established in 1971 (320 UPCs - standard capital units), interest rates would range from one to a maximum of six per cent (on a 320 UPC loan), and families would be allocated houses demanding no more than twenty per cent of their monthly income in repayments. The PLANHAP would serve the 'official poor', those families with an income equivalent to between one and three minimum salaries and with at least one member having regular employment: the excluding implications of even this definition of the eligible population would be great.

PLANHAP did not change the terms on which credit was offered to house purchasers; rather it modified the structure of the popular housing programme and opened new lines of credit for official agencies. The BNH would enter into covenants with State governments to set up a fund for the implementation of an agreed housing programme. The covenants did not themselves have the effect of increasing the funds available for popular housing but of implicating State governments in the provision of associated infrastructural services and of passing to them some of the risks of the operations. COHABs would now be backed by the resources of State governments and could take on loans from the BNH (acting as a second line bank) with as little risk to bank resources as in the case of its other programmes. In fact, certain States, most significantly Sao Paulo, were not prepared to negotiate conventions and here the COHABs (which in the case of Sao Paulo remained municipal) survived only in a condition of unreliable support from State agencies and in a precarious balance between their receipts from purchasers and their debts to the bank.

The frustration of this attempt to resuscitate the popular housing programme did not so much put the programme in question as the income group for which it was intended. PLANHAP had attempted to increase the supply of low income housing without changing the terms for purchasers and hence their capacity to buy. BNH's response (at the end of 1974) was to increase the income range served by PLANHAP to include families with incomes up to five minimum salaries and to increase the maximum loan which could be offered to 500 from 320 UPCs.[17] Since the 'housing need' of the originally defined income group (from one to three minimum salaries) could by no means be said to have been abolished, the extension of the income range was in effect an admission that the COHABs would be shifting their operations to serve primarily the higher end of the new income range from about three to five minimum salaries. Even if we took the lowest eligible family income as two minimum salaries, this would still render large proportions of the population ineligible – almost a quarter of the families in one of the richest urban areas, the metropolis of Sao Paulo, would be excluded (table 4.2).

At the same time interest rates were reduced for all but the smallest loans which were already only charged one per cent per annum (plus inflationary correction). The maximum charge on the highest loan under the popular housing programme remained six per cent, but of course the loan itself had been lifted to take account of increased building costs. The effect was to benefit existing purchasers who might have their interest reduced, and to keep interest rates low for the new higher income purchasers who were now entering the programme.

The 'popular' housing programme's move up market was one response to its inability to serve the originally defined income groups; another response was the introduction of new, cheaper sub-programmes. The plan inaugurated in 1975 for site and service schemes limited loans to the costs involved in the acquisition and preparation of building sites, the planning and administration of schemes, and the provision of drainage, sewerage, electricity and water. The work and the costs of house construction would fall to the site purchasers, but the terms of finance would be exactly as in other BNH loans, except that the rate of interest would be zero. However, this programme ran at a very low level allocating about 8000 serviced plots per year, accounting for about five per cent of 'popular housing' in 1979 (BNH 1980). In that year, the launching of a further programme, this time for the improvement of existing housing in shanty towns, offered new hope for a housing programme which could effectively reach the mass of the population with an income of less than three minimum salaries. The effectiveness of that initiative is beyond the scope of this study.

NEW INCOME LIMITS AND SUBSIDIES

The raising of income limits and of maximum loans and the introduction of more favourable repayment terms were happening at the same time throughout the housing finance system. As a result, while the bending of BNH's firm anti-subsidy principle may have had the intention of keeping lower income groups in the system, the effect was to extend benefits to more affluent groups of the population. In place of the division of the housing market into three categories (popular, economic and intermediary) with their respective agencies (to simplify, the COHABs, cooperatives and SBPE agents) serving their respective income groups with loans up to maximum values, the system was slowly opened up so that eventually the only limit on any agency was that it had to ensure that the loan was compatible with the income of the purchaser. This calculation was made according to BNH tables which were designed to ensure that no purchaser took on repayments beyond twenty five per cent of his monthly income. Except for COHABs, the upper income limits on applicants were abolished and agencies (whether of the SBPE savings and loans system or of the BNH) could offer loans up to a universally applicable maximum. This maximum loan was itself raised from 900 to 2250 standard capital units (UPCs) and, then in 1975, to 3500 UPCs[18] for all programmes except that operated by the COHABs.

Paradoxically, the raising of loans and the extension of markets into higher income groups was defended as one way of 'increasing the

viability of attending the housing needs of low income populations'
(Hungria 1975 p.10). In effect, programmes were preserved, on the one
hand, by redefining their markets and, on the other by alleviating
the terms of repayment applied to purchasers. One important subsidy
which applied only to higher income groups came from outside the
housing finance system: the interest payable on loans was totally free
of income tax (Costa 1972a p.19). From 1971, this benefit was
accompanied by the deduction of the value of twenty per cent of the
annual mortgage repayments from the mortgagee's tax bill. This meant
that the higher interest rates paid on higher loans (by higher income
mortgagees) were compensated for by tax deductions, while lower income
groups who were not liable to tax received no rebate.

While the interest remained tax free, in later legislation in 1974
(Sande 1975 p.9) the regressive effects of the tax deduction were
modified by the introduction in its place of a yearly reimbursement to
all mortgagees of ten (later twelve) per cent of their annual mortgage
repayments. This subsidy again was paid out of the national treasury
rather than at the expense of the housing finance system. It was in
principle less regressive than the previous system because all
mortgages received some reimbursement and because a minimum and maximum
were set on the sum. But the reimbursement was only made if the
purchaser was up to date in his monthly payments. In that way, the
scheme acted not only to alleviate the terms (for all income groups)
but also to stimulate repayment.

The case for introducing new forms of subsidy was presented by BNH
as part of a 'constant attempt to equate the purchasing power of this
/low income/ group of the population with the price of the housing unit'
(Sande 1975 p.5). But this was not just in pursuit of BNH's (low
income) housing objectives; it was also a necessary response to the
unwillingness or incapacity of many purchasers to maintain their
payments. For that reason, the easing of terms of repayment had to
apply to all and not only to lower income groups. Lower interest rates,
longer mortgage periods and the rebates (at least in proportional terms)
marginally favoured those with smaller loans; the tax relief on
interest wholly favoured higher income groups. Most benefits applied
indiscriminately in order to maintain the viability of programmes.
Thus, in 1973, the basis for the indexation of repayments was changed
throughout the system with the introduction of an artificially low
minimum salary as the factor for inflationary correction.[19]

Formally, BNH argues that it does not apply subsidies in the housing
finance system except in the sense that 'The BNH in all its financing
applies the principle of income distribution, in which the richest
subsidise the poorest' (Sande 1975 p.5). In fact, the benefits which
were introduced into the system were in general made at the expense of
investors and taxpayers. In absolute terms, these benefits accrue most
to borrowers of higher sums and to higher income groups. If cross
subsidisation can be observed, it is only in the differential interest
rates where the highest loans pay above, and the lowest loans below,
the interest which FGTS and SBPE investors earn. But even here the
cross subsidisation is largely illusory: lower interest on smaller
loans is subsidised much more by the lower return of FGTS (over SBPE)
investors than by the higher interest on higher loans (which largely

stay within the SBPE).

CONCLUSION

At a general level, these adjustments (changes in the organisational structure, modifications of the repayment and readjustment schemes, the extension in the range of programmes and markets, and the introduction of new subsidies) were necessary to the maintenance of the system and logic on which savings policy rested.  They had the effect of reducing the risk and guaranteeing or increasing the return of the savings and loans system and of the BNH and its financial agents, largely at the cost of captive (FGTS) investors and of low income participation in the programmes.

Increasingly reflected in the investments of the bank as well as of the SBPE agencies was an orientation to the demands of groups whose purchasing power was growing with the concentrative momentum of economic growth;  at the same time BNH resources were progressively a source of direct and indirect investments in infrastructural and industrial development.  With the establishment of the new economic model, the need to conciliate and even symbolically incorporate excluded groups could give way to the satisfaction of the (housing) demand of the model's constituency of beneficiaries.  The movement in this direction relieved, but did not remove, the incompatibility of BNH's roles as an instrument of economic policy and as an instrument of compensation for its effects.

This is not to argue that these changes were part of some 'technocratic' plan;  rather they took place in a step by step logic of response to constraints and pressures which the BNH experienced as crises of internal consistency between the interests of parts of its organisation, between the rates of capital deposits, loans and returns, and between its roles as the manager of social security funds, invest-ment bank, and low income housing agency.  The participant organisations survived, even the programmes survived though new ones were created, but the recipients and what they received changed.  Because the changes were step by step they could at each stage be justified in terms of first principles;  so the service of higher income groups was said to have the effect of 'increasing the viability of meeting the housing needs of low income populations' (Hungria 1975 p.10)  and of 'widening the portion of the population attended by PLANHAP' (BNH 1975 p.31) :

> 'The raison d'etre of the bank, the only objective which keeps
> us working in the bank is effectively to find the solution to
> the housing problem of low income families.  Whatever the
> Bank does is in order to have funds for this and in order to
> deal with the problem as a whole'. (Schulman 1975 p.21)

The orientation of BNH's provision to other sectors than low income housing was seen by some officials as a product of the bank's success in these other fields rather than of its failure in the 'popular' programmes.  Two senior officials interviewed by the writer argued that BNH had equal responsibility to service the middle and upper income markets.  In that case, the problem was not one of misapplication of funds (of which there was no shortage) but the inadequate performance of the agencies responsible for low income housing.  Where this failure was explained, in official publications and by BNH officials who were interviewed, it was generally in terms of external costs (for example of land and materials), the decline of purchasing power, financial difficulties of housing agencies and beneficiaries, the lack of competent personnel, bureaucratic complexity and the incapacity of BNH as a second line bank to control its own agents and the private financial agencies. The common characteristic of these explanations is not that they are wrong, but that they pick out separate and isolated phenomena as 'obstacles' to the fulfilment of the objectives of the programme as a whole. This chapter, on the other hand, has suggested a systemic relationship between the structure of the housing finance system, modifications in the structure and the move away from low income provision. For example, the incorporation of private financial agents into BNH's own operations was not an accident, a mistake or an aberration but followed logically (though we are not arguing it followed necessarily) from BNH's own role as a centralised instrument of savings policy. Once the connection between housing policy and economic (including savings) policy had been established and structured, each step away from the compensatory principle represented a response to the logic of organisational survival; that is, each step was legitimate in terms of the major requirements on organisations. The definition of the housing problem was inseparable from the definition of the national political and economic problem; the government's response to the housing problem was a part of its response to the economic problem. As instruments of the voluntary and compulsory savings scheme, of inflationary correction, of the accumulation and investment of finance capital, BNH and its agents were part of the economic model for the concentrative effects of which they were also expected to compensate. In that sense, at least, the solution was itself the problem.

But the complexity of the housing finance system, and the continuance of 'low income' housing programmes (in name at least) are not to be explained simply in this way. The system we have discussed provided a framework for local COHABs and INOCOOPs and their applicants; it was at that local level that the contradictory constraints to act both on a commercial basis and as a social service were most acutely felt. Much of the adjustment at the centre was in response to this local experience of the contradictions. Agencies must serve low income groups but offer a return on credit from BNH; eligibility for housing must be on the basis of need but also of capacity to pay. It was at the level of the local agency that both the promise and the scarcity of low income housing had to be managed. The myth of availability survived the decline of low income housing. From BNH's point of view, there was no shortage of funds and no lack of programmes. Locally too, there was no shortage of access routes for would be house-owners, but complex procedures grew up for the allocation of housing which were not solely a product of the pressures emanating from BNH.

In the following chapters we will turn to the experience of some of BNH's programmes in the metropolitan area of Greater Sao Paulo, the principle conurbation in Brazil.

NOTES

1. Anais da Camara dos Deputados 12: pp.5-24, Sessoes 18-25, Brasilia, June 1964.

2. These figures which are so constantly quoted in BNH documents were disputed by an opposition member of the Senate in discussion

with the President of BNH (Schulman 1975 p.13).

3. See annex for full text of letter from Cavalcanti to Castelo Branco dated 18 April 1964.

4. Interviews by the author with a later president of BNH, Rubens Vaz da Costa, and one of the first BNH officials support this interpretation.

5. The logic in favour of sale depended on speed of return on capital, minimising administrative and repair costs, avoidance of political pressure for uneconomic rents, the expected short life of houses built, and, according to Bolaffi (1975), awareness of the conservatising influence of home ownership.

6. Law 4380 Article 4 21 August 1964.

7. Other agencies involved in the implementation of the low income housing programme were the military and public servants' providential or social security institutes.

8. Minimum salaries or wages are fixed by government and vary by region of the country.

9. This FGTS rate was significantly modified in 1971, when the interest on new accounts and on change of employment was reduced to three per cent, while old accounts received variable interest rates dependent upon the period with one employer (ranging from three per cent to a maximum of six per cent for more than ten years' service) - see Law 5705 of 21 September 1971 and IBMEC (1974 p.42).

10. The standard capital unit is a reference unit which expresses the asset and liability operations generated by BNH. The value of the unit is reviewed every quarter and coincides with the value fixed for readjustable national treasury bonds (ORTN).

11. Approximately five per cent of the families of the population of Greater Sao Paulo fall into this category (see Chapter 4).

12. The following draws partly on Valladares (1974, 1978a and b). See also Parisse (1969) for a history of attitudes and interventions with regard to favelas, and Perlman (1976).

13. Interview with Rubens Vaz da Costa, ex president BNH, 11 August 1976.

14. Interview with Rubens Vaz da Costa confirms these intentions: 'We reduced and divided the risk... we paid others who were better experienced than ourselves to take the risk'.

15. See Ministerio de Trabalho e Previdencia Social (1968, 4:3), Trindade (1971) and Costa (1972b).

16. Among the economically active urban population in 1976, 77 per cent earned less than the COHAB income maximum at that time (Fundacao IBGE 1976). Among families (the real unit of assessment for housing

eligibility) rather than workers in Greater Sao Paulo in 1970 62
per cent earned less than this maximum of five minimum salaries
(see table 4.2).

17. At the end of 1975, five minimum salaries amounted to 2664
    cruzeiros (approximately £148 or US $ 290) monthly and 500 UPCs
    amounted to 62850 cruzeiros (approximately £3492 or US $ 6983).

18. At the end of 1975, 3500 UPCs amounted to 439950 cruzeiros
    (approximately £24450 or US $ 48883).

19. Known as the 'housing minimum salary, this constituted the highest
    regional minimum salary less the factor for productivity increases
    included in the salary's calculation.

ANNEX

Translation of letter dated 18 April 1964 from Sandra Cavalcanti to President Castelo Branco. With the letter was sent the first draft of the 'Law of the Housing Plan' as Cavalcanti called it.

Dear friend President Castelo,

This is how the work about which we were talking is going. It was going to form a part of the presidential campaign of Carlos /Lacerda/, but we think that the Revolution is going to need to act vigorously with the masses. They are orphaned and hurt, and we will have to give them some happiness. I think that the solution of the housing problem, at least in the big cities, will have the effect of applying balsam to their civic wounds.

As I told you, I am still working on the idea. For this reason I am sending you a draft for debate and discussion by the specialists who will make up your governing team. In any case, as this will have to be transformed into a legal text, I would like to offer a few observations and warnings, which it seems to me are of great importance.

First: the Plan will be difficult to implement in a turbulent time. For this reason, I believe that the legal text must be the least complicated as possible. Our legislators have the awful habit of making casuistical little laws, which require further resort to the legislative each time that a tiny little point needs to be corrected or perfected. I think that the enclosed suffices. It consists only of 55 rather wide ranging articles. I tried only to indicate the philosophy of the Plan and to lay down powers, duties, attributions, resources and jurisdiction. More than this seems to me superfluous.

Second: I think that it is indispensable that the Housing Plan should be based on a Financial System. My experience in Guanabara allows me to assure you that the difficulties of the residential market lie in: (1) the inadequate supply of dwellings, (2) the lack of interest of investors in building for rent. All this is the result of inflation. Housing credit is generally what requires, in everybody's life, the longest period of repayment. At least ten years. Who will take on ten years with this inflation? Even the favela population responded well to our project. They are making their repayments perfectly in Vila Kennedy, even though these are readjusted /for inflation/ 'illegally' by us, as you know....

I know that in the Chamber and in the Senate the discussion will be reopened on the sociological, urban planning and social security aspects of the question. Without a healthy currency circulating in the Housing System there will be no output. The central choice must be for a bank. Close the discussion on this, Mr President.

Third: do not omit to pass on a message about rented housing. All that I have already written applies also to rents. Nobody any longer, in the big cities, is constructing housing for rent as a normal way of investing savings.

Fourth: I think that the question of house values and inflationary indexation should not appear in the legal text. I am afraid of the

98

technicians who will offer their views on this. They love mathematical formulae... If one should appear in the law and it should later become necessary to make a small adjustment, instead of simply decreeing  the change it will be necessary to go back to Congress!

Five:  when the Plan speaks generically of 'urban infrastructure' it means that the bank should act in the areas of basic sanitation and mass transport. Our cities are chaotic with regard to essential services, Mr President. It is no good building enormous housing estates where there is no water, electricity, sewerage, police and transport. In Vila Kennedy we even had to provide a bus service...

Six:  last, but not least, the favela population must not be abandoned. In reality, it is much bigger than can be seen in the favelas themselves, because to them must be added the tenements, basements, shacks etc. These people have minimal spending power, but they are people. For them there must be maintained the Social Assistance Fund which is proposed more fully in the text but which should later be studied and elaborated. If this section of the population is not attended, the Plan will fail. It may help the country's construction industry to recover;  it may have a marvellous effect in opening up new areas of work;  it may improve the medium and small sized firms involved in the production of construction materials and it may give a better location for the savings of the much better off. But, without attending the proletarian population (with an income around the minimum salary) it will have failed in its social objectives. The resources of the Plan will be fatally diverted if they go only to those who can cope with the 'inflationary compensation' which is to be introduced.

Also included in the text is the idea of creating a service centre for research and studies on urban planning and housing, so as to see whether our cities can organise themselves better and whether our civil construction industry can leave behind its rudimentary craft stage.

I think that we should use the private banking network and the savings banks and insurance funds. Let us not create another state bank to compete with and asphixiate private initiative in this country.

The state's presence should be through COHABs like the one we created in Guanabara and through the application of resources to infrastructure. As for urban land, this is the other question. There must be some reform, Mr President, to prevent speculation and to oblige the public authorities to improve their planning of urban development. But I think that this is a matter for a quieter time.

I hope that I have fulfilled my commitment. I am at your service to help in discussing the idea, in carrying it through Congress and in bringing it to victory. A friendly embrace from Sandra.

Note:  Sandra Calvacanti released the letter on 4 March 1974 describing it as follows: 'The President returned the originals of this and other documents in 1966. It is historic in the life of BNH. The marking of the passages /the underlinings shown in this translation/ was done by him'.

# 4 Administration and the housing market

INTRODUCTION

Besides the administrative framework established by the housing bank, local agencies work within the context of the market. Administrative allocation of housing is an alternative procedure to that of the market but it takes place under the influence of a series of markets - at least those for capital, land, labour and materials. For the applicant too, administratively allocated housing is just one of a series of possibilities which present themselves if not as a choice at least as a chance. Each of the housing possibilities is, in varying ratios, market controlled and administratively penetrated; for many of the possibilities there is a mix of market and bureaucratic aspects in the procedures the applicant has to go through to win shelter.

The housing finance system set up by the housing bank (BNH) apparently embraced the whole field of housing need, setting up forms of provision for everyone within several administratively defined categories. First there was the broad distinction between the nominally low-income programmes of the BNH itself and the market operations of the savings and loans system (SBPE), each with its institutional apparatus. Second, there was the repeated emphasis on the existence of programmes for distinct income categories - popular, economic, intermediate. In practice, these administrative distinctions did not retain the clear boundaries which were claimed for them. There was a process of fusion and overlap; the administrative boundaries became unclear. Income categories were redefined to fit the facts of the housing finance system's incapacity to reach certain groups; agencies reached beyond their income boundaries; the BNH launched the mortgage programme to serve populations which were apparently already attended by the private market. In other words, experience showed that there was not a series of distinct and neatly compartmentalised housing markets each of which could be treated separately. The market is not divisible but continuous. This continuity affects the capacity for administrative control at least in the following ways:

a) Action in one part of the housing market affects other parts, for
   example by shifting costs or demands. This may be mediated through
   the housing market's relation to other markets; for example,
   large scale investment in luxury apartment building may at least
   in the short term increase the costs of land, labour, finance and

materials also for all other sectors.[1]  Indeed, the housing finance
system was designed to exploit these links of housing with other
markets:  investing in construction to promote employment, boosting
the economy through the materials and construction industries, and
offering a resort for savings.  The concomitant is that these
linkages and therefore pressures to shift are built· into the housing
system as part of it.  Public and private agencies compete with
each other and the market in general for capital, land, materials,
labour, public services and certain customers.

b)  Clients have, in varying degree, options about where their demands
are attended.  The capacity of choice affects the level of reliance,
or dependence, upon any particular agency for a solution to housing
problems.  The applicant has more or less freedom to exercise his
'voice',[2] to seek alternative arrangements or modifications in the
terms on which he is served.

c)  So also administrative agencies have varying degrees of choice
about which clients they attend.  If the market is continuous
rather than administratively boxed there will be no clear cut off
point between acceptable and unacceptable applicants.  Where the
agency is also expected to reduce risk and ensure returns, all the
pressure is for shifts towards more credit-worthy groups of the
population;  a continuous market makes these shifts imperceptible
as well as difficult to resist.

The best willed plans and administrative intentions are therefore
exposed to these market constraints not from outside but from within
the housing system.  On the other hand, there is no more a pure market
than there is administrative allocation exclusive of the market.  Public
administration itself affects the operation of the market and the
options which are open to applicants and agencies.  This is partly in
the general sense that governmental action seeks to transfer resources
into and out of housing and to regulate aspects of the market - for
example, in the Brazilian case, by setting up institutions to allocate
credit, by promoting investment in the construction and materials
industries and by urban planning to zone residential and industrial
development.  But these and other controls and resource transfers are
also particular in their effect, in the sense that they discriminate
between and even create options within the housing market.  People,
depending for example on income or housing type, are more or less able
to claim or avoid the administrative categorisation which renders them
eligible, on the one hand, for cheap credit, public services,
residential zoning, security of tenure and controlled repayments, or,
on the other hand, for penalties, insecurity, harrassment and eviction.
Although the housing market is continuous, the terms which operate
within its parts are distinct, and administrative action contributes
to the distinctions.  The encounter between the agencies of BNH and
their applicants therefore takes place in the context of market
pressures, constraints and options which are themselves influenced by
public policy.  In other guises, BNH may itself affect the conditions
which applicants bring to housing agencies for solution.  The division
of the market between BNH agencies by income groups means that
institutions confront applicants whose market situation gives them a
particular range of possibilities, experiences and degrees of reliance
upon administrative solutions.

This chapter examines this market context outling the housing types and options which exist in Sao Paulo, the way in which their terms and conditions are affected by administrative action and the association of income with housing types.

HOUSING OPTIONS

*The spatial distribution of population increase and income*

The population of Greater Sao Paulo (map 4.1) which stood at 4.8 million in 1960 exceeded twelve million by 1980. The annual rate of growth was about 5.5 per cent between 1960 and 1970 compared to six per cent during the previous decade. Something of the order of half a million people were joining the population of Greater Sao Paulo during the 1970s - about sixty per cent of them by migration.

The highest rates of increase were taking place in the outer municipalities of the metropolis, in spite of the fact that large tracts of vacant land existed in the central areas (EMPLASA 1975 p.9). The areas of greatest population expansion were those which contained the highest proportions of low income groups. The most rapidly expanding municipalities[3] and districts[4] of Greater Sao Paulo were also areas in which more than half of families earned less than three minimum salaries[5] in 1970 (maps 4.2 and 4.3). But this was not simply a matter of the settlement of poorer newcomers in the expanding periphery; only the most central districts had a relatively stable or declining population. Beyond the centre, the populations of most areas of the city more than doubled between 1960 and 1970, while some, in the east (Itaquera), south (Diadema) and west (Taboao), quadrupled.

Rapid growth was normal; what has to be explained is the relative stability of the central and inner suburban areas and their relationship with the rest of the city. In one obvious way they were distinctive; while they contained only seventeen per cent of metropolitan inhabitants, in these areas were concentrated the wealthiest groups of the population. A special run of the 1970 census demonstrated that over three quarters of families in the top income bracket (those earning over about US $ 1100 monthly in 1970) lived in seven districts within a radius of approximately 7 kilometres to the south and west of the city (Fundacao IBGE 1973b).[6]

The picture that seems to emerge is of an island of calm surrounded by a turbulent sea of urban development. This picture would, however, be false; there is no island of calm. The relatively slow population growth of the central districts of Sao Paulo is due to the form rather than to the absence of urban development in those areas. Indeed, the higher income districts of the city are the areas of most obvious 'modern' construction and the constant replacement of older buildings by roads, offices, shopping centres and newer, higher apartment blocks. Behind the relative stability in population numbers was a process of considerable change promoted by the investments of financial institutions and large-scale construction firms.

What was being built in the centre and the inner suburbs was certainly not accessible to the mass of the population; indeed, it positively contributed to their expulsion. The continuous process of urban redevelopment, backed by high-income demand and institutional finance,

102

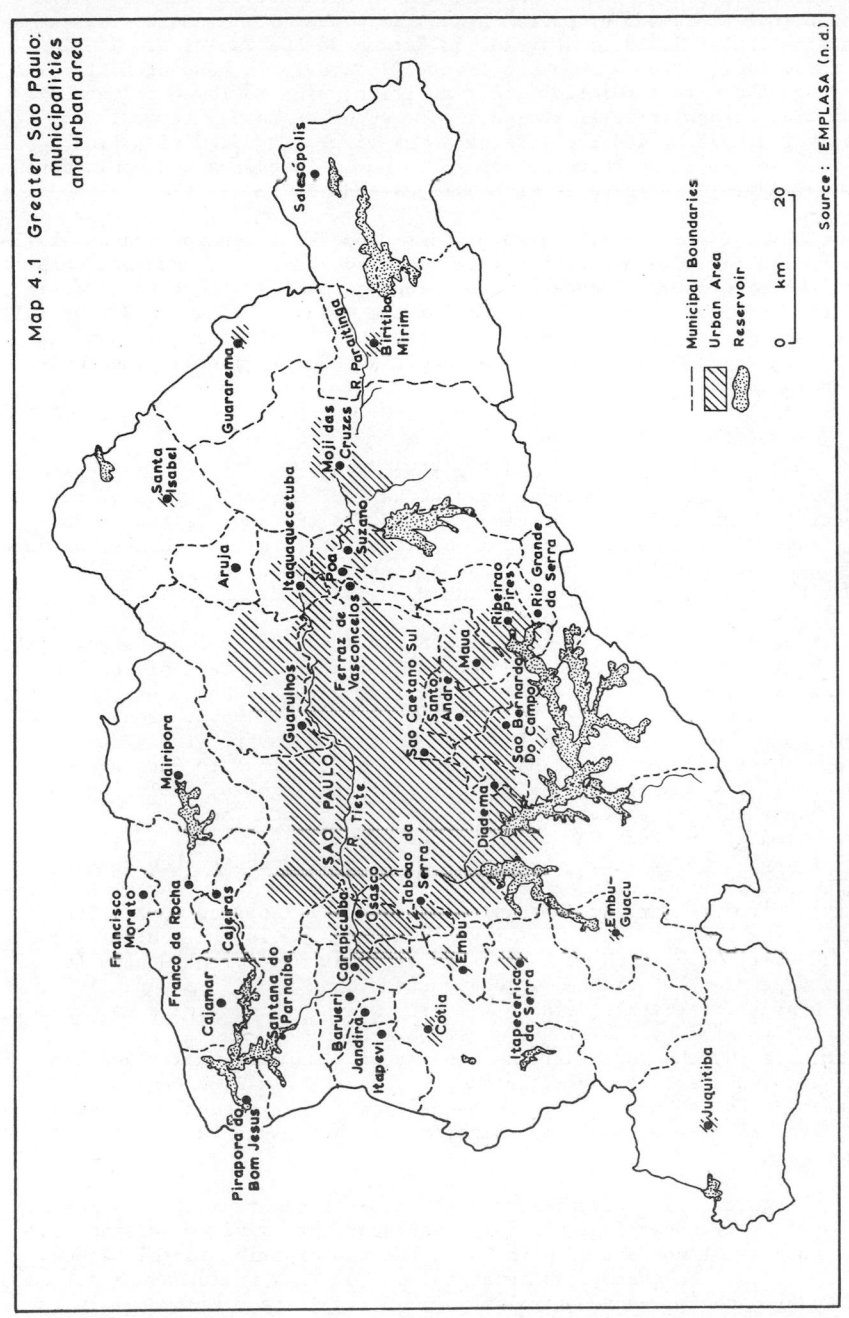

Map 4.1 Greater Sao Paulo: municipalities and urban area

Municipal Boundaries
Urban Area
Reservoir

0   km   20

Source: EMPLASA (n.d.)

Salesópolis

Biritiba Mirim

R. Paraitinga

Guararema

Santa Isabel

Moji das Cruzes

Itaquaquecetuba

Aruja

Poa

Suzano

Ferraz de Vasconcelos

Guarulhos

Ribeirao Pires

Rio Grande da Serra

Sao Caetano Sul

Santo André

Maua

SAO PAULO

R. Tiete

Sao Bernardo Do Campo

Mairipora

Diadema

Embu-Guacu

Francisco Morato

Franco da Rocha

Cajamar

Cajiras

Santana do Parnaiba

Taboao da Serra

Osasco

Carapicuiba

Barueri

Jandira

Itapevi

Cótia

Embu

Itapecerica da Serra

Juquitiba

Pirapora do Bom Jesus

103

stimulated rapid increases in land and housing prices in the centre
and the displacement of poorer groups from previous areas of low income
housing (Bolaffi, 1975; Governo do Estado de Sao Paulo, n.d.).  The
removal took place through the eventual increase in housing costs or
through the direct eviction and demolition which followed private
building or public works projects.  For poorer groups, removal from
central areas implied the loss of a relatively favoured situation
almost certainly in terms of access to public services and employment
and probably also in terms of housing standards.

In chapter six, we will examine this process of renewal and expulsion
as it applied to a particular neighbourhood, Bras.  The present chapter
has the more general concern of showing how public sector intervention
contributes to the differentiation of the urban property (and especially
housing) markets.  First we examine the impetus given by the savings
and loans system (SBPE) to the high class redevelopment of the central
areas.

## Income distribution and the SBPE

The mechanism by which the housing finance system attains the apparent
universality of its coverage, beyond the 'sub market' levels of the
population which are the province of BNH, is the savings and loans
system.  Operated on a commercial basis by state savings banks, private
savings and loans associations and property companies, the SBPE's
operations are supported by BNH through loans and guarantees.

Output by the SBPE has clearly been too small to have any significance
in the face of Sao Paulo's population increase.  In each of the two
years 1973 and 1974, the number of housing units financed by the SBPE
in the municipality of Sao Paulo amounted to about 9500;  roughly 8000
were completed in 1975 (BNH 1974 and 1975).  However, its market and
geographical concentration has been held by critics[7] to have worsened
the housing situation of the mass of the population by inflating land
and house prices, elevating construction costs and focusing the
attention of builders on higher income groups.  Practically all the
loans made by SBPE go to the purchase  of newly constructed housing
which, in the case of Greater Sao Paulo is nearly all (ninety per cent)
in the form of apartment blocks.  Construction financed by the SBPE
during the 1970s was overwhelmingly concentrated in the central areas
of the city;  the richest core areas shown in map 4.3 accounted for
eighty per cent of the units constructed through SBPE up until 1975.[8]
Any hoped for 'trickle down' effect (by which poorer groups move into
housing vacated by the richer) must have been reduced if not
eliminated by the fact that the construction usually took place in
established areas of higher income housing which was destroyed to
make way for the new.  Increased densities may have been achieved but
at rates which were small by comparison with the general population
increase.[9]

The average price of units, and the cost of downpayments and monthly
repayments is shown in table 4.1 translated into minimum salaries for
the purpose of comparison with the level and distribution of incomes
in the city.  An average house at the end of 1974 would have required
not only a downpayment equivalent to 270 times the minimum salary but
also a monthly payment equivalent to six salaries.  The standard BNH
requirement is that monthly repayments should not exceed a quarter of

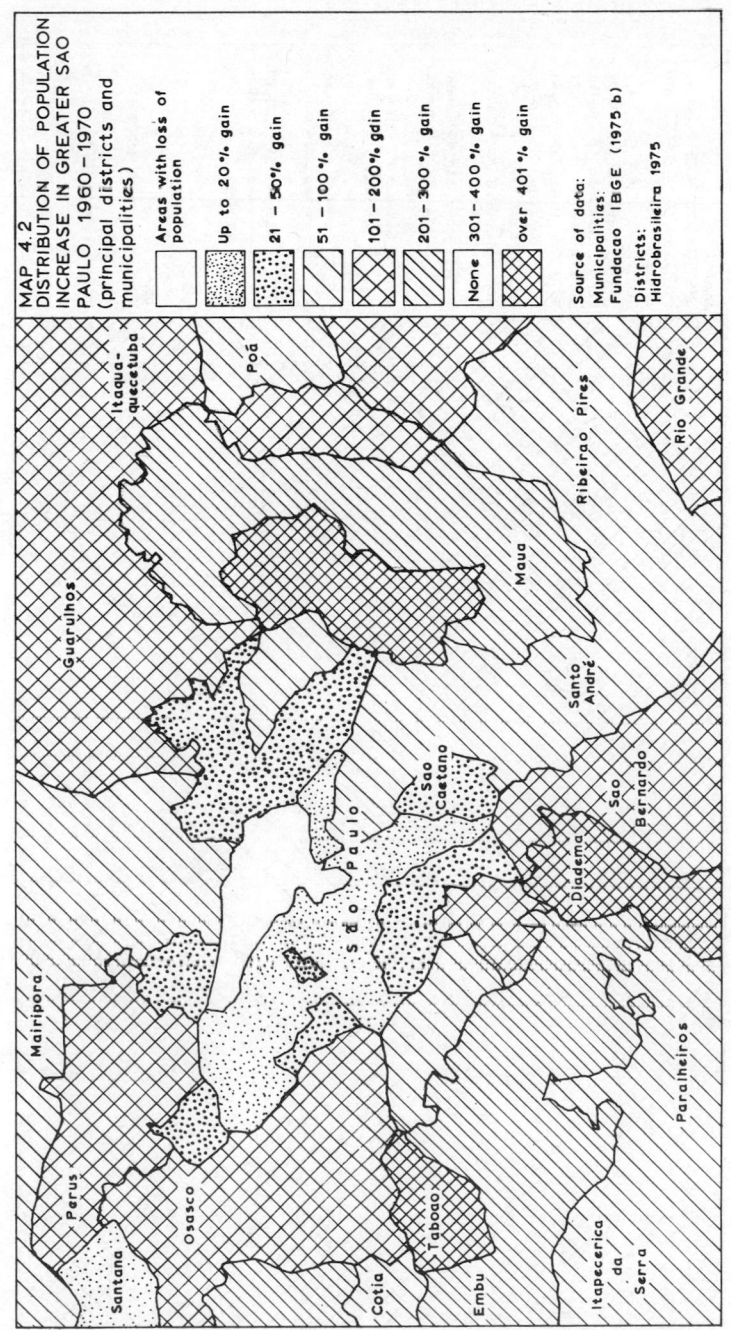

MAP 4.2
DISTRIBUTION OF POPULATION
INCREASE IN GREATER SAO
PAULO 1960-1970
(principal districts and
municipalities)

Areas with loss of
population

Up to 20% gain

21 – 50% gain

51 – 100% gain

101 – 200% gain

201 – 300% gain

None

301 – 400% gain

over 401% gain

Source of data:
Municipalities:
Fundacao IBGE (1975 b)

Districts:
Hidrobrasileira 1975

Itaqua-
quecetuba

Poá

Ribeirao Pires

Rio Grande

Guarulhos

Maua

Santo
André

Mairipora

São Paulo

Sao
Caetano

Sao
Bernardo

Diadema

Perus

Osasco

Taboao

Santana

Cotia

Embu

Itapecerica
da.
Serra

Paralheiros

105

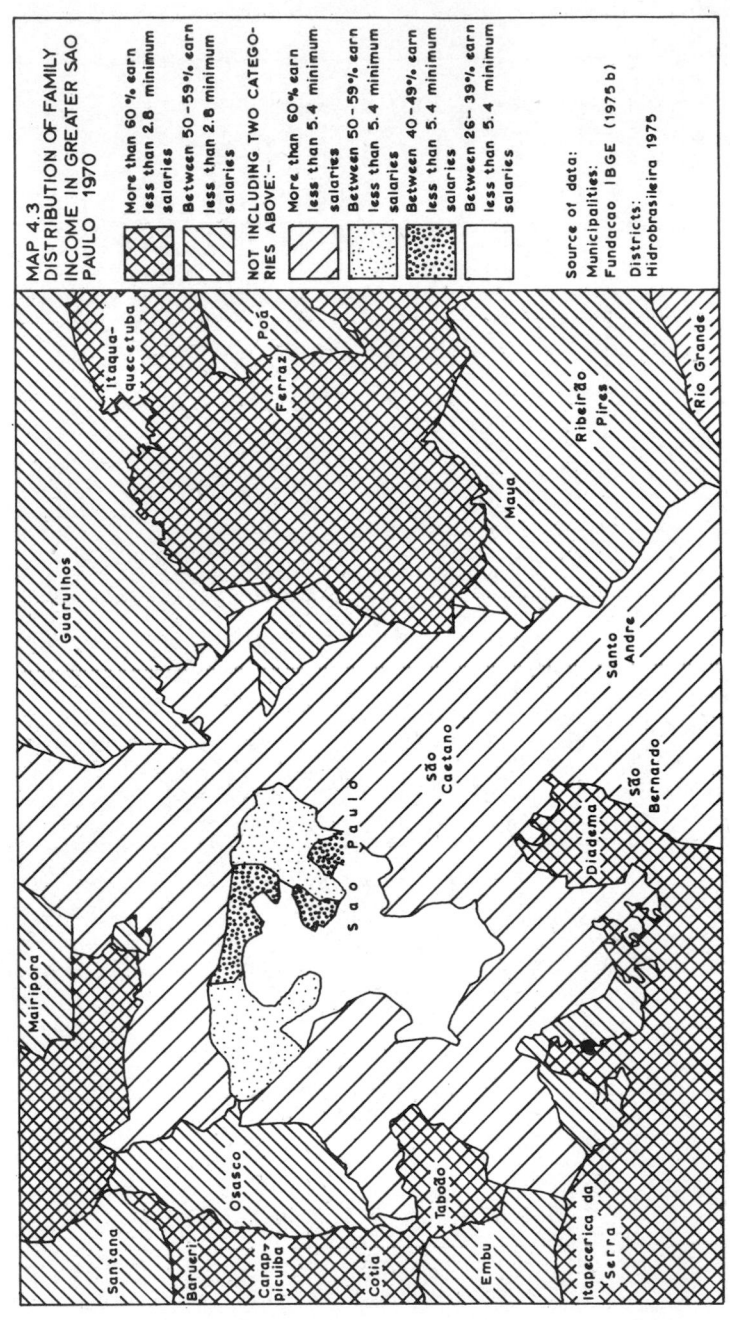

MAP 4.3
DISTRIBUTION OF FAMILY
INCOME IN GREATER SAO
PAULO 1970

More than 60% earn
less than 2.8 minimum
salaries

Between 50-59% earn
less than 2.8 minimum
salaries

NOT INCLUDING TWO CATEGO-
RIES ABOVE:-

More than 60% earn
less than 5.4 minimum
salaries

Between 50-59% earn
less than 5.4 minimum
salaries

Between 40-49% earn
less than 5.4 minimum
salaries

Between 26-39% earn
less than 5.4 minimum
salaries

Source of data:
Municipalities:
Fundacao IBGE (1975 b)

Districts:
Hidrobrasileira 1975

Itaqua-
quecetuba

Poá

Ferraz

Ribeirão
Pires

Rio Grande

Guarulhos

Maua

Santo
Andre

São
Caetano

São
Paulo

Diadema

São
Bernardo

Mairipora

Santana

Osasco

Barueri

Carap-
picuiba

Cotia

Taboão

Embu

Itapecerica da
Serra

106

Table 4.1

Average price of SBPE housing units sold in Sao Paulo municipality 1973-1975.
(prices in standard capital units (UPCs) and minimum salaries)

| | Prices in standard capital units | | | | | | | | | | Prices in minimum salaries | | | | | | | | | |
|---|---|---|---|---|---|---|---|---|---|---|---|---|---|---|---|---|---|---|---|---|
| | 1973 | | | 1974 | | | | 1975 | | | 1973. | | | 1974 | | | | 1975 | | |
| | in quarters | | | in quarters | | | | in quarters | | | in quarters | | | in quarters | | | | in quarters | | |
| | 2 | 3 | 4 | 1 | 2 | 3 | 4 | 1 | 2 | 3 | 2 | 3 | 4 | 1 | 2 | 3 | 4 | 1 | 2 | 3 |
| Average Price | 1951 | 2229 | 2948 | 2548 | 2993 | 2749 | 2969 | 2785 | 4192 | 3096 | 457 | 542 | 686 | 658 | 665 | 655 | 749 | 789 | 883 | 693 |
| Average proportion of price in downpayment | 26% | 30% | 34% | 35% | 39% | 35% | 36% | 37% | 44% | 33% | 26% | 30% | 34% | 35% | 39% | 35% | 36% | 37% | 44% | 33% |
| Average downpayment | 504 | 657 | 932 | 879 | 1170 | 950 | 998 | 1026 | 1825 | 1015 | 118 | 160 | 233 | 227 | 260 | 226 | 270 | 290 | 384 | 227 |
| Average monthly payment | 23 | 24 | 25 | 23 | 27 | 25 | 24 | 24 | 28 | 31 | 5 | 6 | 6 | 6 | 6 | 6 | 6 | 6 | 7 | 7 |

Source: Calculated from BNH (1974 and 1975). Figures adjusted from UPCs into cruzeiros (Fundacao Getulio Vargas 1976 p.173) and from cruzeiros into minimum salaries for Sao Paulo.

family income; on this basis a family income of twenty four minimum
salaries per month would have been required to buy the house.[10] Less
than eight per cent of houses were sold at under 1351 standard capital
units (UPCs) which, on the same basis, required family earnings of
twelve minimum salaries. The income table (4.2) shows that few
families reached this level.

Table 4.2
Income distribution in the major municipalities of
Greater Sao Paulo 1970, by household
(Per cent)

| House-hold income in sm (minimum salary) ranges | Sao Paulo | Santo Andre | Osasco | Guarulhos | Sao Bernardo | Sao Caetano | Daidema | Total |
|---|---|---|---|---|---|---|---|---|
| up to 1sm | 5.1 | 5.3 | 8.4 | 9.4 | 5.3 | 3.9 | 9.3 | 5.4 |
| 1-2 | 16.0 | 15.0 | 24.9 | 24.1 | 14.9 | 11.1 | 29.9 | 16.5 |
| 2-3 | 17.2 | 19.8 | 22.5 | 21.2 | 17.8 | 16.3 | 22.9 | 17.7 |
| 3-5 | 22.4 | 25.5 | 21.2 | 21.4 | 24.3 | 26.1 | 20.0 | 22.6 |
| 5-7 | 11.9 | 12.4 | 8.8 | 9.2 | 13.3 | 15.3 | 7.3 | 11.8 |
| 7-10 | 8.2 | 7.3 | 4.3 | 4.5 | 8.9 | 10.7 | 3.4 | 7.9 |
| 10-15 | 6.8 | 4.3 | 2.1 | 2.7 | 6.0 | 6.0 | 1.3 | 6.3 |
| 15-20 | 3.1 | 1.4 | 0.5 | 0.8 | 1.5 | 1.9 | 0.3 | 2.7 |
| 20+ | 4.0 | 1.2 | 0.4 | 0.4 | 1.4 | 1.1 | 0.2 | 3.8 |
| no declaration | 5.3 | 7.8 | 6.9 | 6.3 | 6.6 | 7.6 | 5.4 | 5.3 |
| | 100.0 | 100.0 | 100.0 | 100.0 | 100.0 | 100.0 | 100.0 | 100.0 |

Source: calculated from a special run of the 1970 census for Metro,
made available by CECAP.

According to the census figures, eighty two per cent of families in the
Sao Paulo population earned less than ten minimum salaries. In any
case, it is clear that the vast majority of the population is excluded
from the private agency operations of the housing finance system.
Unless they have access through the BNH's popular and economic
programmes (which are marginal in their scale as chapter three showed),
they are therefore excluded from the officially approved programmes of
financing for house purchase which bring not only housing and public
services but also subsidies in the shape of tax relief on loan interest
and capital repayments. A study by the Sao Paulo State housing
organisation (CECAP) in the areas to the north and east of the centre of
Greater Sao Paulo showed that of the half of the sample who wished to buy
a house more than two thirds were prepared to pay less than one minimum
salary monthly and eighty two per cent were able to offer no more than
seven minimum salaries as a downpayment. These aspirations contrast
sharply with the requirements of SBPE financing, and the contrast was
growing. Table 4.1 shows how the average price of units increased over
the period 1973-1975 in real (UPC) terms by nearly sixty per cent, and
how this pushed up the cost in downpayments and monthly repayments on
loans.

The scale of the increase led the national housing bank cautiously to suggest that it was not possible to exclude the hypothesis that the rise was due to 'property speculation' (BNH 1975 1st quarter p.21) as well as to increased demand. Indeed it reported a growing difficulty in the marketing of units. In a city experiencing a rapid growth of population, it was nevertheless necessary for constructors and developers to undertake television advertising and street leaflet campaigns to attempt to sell housing in new developments. The saturation of the upper income market contributed to the crisis in the construction industry which was evident by 1978. Chapter three (tables 3.8 and 3.9) showed that it was in exactly that year that BNH's low income housing programmes began to expand after a long period of contraction. The possibility of moving into publicly sponsored 'popular' housing rescued some large construction firms and allowed the BNH for the first time to overshoot its construction targets.

*Housing alternatives*

The mass exclusion from officially sponsored forms of house purchase does not imply that in Sao Paulo there is any homogeneity in the solutions adopted by the population. There is, especially, relatively little collective action to break the procedures of the market. Popularly organised invasion of land is not common place as it is, for example, for thirty per cent of the population of Lima; nor is accretive occupation of land without the owner's permission the norm as it is for forty per cent of the population of Caracas (Batley 1978). Low income housing in Sao Paulo on the whole respects the market's principles and rules, even if landowners and developers frequently themselves break the governmental rules in the division and sale of their land.

There has therefore grown up a variety of forms of popular housing which depend, as Leeds (1974) has suggested, on the household's position in the labour market, on the household cycle (different needs associated for example with single people and established families) and on the capacity to make institutional connections which bring with them access to housing opportunities. Leeds (1974 p.78) argues that the underlying conditioning factor is the position of households in the wage-labour market, according to which they 'confront a system of institutional and financial constraints.... which set the parameters of the choices they can make among the arrangements for living'. Employment determines not only (i) wage levels and hence capacity to pay, but also (ii) the level of job security and availability of alternatives and hence the need for proximity to labour markets, and (iii) the sorts of institutional connections (trade union, providential association, government department) which go with certain employment and which may be avenues to occupational-residential enclaves. For Rio de Janeiro, Leeds identifies eight 'proletarian' settlement types varying by tenure, location, cost, form of access, quality of construction and services: rooming houses, single storey terraced rooms (*vilas*), governmental emergency shelter, multi-storey apartments built by occupationally associated organisations, governmental 'popular' housing, small private houses in outlying areas (*suburbios*), central slums (*corticos*), and squatter settlements (*favelas*). About '70 per cent of the population of the city of Rio de Janeiro... live in housing, which, with the exception of a few more evolved squatments, is almost exclusively proletarian' (Leeds 1974 p.73).

The Sao Paulo State metropolitan planning organisation (EMPLASA), anticipating the housing alternatives of the 757,000 families which it estimated would join the metropolitan area between 1975 and 1979, grouped the possibilities for the majority of the new population into two - slum housing in the central areas or self-built housing on the periphery. It estimated that two thirds of the new families would earn less than five minimum salaries and that

> '... the larger part of this population will be forced to choose between installing themselves precariously and clandestinely in the most central urbanised areas (in favelas or corticos), or seeking to accommodate themselves in rustic houses made with their own hands, in the distant periphery, without urban services, where there are the worst conditions of sanitation, transport, provisioning and social service'. (EMPLASA 1975 pp.1-2)

Favelas and corticos represent an extremity in bad housing conditions and visibility which has led them to be more studied than other more prevalent forms of housing for the mass of the population. The most thorough of these studies in Sao Paulo are those carried out by the municipality's welfare department (Secretaria de Bem Estar) and housing and labour department (Departamento de Habitacao e Trabalho) - but they apply only to the municipality.

Corticos are forms of collective housing, 'involuntarily cohabited', subdivided into rented (or sub let) rooms and sharing domestic services. They are usually old decayed houses in the inner residential areas of Sao Paulo and therefore hardly overlap with the favelas (see map 4.4). The municipal study (Boletim Habi 1975) estimated a total of 20,600 corticos with a population of 554,000 people, equivalent to about nine per cent of the municipal population in 1973. Taking into account newer collective housing in the periphery of the city, the proportion reached twenty three per cent. While eighty per cent of cortico inhabitants originated from outside Sao Paulo, it appeared that they were much longer established in the city than favelados (table 4.3) and that half had lived in the same cortico more than five years. The evidence suggested that the population of the corticos arose from earlier waves of migration (during the 1940s and 1950s) and that the cortico turned out to be a less provisional housing solution than the inhabitants had hoped.

Table 4.3
Distribution of favela and cortico population by length
of residence in the municipality of Sao Paulo,1973

| Period of residence Years | Favela population % | % accumulative | Cortico population % | % accumulative |
|---|---|---|---|---|
| less than 1 | 18 | 18 | | |
| 1-3 | 24 | 42 | 16 | 16 |
| 3-5 | 17 | 59 | | |
| 5-7 | 9 | 68 | | |
| 7-10 | 9 | 77 | 15 | 31 |
| 10+ | 23 | 100 | 69 | 100 |
| | 100 | | 100 | |
| Base No. | (42,247) | | (153) | |

Sources: Boletim Habi (1975 p.54), Boletim Habi (1974 p.81)

110

In several respects, this slum accommodation demonstrates a match between the labour and housing markets: (a) Practically all heads of families were in work, seventy three per cent of them with registered employment[11] but with very high instability in work:- seventeen per cent had been in their last employment only six months, and sixty two per cent for less than two years. A central residential location helps to meet this situation by offering alternative employment within easy reach - two thirds of the sample lived within half an hour of their work. (b) The connection between the labour and housing markets operates also in the other direction: the study shows how corticos occur in areas of declining residential value which is itself associated with the penetration of industry, commerce and services. (c) Incomes are low (table 4.4) but rents approximately match, at least in the sense that seventy per cent of cortico families pay less than thirty per cent of their income in rent.

Cortico housing is relatively cheap, well located for work and offers access to the basic urban services which a large part of the urban population lacks. Practically all cortico residents have access to piped water, drainage, electric light and rubbish collection (Boletim Habi 1975 p.45). The costs are in the decayed buildings, shared services and overcrowded space (table 4.5). Two thirds of residents wish to leave the corticos for these reasons. However, the evidence suggests that there is no alternative available which matches their employment needs and income capacity. This is the accommodation which their market position earns them. As will be shown later, there is little if anything which the BNH's popular housing programme does to change this reality, although this is precisely the income group which it sets out to serve. Most of this group will only leave their present cortico accommodation if land values in their area rise and redevelopment forces them out.

Table 4.4
Distribution of favela and cortico households by family
income ranges in minimum salaries, Sao Paulo

| Family income ranges in minimum salaries | Favela households (1973) % | % accumulative | Cortico households (1973) % | % accumulative | Sao Paulo households (1970) % | % accumulative |
|---|---|---|---|---|---|---|
| up to 2 | 80 | 80 | 28 | 28 | 22 | 22 |
| 2-4 | 17 | 97 | 41 | 69 | } 52 | 74 |
| 4-7 | } 3 | 100 | 22 | 91 | | |
| 7+ | | | 9 | 100 | 26 | 100 |
| | 100 | | 100 | | | |
| Base No. | (8669) | | (153) | | (1,538,843) | |

Sources: Boletim Habi (1975 p.70)
         Boletim Habi (1974 p.115)

Favelas are probably the cheapest form of housing and their residents are concentrated among the lowest income groups. By one official definition they are '... groups of small dwellings constructed with inadequate materials (old wood, zinc, tin cans and cardboard) distri- buted irregularly almost always on land without urban services and facilities...' (Prefeitura 1972). The occupation of the land is never

111

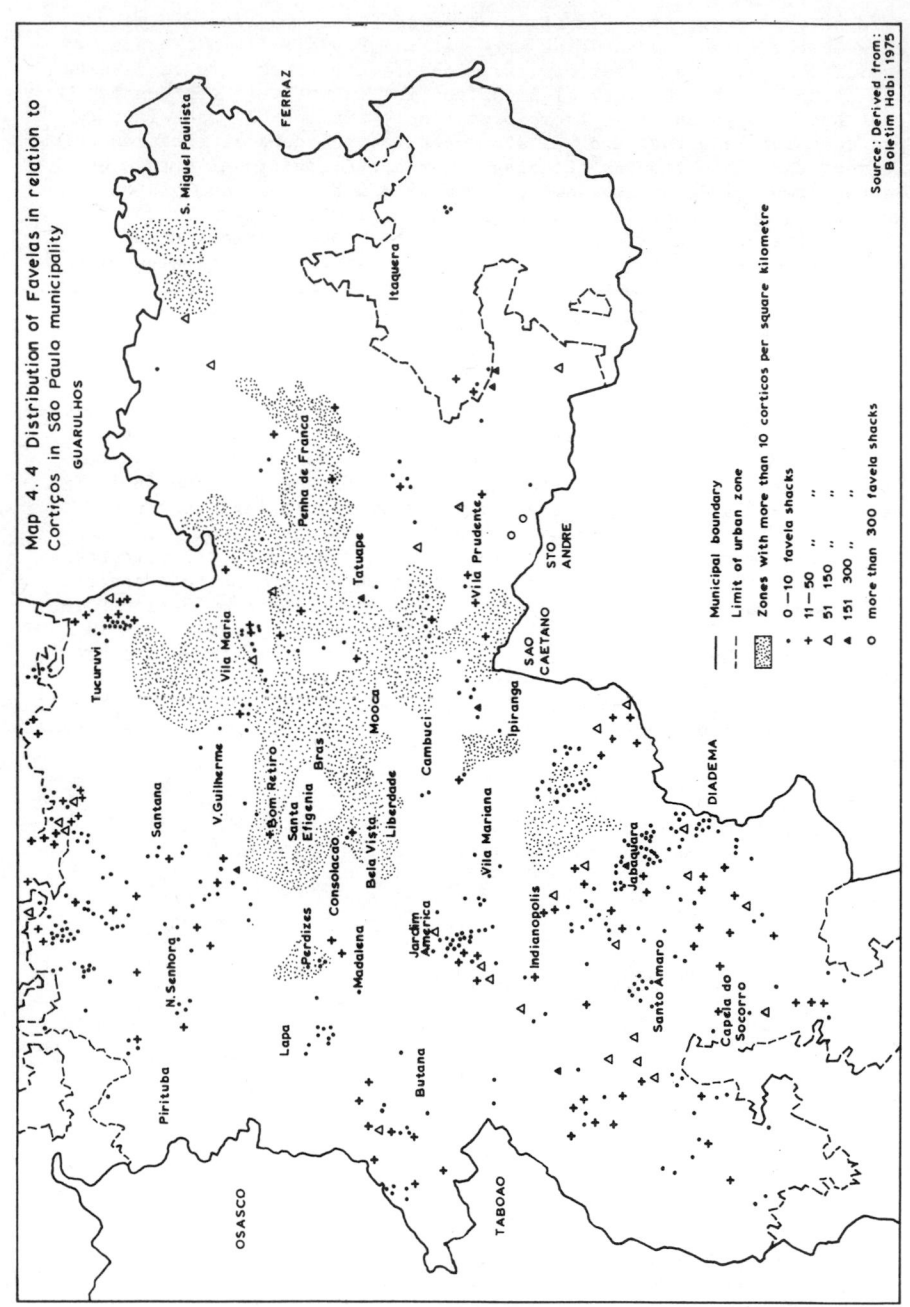

Map 4.4 Distribution of Favelas in relation to Cortiços in São Paulo municipality

Source: Derived from:
Boletim Habi 1975

Municipal boundary
Limit of urban zone
Zones with more than 10 cortiços per square kilometre
•    0—10  favela shacks
+    11—50   "    "
△    51  150   "    "
▲   151  300   "    "
○   more than 300  favela shacks

GUARULHOS

FERRAZ

S. Miguel Paulista

Itaquera

Penha de Franca

Tatuapé

Vila Prudente

Tucuruvi

Vila Maria

SAO CAETANO

STO ANDRE

Santana

V.Guilherme

Bras

Santa Efigenia

Bom Retiro

Mooca

Cambuci

Liberdade

Bela Vista

Ipiranga

Consolacão

Perdizes

Madalena

Jardim América

Vila Mariana

Indianopolis

Jabaquara

N.Senhora

Lapa

Santo Amaro

DIADEMA

Capela do Socorro

Pirituba

Butana

OSASCO

TABOAO

112

Table 4.5

Rates of occupation of housing in favelas, corticos, (1973)
and all Sao Paulo households (1970)

| | Favelas | Corticos | All Sao Paulo municipality |
|---|---|---|---|
| Persons per room | 3.1 | 3.6 | 1.0 |
| families per room | 1.3 | 1.6 | 0.2 |
| square metres per person | $1.1m^2$ | $3.1m^2$ | - |

Source: Boletim Habi (1975 p.47)

formally legalised and registered but,according to a Sao Paulo
municipal study (Boletim Habi 1974), it does not take place only by
unpermitted settlement (47 per cent of favelas) but also by the owner's
verbal concession (24 per cent of favelas) or by other means including
renting (29 per cent of cases). More than half the settlements are
on private land, the rest (44 per cent) on land belonging to a public
authority (usually the municipality). They are not located as centrally
as corticos (map 4.4) but are still within rather than at the periphery
of the urban system, near or with access to centres of unskilled
employment. The land occupied has low alternative use value due to its
proximity to main roads (80 per cent of favelas), steep slopes and
proximity to streams (60 per cent), proximity to rubbish tips (64 per
cent), or subjection to flooding (32 per cent). Their illegality and
location near urban employment centres put favelas permanently under
the threat of removal if an increase in property values makes the
recovery of land viable.[12] The threat is permanent but the municipal
study shows that in the case of most favelas (88 per cent) there had
never been any realisation of the threat.

The study estimated the 1973 favela population as 72,000 people (just
over one per cent of the municipal population) living in 527 settlements.
By comparison with corticos, these settlements were recently established
- 44 per cent had existed for less than five years, 90 per cent for less
than fifteen years. The Sao Paulo favelas contained a largely migrant
population of recent arrival (63 per cent of household had arrived in
the municipality over the previous ten years). However, the favelas are
not simply explained as the product of the migration of the poor. The
evidence is that a large proportion of the favela (41 per cent) as of
the cortico (58 per cent) population previously had a better housing
situation in Sao Paulo (Boletim Habi 1974, 1975 and Taschner 1978).
Apparently, for many their present housing represents a worsening of
their circumstances during their time in the city itself. There is
a process of removal and relocation from more central parts of the
city towards the outlying areas - a process which we will examine in
more detail in chapter six. By 1980, the national census showed that
the proportion of the Sao Paulo population living in favela shacks had
risen to more than four per cent.

Favela dwellings are small, fragile and practically without public
services (table 4.6). Most (93 per cent) are constructed of old wood
and consist of one room (52 per cent) or two (35 per cent). The level
of overcrowding approaches that of the corticos (table 4.5).

Table 4.6
Distribution of dwellings without urban services in
favelas, corticos and all Sao Paulo households
(Per cent)

| Public Service | Favelas[a] 1973 | Corticos[b] 1973 | All Sao Paulo municipality |
|---|---|---|---|
| water system | 80 | 5 | 36 (1970) [c] |
| sewerage system | 99 | 14 | 37 (1970) |
| rubbish collection | 85 | 1 | 16 (1968) [d] |
| Base no. | (8673) | (118) | (1272279-1970) |
| | | | (2409-1968) |

Note: households within corticos will practically always share water
and sanitation facilities.

Sources: (a) Boletim Habi (1974 p.60) per dwelling.
(b) Boletim Habi (1975 p.45) per cortico.
(c) Fundacao IBGE (1973) per dwelling in 1970.
(d) Prefeitura (1969) per dwelling in 1968.

As in the case of the corticos, the favelas demonstrate a match
between the labour and housing markets. The low income of the favela
population is matched by the free occupation of land and the rent free
occupation of self built housing. The municipal study shows that 82 per
cent of shacks are 'owned' (without title) by their occupants (Boletim
Habi 1974). The location of favelas reflects the need for proximity
to alternative employment opportunities. The precariousness of the
favela's legal security and physical survival is a reflection of
residents' intermittent and insecure employment. Most favelados are
in casual, unskilled work (73 per cent) and a large proportion (42 per
cent) are in unregistered employment. A far higher proportion (56 per
cent) of favela residents aged over ten are economically active than
of the municipal population as a whole (39 per cent). It is not, then,
that they are unintegrated with the urban economy any more than that
they are outside the land and housing markets. But they live and work
beyond the fringes of official recognition, formal regulation and
protection.

The population of the favelas is growing faster than that of the
city,[13] with evidence that they are increasingly recruiting from among
people who have fallen out of better housing categories in the city
(Taschner 1978). But favelas with corticos still only account for the
housing 'solutions' of about fifteen per cent of the municipality's
population. Such housing categories can, however, be too finely drawn.
Aspects of the favela and cortico situation - overcrowding, insecurity
of tenure, lack of public services, inadequate construction - are shared
much more generally by the majority of the poor (say those earning
less than five times the minimum salary), but often without the
advantages of cheapness and proximity to work. A working paper
contributing to the State government's diagnosis of the metropolitan
situation described the characteristics of two 'distinct cities' within
one:

'On the one hand, there is the dispersed, outlying city, with
public services (such as sanitation) which are unreliable,

non-existent or difficult to get access to. It contains a
low income population with alarmingly low levels of health
and with inadequate material conditions (income, time, mobility)
for integrating themselves into metropolitan life. This is the
situation of more than 40 per cent of the metropolitan population.
On the other hand, there is the central city....' (Governo do
Estado de Sao Paulo n.d., Condicoes Urbanas p.11)

This dualistic view is acceptable at the level of summary description
rather than analysis. As has been argued earlier, parts of the land
and housing markets, as of the labour market, are continuously
connected and not 'distinct'. Numerous studies have reported on the
grades of housing which shade from the favela situation into a state of
housing 'normality' or adequacy (Valladares and Figueiredo 1982). A
study of the municipal area of Sao Paulo (Prefeitura 1969) classified
a quarter of its housing stock as 'precarious', that is inadequately
constructed, overcrowded and under-serviced. The 1970 national census
defined seven per cent of the housing stock of Greater Sao Paulo as
'rustic', that is 'buildings in which predominate mud walls, thatch,
unprepared wood, used packing material and earth floors'. Such overcrowded and inadequately constructed housing occurs in the highest
proportions outside Sao Paulo municipality in the outlying areas of the
metropolis (table 4.7).

Rustic housing is one sign of the process of self building which goes
on especially at the periphery of the city. Plots are sold
'clandestinely' by land developers – that is without official permission
or registration – and purchasers build their own house, again without
official permission. There is no firm data on the scale of this activity
but Maricato (1979) estimates that outside the central municipalities
(Sao Paulo, Santo Andre, Sao Caetano and Sao Bernardo) more than half
the houses in Greater Sao Paulo were built by their inhabitants
although often with the support of paid labour. Self-built housing
provides the possibility of ownership to a much wider section of the
population than could find a place in the formal housing market.
However the legality of the claim to ownership is usually dubious.
A survey in 1976 by the Sao Paulo metropolitan housing company of one
area of clandestine plots showed that only sixteen per cent of occupants
had any formally registered claim to ownership of the land although
ninety per cent were paying for their site.

As a result of this informal market, ownership is fairly evenly
distributed across the population of Greater Sao Paulo at between half
and three quarters of all income groups, according to the 1970 census.
Indeed for many it appears that ownership through the informal market
is the way in which the costs of officially approved and financed
housing are avoided. Table 4.8 shows how most purchases take place by
direct arrangement with the vendor or by self-building rather than
through financial institutions. Procedural complexities are minimised,
instalments are based on what purchasers can actually pay, a downpayment
is not always required, the repayment period is limited and negotiable
(Chinelli 1980).

The existence of cheaper and more direct means of purchase  than those
offered by BNH or the formal private market means that housing is
usually owned outright rather than in the process of acquisition (table
4.9) Outright ownership, which is the most common form of occupancy,

Table 4.7
Housing conditions, Greater Sao Paulo 1970

| Municipalities | Percent of dwellings(b) over-crowded (a) | rustic | Percent of dwellings served by piped water | sewerage | No. of Dwellings |
|---|---|---|---|---|---|
| Sao Paulo | 26 | 5 | 64 | 63 | 1,272,279 |
| Osasco | 38 | 11 | 26 | 0 | 57,841 |
| Guarulhos | 37 | 12 | 28 | 9 | 47,059 |
| Sao Bernardo | 28 | 13 | 78 | 65 | 39,833 |
| Sao Caetano | 27 | 2 | 99 | 90 | 34,129 |
| Santo Andre | 30 | 7 | 73 | 54 | 89,317 |
| Itaquaquecetuba | 35 | 12 | 12 | 0 | 5,593 |
| Barueri | 44 | 21 | 1 | 0 | 7,370 |
| Moji ·das Cruzes | 28 | 12 | 37 | 32 | 27,874 |
| Carapicuiba | 40 | 12 | 5 | 0 | 10,733 |
| Cajeiras | | | 65 | 40 | 3,002 |
| Cotia | | | 22 | 0 | 5,994 |
| Diadema | 41 | 28 | 2 | 0 | 15,452 |
| Embu | | | 16 | 8 | 3,561 |
| Ferraz | 43 | 8 | 20 | 9 | 4,796 |
| Itapecerica | | | 17 | 0 | 5,175 |
| Itapevi | 43 | 12 | 2 | 0 | 5,382 |
| Jandira | 47 | 16 | 5 | 0 | 2,423 |
| Mairipora | | | 24 | 12 | 3,890 |
| Maua | 45 | 12 | 17 | 9 | 19,922 |
| Poa | 39 | 4 | 55 | 0 | 6,083 |
| Riberao | 27 | 11 | 35 | 28 | 5,986 |
| Rio Grande | | | 3 | 0 | 1,585 |
| Santana | | | 26 | 22 | 1,174 |
| Suzano | 23 | 13 | 34 | 13 | 10,683 |
| Taboao | 47 | 8 | 6 | 0 | 8,130 |

Notes (a) overcrowding = more than three people per bedroom
(b) the term dwelling is used for the Brazilian census 'domicilio' which is a 'structurally independent dwelling place formed of one or more rooms with a private entrance' (Fundacao IBGE 1973b
Source:    EMPLASA (1975) and Fundacao IBGE (1973b)

Table 4.8
Means of access to house ownership in Greater Sao Paulo, 1971
(Per cent)

| | Total Sample | Owners |
|---|---|---|
| Direct from owner | 40 | 62 |
| Financed but not through BNH | 4 | 7 |
| Financed through BNH | – | 1 |
| Inheritance | 2 | 3 |
| Self-building | 15 | 24 |
| Living in rented property | 35 | – |
| No response | 4 | 3 |
| Total | 100 | 100 |
| Base No. | (1182) | (764) |

Source: Instituto Gallup (1971)

Table 4.9
Ownership and tenancy in Greater Sao Paulo, 1972

| Condition of tenure | Percent of Households |
|---|---|
| Owned | 43.5 |
| In acquisition | 8.6 |
| Rented | 37.8 |
| Ceded etc. | 10.1 |
| Total | 100.0 |
| Base No. | (2035327) |

Source: Fundacao IBGE (1973)

not only avoids the costs and long term commitment of credit for purchase but also the cost, vulnerability to payment increases and insecurity of tenure inherent in renting.[14]

Renting is most common near to the central areas of the city where there is the least possibility for the mass of the population of buying or constructing their own house. Land prices in these areas are high, but the existence of older and decayed buildings means that there is some rented accommodation within the reach of the relatively poor. Two surveys (Instituto Gallup 1971 and CECAP 1972) showed that about three quarters of those families earning less than four minimum monthly salaries paid less than one minimum salary in rent. The subjection of central areas to redevelopment, in order to realise potential land values, contributes to the process of clandestine land occupation and self-building on the periphery. Recent studies have shown that, as this pressure on the peripheral areas increases, there is even there, a growing rental market often in rooms let by the owner occupier. Monthly rents in these areas, though low by comparison with instalments for formal house purchase, could reach up to twice the minimum monthly salary (IPT/FUPAM/CNPq 1979).

The costs in cheap rented housing as in cheap purchase or self-building are in overcrowding and (outside the central areas) poor services, distance from work and transport problems. The further cost for those buying 'clandestinely' or who fail or are unable to register their title is the threat of eviction (by landlord or public authority) without compensation. Overcrowding at rates of more than three per bedroom occurs in more than a quarter of the housing in Greater Sao Paulo and at much higher rates in the outlying areas (table 4.7). Urban services (piped water, public sewerage and domestic electricity)have at best kept pace with urban expansion in the municipality of Sao Paulo (table 4.10). But services of water and sewerage remain very scarcely distributed in the outlying areas of the municipality and in most of the other municipalities outside the core of Sao Paulo, Sao Bernardo, Santo Andre and Sao Caetano (table 4.7).

Alternatives to officially sponsored housing do exist; indeed housing promoted through the housing finance system is marginal to the scale of housing demand. The alternatives exist at rates which conform to the spending power of the mass of the population but the costs are in legal insecurity, overcrowding, poor construction materials and deficient public services. These are on the whole the options available to the people who confront the housing services offered through BNH.

Table 4.10
Percentage of dwellings served by public urban services
1950, 1968 and 1970, Sao Paulo municipality

| Service | 1950 | 1968 | 1970 |
|---|---|---|---|
| Piped water | 58 | 78 | 64 |
| Sewerage system | - | 61 | 63 |
| Domestic electricity | 85 | 98 | 96 |

Note: piped water includes internal and external connections.

Sources: from 1950 and 1970 Censuses and Prefeitura (1969) reprinted in Prefeitura (1973).

## HOUSING AND ADMINISTRATIVE EFFECTS

The previous section has treated the options available to the population of Greater Sao Paulo as if they were pure market alternatives free of administrative (or governmental) influence. It is true that the housing which is financed and distributed through the savings and loans system and the BNH's own programmes is relatively unimportant in numerical terms. BNH does not even claim to be able to do more than meet a quarter of 'popular' housing demand. Between 1968 and 1976, the cooperative housing scheme administered by the Sao Paulo INOCOOP built 24000 housing units in the whole area of the State; the metropolitan COHAB, offering 'popular' housing, built 6000 units in the metropolitan area; CECAP, the Sao Paulo State housing agency, constructed 4000 units in its territory. According to a Gallup survey in 1971 only seven per cent of the Sao Paulo metropolitan housing had ever attempted to buy through the national housing bank; according to a survey by CECAP in 1972 only eight per cent of respondents had ever heard of the State agency.

However, in less direct ways, whether or not the population is aware of it, governmental policy has a serious effect on the housing market. The distribution of government benefits and controls has the general effect of enhancing and even creating the differentiation between parts of the housing market in the following ways:

a) The existence of the housing finance system affects even those who are outside it. A working paper contributing to the State housing plan argued that the selectivity of the housing finance system in favour of the relatively well off, by concentrating available finance, had increased construction, land and material costs also for those included from the system (Governo de Estado 1975). The competitive position of the relatively well off was strengthened.

b) The effect of the housing finance system on prices and on the relative position of income groups is not one which is restricted to the internal operation of the housing market; it is also a product of the incorporation of the housing into the financial market. Chapter three showed how the housing finance system had been developed as an important part of the attempt to build up and rationalise a system of savings for investment. As a well structured and guaranteed deposit for voluntary as well as compulsory savings, it helped not only to strengthen housing demand but also to make the housing and land markets a safe area for speculative investment in

118

property purchase. Whatever the compensatory or redistributive
intent (chapter 3 p.63),the effect was of a channelling away of
resources from low income groups. On the one hand, in a
situation of growing income concentration high income demand
was enhanced by the privatised nature of the housing finance
system and by its market tendency to respond on an income
selective basis. On the other hand, the property market, backed
by this high income demand and the structure of the system,
became a safe resort for speculative investment in property
holdings with a consequent effect on prices. As Bolaffi (1975
p.23) points out:

> '.... the chronically inflationary state of the
> economy and the absence of a capital market stable
> enough to act as a secure refuge for investors'
> savings, and above all the absence of significant
> taxes on fixed property turned this form of invest-
> ment into practically the only way of accumulating
> and preserving wealth'.

The effect of investment of this sort was to raise land and house
prices at a rate which yet further enhanced its attractiveness
as a 'refuge for savings'.

c) One of the divisions in the housing market is between those who own
and those who rent. The significance of and distinction between
these two forms of tenure have changed with government policy over
time. Since 1964, in brief, owners have benefited over tenants.
Acquisition of housing, before the establishment of the housing
finance system had been effectively subsidised because loan
repayments took no account of inflation. The ending of this form
of subsidy was compensated for in some degree by the increased
availability of capital, tax relief on repayments and subsidies
on interest repayments in the case of officially supported systems
of financing. 'Pre-revolutionary' rent control had similarly
subsidised the costs of tenancy. The progressive abolition of rent
controls and tenancy protection by the new government was not,
however, compensated for by any new forms of subsidy.[15] An initial
general tenancy law (Law 4494, 25 November 1964) set out to govern
all rent increases on urban buildings according to the level of
increase in the official minimum salary until the year 1974. From
that point, there would be no further increases in rent, reflecting
the hoped for monetary stability and balance in the supply of and
demand for housing. The effect of the rent control was progressively
reduced [16] however,first by the exclusion of controls on broad
categories of tenancy agreement (for example practically all those
made after 1964) and then by provisions for the staged increase of
rents which were to have been 'frozen' from 1974. Similarly,
protection against eviction was narrowed down by the limitation
of the effect of the general law 4494. Even within these narrow
bounds, the landlord is entitled to claim eviction for a wide
variety of reasons ranging from non-payment of rent to his
requirement of the property for his own use or development. Outside
the bounds of Law 4494 (for the majority) more limited protection is
restricted to the period of the contract: where the contract has
no term the landlord can terminate it at any time; where there is
no written contract there is no protection.

d) As the last sentence suggests, governmental controls and benefits
   distinguish between sectors of the housing market not only on the
   basis of ownership but also on the basis of the formality of the
   tenure system. Written (post 1964) contracts of tenancy make the
   tenant eligible for some protection though also to automatic rent
   increases; others are freely subject to the landlord's decision.
   The benefits of ownership in terms of security depend on the degree
   to which the ownership is properly registered with the authorities
   and formal title obtained; neither are possible where the occupation,
   sale of the land, site size and construction standards were in the
   first place neither officially approved nor later 'officialised'.
   Such irregularity not only brings the permanent possibility of
   removal without legal rights to compensation, but also (a) lack of
   access to public services and utilities and (b) forms of 'punishment'
   through taxation for failure to obtain legal permissions for
   occupation, construction and improvements.

   The requirement of approvals at different stages of occupation
   gives rise to a range of possible levels of legality and consequent
   confusions. Plots may be approved, registered but not approved,
   'officialised' after registration, or they may remain 'clandestine'
   and illegal in every respect. An unapproved construction may be
   subject to periodic prefectural 'amnesties', but the plot on which
   it stands may remain 'illegal' because of its small size.[17] The
   consequence of selling small and densely packed plots will be of
   less 'waste' and more profit for the sellers of the land; for the
   purchaser it may be the maximum size of property he is able to
   purchase, but it is also one which subjects him (rather than the
   seller) to the possible application of penalties in the shape of
   fines administered by the regional offices of the municipality.
   Thus, for example, failure to register a plot brings the possibility
   of a 100 per cent increase in property tax, a clandestine plot a
   200 per cent increase, building or improving property without a
   licence and permission to occupy it a 200 per cent increase.
   Failure to respect the necessary permissions and taxes itself
   results in the impossibility of obtaining final legal title to a
   property. The housing market is thus further divided according to
   the degree of its legality, or official recognition, and consequent
   subjection to insecurity and punitive costs.

e) Legality (at least in ownership) brings relative security, freedom
   from punishment and the possibility of access to public services,
   but within the legal or formal sector of the housing market also
   there are divisions according to administrative categories. These
   categories themselves have an effect on exchange value, on living
   conditions and ultimately on the development of the city. Permissions
   for development, the zoning of the city by land use, the programmed
   extension of public services are not factors whose effect stops at
   the imposition of order on city growth. The issue of planning
   permission by itself enhances land values and makes gains from
   private development all the greater by the very fact that it restricts
   legal development. For this reason, the municipal planning department
   is subject to pressures for permission from property developers and
   the department's senior employees may be expected to have private
   offices for the channelling of favoured applications. The zoning
   of the city similarly enhances and protects living conditions and

property values in selected areas - the areas of higher income occupation (maps 4.2 and 4.3) are also the 'zone one' areas of 'strictly residential use with low population density'. The city prefect appealed for a system of land use control which was freer of market values but recognised that '/zoning/ will, however, always be subject to economic and political pressures and, in some way, its legitimacy will always be debatable to the extent that it is a factor which directly determines property values' (Setubal 1976).

Selective official recognition also occurs through the operations of the BNH, not only in the sense that they affect the relative purchasing power of income groups, but also in the sense that they discriminate between categories of housing. The availability of credit on favourable terms stimulates market demand and speculation as a whole but with differential effects. The value of new building approved by the officially sanctioned agencies of the housing finance system is increased; the value of buildings which are not eligible for the system's credit will be relatively reduced, although the cost of even sub-standard construction will also be affected by increased land, material and labour prices. The fact that the credit of the housing finance system is available almost only for new building implies a relative down valuation of old stock leading to deterioration, demolition and rebuilding.[18] A similar effect seems likely to result from the application of rent controls only to pre 1964 tenancies and therefore not to rents on new buildings. Similarly, as Bolaffi points out, public infrastructure development (water, drainage, roads, public transport) results in land and house value gains which are appropriated by private owners. Credit allocation, rent control and service extension are among the administrative factors which thus contribute to the speculative development of new areas and the decline and deterioration of existing housing stock and already serviced areas.

The continuous urban redevelopment which results is associated with the expulsion of poorer groups from the areas which have increased in relative value, whether the 'renewal' is a product of private projects of demolition and rebuilding or public sector infrastructural programmes. In either case the change in value is itself partly in response to processes which public policy has helped to generate. Urban demolition and rebuilding then have differential effects on groups of the population according to their market situation and administrative categorisation: the nature of their tenure, the legality of their occupation, their rights to compensation and their capacity to obtain alternative accommodation.

f) Illegality of occupation is, no more than legality, a simple category free of further administrative divisions. As was shown earlier, favelas (and more generally clandestine purchase and occupation), though generally illegal settlements, were rarely subject to any immediate threat of removal. In fact such settlements in Brazil as elsewhere in Latin America commonly receive a level of official recognition. This may be awarded at a post hoc stage, in the shape of amnesties or squatter settlement improvement programmes, but it may also occur at the outset. Land invasions and 'uncontrolled' building which have become the main way of satisfying low income groups' housing needs in, for example, metropolitan Caracas or Lima are not only the product of the breakdown of order, nor simply of official tolerance;  they are also the product of discretely applied semi official policies.  There are striking similarities between the Peruvian and Venezuelan cases in the complicity of private owners and of formal government organisations in the process of the formation and ordering of illegal settlements, whether in response to effectively expressed popular demands or in a more direct bargain for electoral support.[19]  Perez Perdomo and Nikken (1977) show for Caracas that once installed a settlement is practically secure though it remains dependent on the support of government bodies and political parties.  Leeds (1973) argues that Brazilian public policy has never been so positive in its effect on the security and development of Brazilian illegal settlements. It is certainly true that at least under the post 1964 regime the emphasis of Brazilian public policy has been on the removal of illegal settlements or the offering of relief to individual favela families rather than on area improvement.  Nevertheless the law establishes squatters' rights which distinguish between settlements according to the length of their establishment and may even (after thirty years) give them the possibility of access to legal land title (CIDOC 1969).  Until then it is a matter for State or municipal decision and the political connections of settlement leaders what unofficial recognition or protection is awarded to a settlement.  'Illegal' settlements may, then, be differentiated by levels of illegality, official sponsorship or recognition;[20] on this depends the likelihood of removal, of compensation in the event of removal, of protection from harrassment and of the application of punitive taxes.

CONCLUSION

Administered housing programmes encounter their applicants not within the limited context of a programmed world in which clients and housing needs can be simply defined by income groups and solutions tailored to match them, but in a context where

a) need, officially defined according to construction standards, service distribution, legality and overcrowding, is on a massive scale which is quite beyond the scope of programmes.  An estimate by the State housing company for the State housing plan suggested a 'deficit' for Greater Sao Paulo of about half a million housing units in 1975. This deficiency amounted to about one third of the then total housing stock and consisted overwhelmingly (ninety per cent) in estimated demand from 'sub market' levels of the population (below five minimum salaries monthly).

b) there is in fact no 'sub market' level;  all applicants have some alternative to programmed housing.  The nature of the alternatives corresponds broadly to the position of the occupant in the wage labour market, not only in the sense that this determines his purchasing power but also his capacity to make regular payment, his locational and transport needs, and his capacity to raise loans and guarantees and to produce documentary evidence of employment.

According to administrative definitions, the housing need which agencies confront is overwhelming; in a market sense, need at all levels has its solution. The question is whether administrative practice has the capacity to operate according to its definitions and to offer a basis for distribution which is different in its effects from that of the market. The correspondence between housing solutions and market capacity cannot necessarily be bettered by administrative agencies which are themselves operating within market constraints.

Market and administrative factors are closely intertwined. The implication of governmental definitions of the problem facing BNH agencies (see chapter three) is that housing need had little to do with the urban social structure but was rather a product of impacts upon the urban environment. - emigration for higher wages, rapid urban growth, disorderly pressures on land and public services. The data referred to in this chapter have, however, related poor and vulnerable housing conditions to a) highly differentiated market bargaining capacity and b) processes of land purchase and urban development which concentrate the benefits and spread unequally the penalties of construction, demolition and renewal. Administrative practice does not only operate within that market context; it also affects it. Whether administrative definitions and procedures are taken to reflect true or false understanding of the housing or the urban problem, they are categories which influence the operation and effect of the market. Administrative factors clearly intervene when housing is presented as a problem for administrative solution, but they also contribute at earlier stages in the development of the problem by their part in

i) the process of urban concentration and expulsion, through, for example, the financing of development and through the application of permissions, zoning and infrastructure which selectively increase the exchange value of property,

ii) their enhancement of the differentiation between housing alternatives, through, for example, the variable application of rent controls, of ownership benefits, of insecurity and of penalties.

Administrative practice may thus be supportive to the very processes and conditions which lead the poor to seek administrative solutions.

Chapter three showed that BNH and its agents were conceived as part of the economic model for whose concentrative effects they were expected to compensate. This chapter has shown how the housing market, often supported by public policy, itself reflects the concentrative outcomes of the economic model. The additional question which this chapter raises is how far the agents of the BNH can then be free to take action to relieve the effects of the market.

In the following chapter we will examine BNH supported operations which come at various crucial points in this chain of connections between the market and administrative distribution. First, in chapter five we will examine the implementation of the 'popular' housing programme, administered by the Sao Paulo COHAB and set up to offer officially approved alternatives to those otherwise obliged to operate at 'sub-market' levels in the informal housing sector. In a system

designed to accommodate all income groups, COHAB's concern has been
with the poorest and largest group. It has operated on each side of
the margin of regular market viability, on the one hand struggling
with the incapacity of its beneficiaries to meet formal market conditions
and on the other hand intervening in aspects of the control of irregular,
unofficial housing. More typical, however, of the experience of the
majority of the population than the offer of definitive housing
solutions is their involvement in the constant redefinition of their
housing problems which follows from the processes of urban expansion,
demolition and reconstruction. Second, in chapter six we will therefore
examine the effects of administrative action in an area where public
infrastructural works (the building of an underground railway) have
been taken as an opportunity to redevelop a part of the city which
has previously accommodated a low income population and small scale
enterprises. BNH is associated with the two sides of the operation,
both with the financing of the infrastructural investment and with
the future housing of the displaced population.

NOTES

1.  Another extreme example is the case of the sudden and unplanned
    expansion of upper income house construction in Bogota, Colombia,
    during the 1970s.

2.  See Hirschman (1970).

3.  The most rapidly expanding municipalities were Diadema, Taboao da
    Serra, Jandira, Carapicuiba, Barueri, Osasco, Guarulhos,
    Itaquaquecetuba, Suzano, Ferraz, and Rio Grande.

4.  such as Perus, Itaquera, Guaianazes, Sao Miguel Paulista and
    Ermelino Matarazzo.

5.  one monthly minimum salary in 1970 was worth about US $41 or £17.

6.  The seven districts containing three quarters of families in the
    top income group (with 26.7 times the minimum salary) were:
    Jardim Paulista, Jardim America, Ibirapuera, Perdizez, Consolacao,
    Indianopolis and Cerqueira Cesar. More than thirty eight per cent
    of this group lived in the first three districts. These figures
    are from a special run of the 1970 census undertaken for the Metro
    organisation.

7.  These points have been made not only by academic writers but also
    by organisations of the Sao Paulo State government in comments
    contributing to the State's housing plan (EMPLASA 1975 and CECAP
    1975).

8.  Data in this paragraph are based on quarterly construction figures
    for Sao Paulo city published by BNH (1974 and 1975).

9.  Between 1960 and 1970 the population of the richer areas in which
    SBPE investments were focused increased by twenty per cent over
    the whole ten years compared with an annual city increase of six
    per cent.

10. 24 minimum salaries was worth about £6000 or US $ 1200 at the

end of 1974.

11. Registration means that the employer officially records the post and pays the associated taxes and insurance contributions. Non-registration is illegal for the employer but also has consequences for the employee who has no employment card, no labour rights, no insurance and no access to individually provided public services, such as 'popular' housing.

12. Camargo et al (1976 p.37) argue that where expulsion from favelas has taken place in Sao Paulo this has been as a result of increases in land values. A governmental campaign of favela removal took place on a national scale during the 1960s (see chapter three).

13. The favela population of Sao Paulo municipality is estimated to have increased by more than 60 per cent between 1973 and 1975 to reach 117237 and then to have doubled by 1980 to reach 360,000 people (IPT/FUPAM/CNPq 1979).

14. Access to private, rented accommodation also usually requires guarantees which are difficult for the poor to meet, such as a deposit and a legal commitment by a house owner to meet unpaid rent.

15. Bolaffi (1975 p.22) cites a 1969 survey which showed that low income families then spent only six per cent of their income on housing.

16. An authoritative work (Levenhagen 1976 p.64) claims that only fifteen per cent of all rental agreements remained controlled by law 4494 in 1976.

17. According to the Sao Paulo municipal zoning law of 1972 the minimum plot size is 10 x 25 metres. In a survey by the Sao Paulo COHAB (1976) eighty per cent of the sample of households living on clandestine plots occupied less than this area.

18. Bolaffi (1975 p.26) cites figures to the effect that a fifteen year old apartment has thirty per cent of the value of a new one on a neighbouring site.

19. See Collier (1976) on Peru and Ray (1969) on Venezuela; also Batley (1978b) on both Lima and Caracas. In the case of Rio de Janeiro, Valladares (1978b) has shown how the occupation of land may be encouraged by the proprietors themselves or by party campaigners and politicians. Leeds and Leeds (1970) and Leeds (1972) describe the negotiating relationship between favelados and politicians to secure construction, public utilities and legalised street layouts for favelas.

20. The search for official recognition is symbolised in the Lima barriadas by the raising of Peruvian flags over new invasions and in Sao Paulo by the naming of favelas with authoritatively associated titles, such as 'Ordem e Progresso' (the Brazilian national motto). See also Bonduki and Rolnik (1979) and Chinelli

(1980) on the variety of degrees and types of illegality in land occupation and building.

# 5 The allocation of public housing

## INTRODUCTION[1]

During March 1976, 16000 calls were made at COHAB's reception desk.
In April, calls had fallen to a somewhat lower rate of about 350 to
500 people per day.  The point of interest was the possibility of
inscribing on the list of possible candidates for housing units
which were about to become available.  Inscription was to remain open
until July 1976.  These calls were not casual but involved in every
case up to several hours queueing, first for the office to open and
then for the inching forward towards the two officials at the desk.
Before the queue divided in the reception hall, the file of people ran
out of and round the building for perhaps a hundred metres along the
pavement near to the Rua da Consolacao, a main road within the central
area of the city.  After this long wait, each interview could last only
a minute or two.  At the very least three visits would have to be made
before any application would be registered.

Available for allocation at this time were 3500 units at Carapicuiba,
on the periphery of the city.  The units had been built some time
before, had stood empty and had then had to be improved and completed
ready for allocation.  Besides registration for these units, it was
possible to register in the hope of entry onto the waiting list for a
new project at Itaquera where, in a first stage, approximately 1800
units would be built over the following two years.  For the Carapicuiba
project there already existed a waiting list of 3117 families.  It was
expected that about 2000 of these would confirm their interest and
have priority in selection;  a further 4000 families from among those
currently registering would be allowed to go forward to the point that
they would join the pool from which the first selection would be made.
Thus out of about 20,000 families who would make an acceptable initial
application between March and July, about 4000 would be selected for
closer examination.  They would be joined by about another 2000 from
the waiting list, and the total of 6000 or 7000 applicant families
would then be reduced to the successful 3500.  Evidently the chances
of success were poor.

In the face of this overwhelming demand, COHAB's output has been
small.  Since its inception in 1966, the following units had been
built or were planned by 1976:

Table 5.1
Housing units built or planned by the Sao Paulo COHAB

| Project [a] | Units built | Date of Sale | Units in Construction | Units under contract |
|---|---|---|---|---|
| Sao Miguel | 349 | 1967 | | |
| Parque Ype | 251 | 1968 | | |
| Sapopemba | 1088 | 1968 | | |
| Guarulhos | 476 | 1970 | | |
| Carapicuiba | 1296 | 1972 | 3552 | 1485 |
| Guaianazes | 1058 | 1975 | | |
| Borore | 1262 | 1975 | 178 | |
| Itaquera | | | | 1834 |
| | 5780 | | 3730 | 3319 |

Note (a) see map 6.1 for location

Between January 1975 and April 1976, 38740 applicants passed initial scrutiny and were given application forms; 4240 forms were officially inscribed. In the same period, only 2320 housing units in Guaianazes and Borore were sold.

Authoritative persons have found the Sao Paulo COHAB's record poor both in terms of quantity and quality of output. At the opening ceremony of the Borore housing estate, the Minister of the Interior managed only rather grudging praise, commenting that the failure which it manifested had provided a lesson which would help avoid the occurrence of other Borores. The President of the BNH, also present at the event, made more direct criticism of the organisation responsible which he classified as 'the worst COHAB in Brazil':

'There is no population in Brazil which lives in worse conditions than the million poorest people of Sao Paulo'... /However/ to construct housing estates very far from the city is not the solution for these people'. (O Estado de Sao Paulo 4 April 1976)

Whether the Sao Paulo COHAB's competence was at this time peculiarly low or the difficulties it faced were peculiarly extreme, other reports suggested that COHABs in other cities were similarly confronted with the problem of rapidly increasing prices. The Brazilian Association of COHABs in an address to BNH complained that:

'Since mid-1972.... new and grave difficulties blocked the activities of the COHABs which had the almost impossible,almost miraculous task of balancing the value of works and of units against the agonizing limitations originating in BNH's manifestly obsolete finance tables and against the limited purchasing capacity of candidates' incomes'. (Associacao Brasileira de COHABs 1975)

Notwithstanding low output, poor quality and difficult locations, queues continued to form for COHAB housing and, although waiting lists were long, some of those currently queueing did manage to get housing without a long wait. Why and how this occurred is the other main point, besides the quantity and quality of output, which gave rise to press reports and occasional BNH concern. On the one hand, there was the

senior official COHAB view that selection was ordered according to
generally established principles which conformed with norms established
by BNH; on the other hand there was the external view, often expressed
by other voices of authority, that what reigned was organisational
chaos:

> 'Without conducting any selection, COHAB took the nearest
> tramp and gave him a house. This individual, in order to
> eat, finished by selling the water taps of his house...'[2]

There were then at least two views about COHAB's failure to bridge
the gap between expectations and availability. There were those who
found COHAB organisationally incompetent, and those insiders who would
reply that the COHAB was struggling against impossible odds to do what
it was required to do. Only those who queued seemed to have any faith
that COHAB could be a source of solutions. In some sense all these
views were correct: there was a chance of obtaining a house; it would
be difficult to establish that the production and allocation of housing
operated according to any systematic plan; what happened was to a great
extent the product of requirements to which COHAB was exposed by its
organisational structure.

OFFICIAL DEFINITIONS

In most of the States of Brazil, there are COHABs which act as housing
companies with a State-wide responsibility. Sao Paulo State has
preserved its own State housing company (CECAP), limiting the BNH
inspired COHABs to a municipal level of responsibility. The Sao Paulo
COHAB is an exception even to that rule since it has a metropolitan
coverage. It was created however by a law of Sao Paulo municipality
and installed in 1966 with a majority shareholding on the part of that
municipality alone. It therefore lies rather awkwardly across several
administrative boundaries: inter-municipal, State-municipality, BNH-
State, BNH-municipality. The Sao Paulo COHAB is a 'mixed economy society'
meaning that it is jointly owned by private and public shareholders.
The vast majority of the shares (98 per cent) are held by the prefecture
of the municipality. Prefectural ownership does not, however, signify
simple prefectural responsibility. COHAB's working capital comes from
the BNH which finances its projects largely by loaning funds to house
purchasers; COHAB thus stands in the role of 'financial agent' to BNH
with the function of

> '... planning, constructing and selling (at a value set by
> the bank on the basis of the UPC with a small increase for
> administrative costs) houses in the municipality of Sao
> Paulo or in Greater Sao Paulo for the low income population...'.

BNH offers one hundred per cent loans on the price of housing units
including land costs. The maximum total value of a housing unit was
set in 1976 by the BNH at 500 standard capital units (UPCs) of which
a maximum of 320 UPCs was to be composed of house and land costs and
of 180 UPCs for infrastructural and community services.[3] In most parts
of the country the bank has an agreement with the State government for
the latter to finance those services, which are for the most part a
State responsibility. In Sao Paulo, there is no such agreement and the
COHAB therefore frequently has to provide the services itself and
eventually cover its costs with a grant from the prefecture of the
municipality.

As an organisation whose capital is largely owned by the prefecture, the appointment of the directorship of the organisation is subject to the control of the prefect.  This may imply not only changes among the four or five directors but also among the subordinate staff whom they may select.  The particular change brought about by the accession of prefect Olavo Setubal in 1975 was not only the appointment of a new director, Jose Celestino Bourol, but also a decision that the municipal welfare department's functions in the provision of temporary emergency shelter should be linked in a common organisation with COHAB's more regular housing function.  This unification brought with it into COHAB a forceful lady, Marta Teresinha Godinho, and her commitment to a housing policy for the provision of alternative emergency accommodation for the favela population and for new cheap site and service schemes.  Her presence and that of many of the social workers she brought with her lasted only a year before she resigned leaving COHAB with responsibility for the administration of the temporary shelter programmes.

The tension which surrounded this appointment was expressed organisationally:  under Godinho, social workers were brought into the process of interviewing and selecting candidates for housing allocation on the basis of need;  with her departure an ex-member of the legal department was put in charge of welfare and allocation, the two functions were separated as community development and public relations departments and both were made subject to a primary responsibility for ensuring the market viability of projects.  The arrangement of these responsibilities as it was left in 1976 is shown in figure 5.1.

Figure 5.1
Organisational structure of COHAB

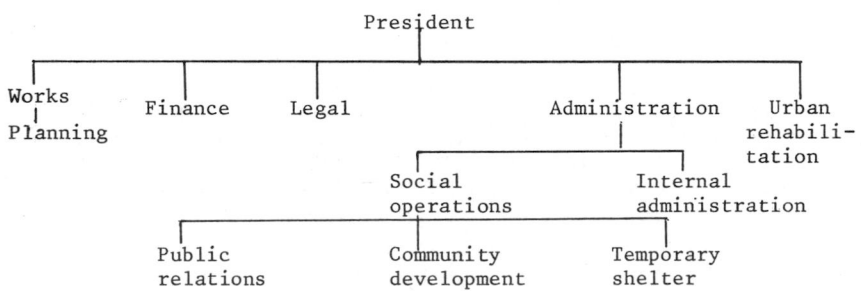

The tension between a welfare and a market orientation is inherent in the basic policy of COHAB (as in the structure and policy of BNH, see chapter three).  On the one hand, it is concerned with 'the most necessitous families';  on the other hand, the housing units are for sale and any repayment failure by the purchasers is reflected in the capacity of COHAB as a financial agent to repay BNH loans.  The dilemma may be dismissed by statements to the effect that from among those who can pay the neediest should be selected but the logic of separate welfare and market orientations has in fact carried COHAB in contradictory directions.

In principle, the procedures and criteria for the selection of applicants are clear and simple.  When the construction of a housing project is initiated, COHAB invites applications and 'inscribes' (that

is, registers) approximately twice as many applicants as there are
places. To be inscribed candidates have to meet the following criteria:

> to have an income up to five minimum salaries
> to be married or to have dependents
> to be between eighteen and fifty four years old
> not to own a house in Greater Sao Paulo
> to have lived or worked in Greater Sao Paulo for at least two years.

In the last stages of construction, a selection is made from among
inscribed applicants on the basis of the information contained in their
application forms. Those selected then enter into a twenty five year
commitment to repay a hundred per cent loan on the price of the house.

## THE APPLICANT'S EXPERIENCE

The applicant does not face such a clear, simple or known set of rules.
Unknown and unstated procedures also apply; the formal criteria leave
areas of doubt, discretion, interpretation, and lead to the erection of
secondary procedures for proof of fulfilment of the main criteria; as
it turns out, different rules apply to different people. The steps
towards application can be set out in some sort of systematic manner,
as they have to be for presentation here, but they do not present
themselves in that way to applicants, nor is it likely that their
totality is seen by the officials who operate the parts within COHAB.
To extract the uncertainty and confusion from the situation is, in a
sense which will be described, to extract its essence.

We will first examine the procedures as candidates confront them and
then see how officials interpret and use the information which is
presented. In some way from among the candidates, numbers have to be
reduced to manageable proportions. The formal, stated criteria are
not enough on their own to achieve this.

The applicant's view of the process of selection is limited. The
process surfaces periodically to involve him directly but for a large
part of the time it is subterranean, an administrative process which
deals with data on him, with chance and with special connections. Even
where the process involves him directly, his involvement must often be
in ignorance of the significance of procedures.

People join the queue to the reception desk of the public relations
department on the basis of little knowledge of what is at the end of
it. There is no attempt made by the organisation to broadcast information about where COHAB is and how it operates, and there is no
published information on what housing is available or how to get it,
except in occasional references in press reports. According to COHAB
files, in 1976 three quarters of applicants had joined the queue for
housing as a result of information acquired from personal contact with
friends, colleagues and relations who had been through the same process[4].
The implication is that those without these connections are on the whole
excluded from the queue. The only way of obtaining official information
on what is available and how to get it is to join the queue to the
reception desk. Except for the relatively few specially channelled
cases this is the only point of entry into the organisation. The queue
which forms every day is therefore composed of people with a variety of
aspirations: there are those requesting information on the housing
available, whether they would be eligible and how to apply; there are

those whose ambition is to acquire a proposal form with which to make an application; there are those returning their proposal forms; and there are those who come to press their cases by inquiring after the progress of their application. The queue contains people with varied circumstances, aspirations and strategies, but the treatment they meet at the desk is standard; even if one only comes with an inquiry he will find himself processed by the same routine procedures.

The business at the desk revolves around the matters of issuing and collecting proposal forms. These replaced a simpler and slower process in which, until 1975, the receptionists had questioned each applicant on his circumstances and documentation and then made a decision about whether the applicant should be inscribed as a candidate for a house in the estate currently on offer. The result was long interviews and delays at the desk, the need for constant return visits with fresh evidence, and a tendency to inscribe an unmanageable number of people for later selection. The proposal form was introduced to allow the selection for inscription to be carried out in the absence of the candidate on the basis of the information given by him. It also, however, introduced a new selection stage: the applicant's success in obtaining a proposal form in effect represents the gate to later tests of eligibility in the following sequence.

## *Application for proposal form*

Depending on the advice they receive from their source of information on the availability of COHAB housing, applicants are likely to arrive at the desk ignorant of what is available and of official requirements about how they should demonstrate their eligibility. In the few minutes allowed for the initial interview with each applicant, it is apparently for the officials to decide whether to allocate rather than for the applicants to decide whether to apply; there is no time to describe the housing and estates on offer. Individual cases are reduced to a routine procedure in a rough attempt to anticipate candidates' conformity with official requirements. The question is not whether applicants can demonstrate their need for housing; chapter four showed that measured against official standards most of those in the COHAB income range would be living in 'inadequate' or insecure housing. Need is general; the point at this stage is to establish whether the applicant roughly meets official definitions of the eligible candidate, can prove his circumstances through documentation and possesses the documentation necessary to a law abiding citizen.

The receptionist asks all applicants the same questions in roughly the same order: are you married? do you have other dependents? who are they? do you own a house? does your wife work? do you have children? are they minors? how long have you been in Sao Paulo? He asks to see the applicant's identity card, work card (or social security registration for self employed workers) and last monthly payment slip. He may ask whether a salary increase is due.

The candidate may have doubts about the meaning of terms (how are marriage or a dependent defined? what is counted as a period of residence?) and about the answers which will favour his application - should he maximise or minimise his income and the number of people dependent upon him? There is in fact a good deal of official flexibility about the meaning of income, marriage, dependence, house and residence. Officials may sometimes hint to applicants how they might prepare their situation so as to modify their response to questions in the future – for example, by including or excluding the wife's salary, by getting married, by getting their parents' dependence or their residence certified, by registering their self-employment and paying into the social security system.

Within the limits of official discretion there are, however, correct answers: the applicant who succeeds in obtaining a proposal form is married or has children or other dependents, owns no other house, has an income between two and five minimum salaries, has worked or lived in Sao Paulo for the past two years and is aged between eighteen and fifty four. He also gives evidence of having the basic work and identity documents. The applicant who fails may apply again but, with little eventual chance of success, it will be at the cost of another lost day's work and at the cost of 'regularising' his situation (for example by obtaining registered work, paying into the social security fund, and acquiring personal documents).

## Submission of proposal

The applicant is given a date a month later to return to the same desk through the same queue with his completed proposal form and with any other document that the receptionist required to see. The proposal form contains questions which relate merely to COHAB's market research (in what State were you born? in which neighbourhood would you like to live?) and others which are crucial to the applicant's success (birth date, marriage status, number of dependents, income, address for correspondence,whether work is registered, and whether land or another house are owned). The candidate has to distinguish the crucial questions and the basis on which judgement will be made. Will the ownership of a small plot of land on the periphery of the city indicate provident forethought or unnecessity? Many dependents may help to prove need but may on the other hand render the family too large for the available houses. Above all, there is a delicate balance between having too much and too little income and great uncertainty about whose income will be counted. The applicant's interpretation of his circumstances is to a great extent a matter for his (informed or ignorant) discretion.

No more than about one in five of those who make the first visit to the reception desk will return to successfully lodge their proposal form in the second visit (see figure 5.2). In any case, getting to this point in the process signifies little about the eventual chance of success. For any particular estate, about six proposal forms would be collected for every place available, and besides these there are the priority cases stored in the waiting list for the same estate. As the proposal form states, 'this is only a proposal and not an inscription'; there is no official recognition that the candidate has any claim on COHAB. He may press his case by repeat visits to the reception desk, but special pleading, which later becomes crucial, is at this stage useless since no record is kept of visits made; the applicant has no means of knowing whether his pressure is useful, useless or an irritant.

## Inscription

The third stage in the process of selection follows the official call to chosen candidates to come to the COHAB office to make their

133

Figure 5.2
Applicants' experience in stages of processing
1 January 1975 to 31 March 1976

|  |  | No of applicants |
|---|---|---|
| 1. | First visit to reception desk to request proposal form | 49,347 |
| 2. | Second visit to reception desk - proposals accepted | 8,517 |
|  | Applicants considered ineligible to submit proposal form on first or second visit | 2,067 |

- reasons:

| already owns | 63 |
|---|---|
| income too big | 110 |
| income too small | 374 |
| period of residence in Sao Paulo | 344 |
| age too high | 199 |
| age too low | 36 |
| non-family situation | 941 |

Applicants considered eligible to submit proposal form on 1st or 2nd visit but who decide not to continue      1,814

- reasons:

| prefers other area | 1,597 |
|---|---|
| not allowed to use social security as deposit | 180 |
| estates too far away | 27 |
| houses too small | 7 |
| repayment period too long | 3 |

3. Inscriptions in public relations office      3,094

Source: COHAB records.

inscription. In the case of the Carapicuiba project about one in five of those who had successfully submitted proposals would be called to inscribe about five or six months later, after a period of administrative selection. In fact, there is also a selective effect implied in the way the call is issued by post to the candidate's residence, where he has a postal code, and otherwise to his place of employment. There is a strong but unquantifiable possibility that candidates living outside the central city and working for small firms would not receive the letter giving them a date for interview.

The applicant fills in the inscription form with a social assistant in the 'public relations' office of COHAB in a room, divided into cubicles, above the reception hall. This form becomes the record of his case history including a note of visits to the office, personal judgements by staff about the case, basic document references (numbers of identity card, income tax, work card, certificate of marriage, separation and death) and personal data: sex, religion, education, nationality, age, marriage status, residence in Sao Paulo, stability and legality of married relationship, employment, family income by members of household, household budget, ownership of land or house, health situation, social and community activities, and present housing situation (number of rooms, access to services, tenure, construction standards, overcrowding, insecurity). Any of this data may require documentary proof and applicants are furnished with a list of twenty four personal documents (ranging for example through certificates of residence, occupational card, declaration of income, birth certificates, and proof of social security payment) which they may have to produce.

Documentary proof for some candidates represents no problem; for others it is an almost insuperable hurdle. If birth certificates or marriage certificates were not obtained at the event or were since lost, the candidate or someone acting legally for him has to return to the municipality of origin (possibly 2000 miles away) to obtain them. These documents (among many others) are necessary as a condition for obtaining identity or work cards. Work (or professional) cards and approved salary slips can only be obtained if the employment is legally registered by the employer. Self-employment to be regularised requires registration with the social security system.[5] All these documents and many more are necessary to the obtention of an income tax number.

The least of the problem in acquiring official documents is the official expense: in 1976, a reissued birth certificate cost 114 cruzeiros (US $ 13), a marriage certificate 100 cruzeiros (US $ 11), an identity card 22 cruzeiros (US $ 2); there were also penalties for non-voting and penalties for avoidance of military service which had to be paid off before other documents were acquired. The worst of the problem was in the frustration, loss of working time, expense on private payments and on supporting photographs, photocopies and X rays for documents. The municipal service(PRODOC) which exists to help poor people to obtain documents does not advertise its existence in case it should attract an overwhelming demand.

In response to the social assistants' questions, the problem for the applicant is again how he should present himself: does the successful applicant maximise his health, housing and income difficulties or does he attempt to demonstrate his capacity and competence to earn and provide for his family? At the end of this interview, he is told to 'await a call' for the allocation of housing: in the intervening period, should he attempt to improve his housing situation or will this prejudice his chances? The chances of success are unclear: should he press his case or wait dutifully? Should he report changed circumstances if they indicate an improvement in his income or housing situation? While most waits from inscription to allocation are for less than two years (reflecting the fact that inscriptions are made for specific, available, estates), examination of the records for one estate showed that some successful applicants (and others still on the waiting list) had maintained hope and an 'active file' for up to six years by continuous revisits.

Persistence and chance exclusion at the crucial moment are illustrated
by the case of an applicant with a wife and three children who inscribed
in January 1969. He was able to support his case with medical evidence
that his wife suffered nervous problems. He called at COHAB's office
five times between 1969 and 1974 to update the information on his file.
In March 1974 he was told to 'await the call' for allocation. He
called twice more for information in April and June, but when in
September he was called to choose a house he failed to appear. His
file was noted 'displaced due to non-appearance'.

In principle, within the six months before completion of construction
all those inscribed for an estate should be called for a final check
of their documentation and current salary and for the allocation of
streets and houses. In practice, some are called but never respond;
others may never be called or may only be called when there are no
more houses to allocate and their only choice is whether to go on to
the waiting list for the next estate to be allocated. Other candidates
prove ineligible upon arrival when it is found that they still do not
possess all the required documents or that their pay does not meet the
minimum required for the housing on offer. Other candidates find on
arrival that during the waiting period, COHAB, upon checking their
credit-worthiness with the 'credit protection service' of the Sao Paulo
Commercial Association, has found that they have debts (with companies
which sell under hire purchase) which must be cleared before house
allocation is made.

The Borore project records show that of those inscribed for the
estate, 1190 candidates were successful and 2265 were unsuccessful.
Of the unsuccessful, 1322 did not respond to the call to appear and the
remaining 943 joined the waiting list for Borore or another project.
Of the successful applicants, thirty eight per cent were required to
clear debts before they were allowed to take up places; more fruitlessly
one quarter of those who joined the waiting list cleared debts before
they learned that their application would go no further.

To the successful applicants, the allocation procedure apparently
offers choice of street and house,but this is within the limits of (a)
what is still available and (b) the parameters of family size and
income. Within any estate, there is a range of house sizes and prices.
The choice for any particular family is restricted by its conformity
with COHAB standards about the sharing of accommodation and about the
proportion of family income which can be dedicated to monthly payments.
While the principle that children of opposite sexes should not share
bedrooms is not applied rigorously, the dilemma for families at the
bottom end of the income range is that the larger the family size the
less of the couple's income is allowed by COHAB to be committed to
monthly repayments. Larger families (over five members) need to be
better off to afford the same space as smaller families; COHAB
standards will normally require them to buy even more space than
smaller families.

Choice restricted by pre-established criteria would seem to be a
manifestation of the bureaucratic rationality which the applicant
might hope underlies the selective process. The queries, routine

questions, forms and standard requirements he faces imply first that there is a reasonable chance of a favourable outcome and second that allocation, while noting personal preferences, will follow the fair and impersonal application of rules on the basis of the data collected. If the process frequently disappears from view, this would seem to be a necessary feature of a bureaucratic consideration which is properly beyond personal influence.

However, the selection procedures are not only unclear to the candidate when they disappear from view into the administration, but also when he is face to face with officials. He can have no basis for knowing how to present his case, what would be data which favoured his case and how his statements would be interpreted. To all appearances, procedures are bureaucratic, rational and fair; at the same time they are unclear. In these two senses an unsuccessful candidate cannot easily attribute to them the blame for his failure. Failure would then depend on two other possibilities. Either, in the covert administrative world, his case has been assessed as less valid than others, or else through the overt procedures the candidate has failed himself by being less able to present the facts about his case, by queueing too late or by not having normal circumstances supported by the documents held by a proper citizen. The examination of the overt procedures from the viewpoint of the applicant shows, however, that these procedures are not just a neutral route towards a later covert stage where selection takes place. The procedures for making an application themselves implicitly select between candidates through, for example, the differential distribution of information, documentation, registered work, the postal service,and the helpfulness of officials as well as through the differential capacity to wait for a COHAB house and to conform with COHAB family size and income requirements.

OFFICIAL DEMAND MANAGEMENT

Most of the people who first visit COHAB's reception desk conform with the basic selection criteria concerned with income, residence, age, non-ownership of housing and family responsibility. Figure 5.2 showed that by comparison with the number interested in making an application (49000) relatively few (2000) were regarded as ineligible against any of these criteria between January 1975 and March 1976. Part of the necessary reduction in numbers to match COHAB's low supply of housing is effected by the variable capacity of applicants to follow the procedures of application; the other part follows from the more deliberate action of officials. Having considered the applicants' experience of selection procedures, we will now turn attention to the more covert official world in which the formal rules of selection are interpreted, modified, substituted or ignored.

*Rules of eligibility for consideration*

Until 1976, candidates inscribed (ie.registered) directly at the reception desk and were taken on to the list of applicants for the next housing project. The problem for officials was that this led to a vast list of perhaps seven times more applicants than places, many of the applicants with no more income than formal inscription rules required.

The introduction in 1976 of a 'proposal form' narrowed the universe under consideration for inscription from all those who present

137

themselves at the reception desk to all those who return the forms. This represents (as has been shown) a new selection stage; nevertheless the criteria applied at this stage are the minimum, stated COHAB requirements. At this stage also the criteria are interpreted by the receptionists flexibly and liberally. The requirements that candidates be married or have dependents are given wide interpretations. In recognition that a large proportion[6] of candidates are not legally married, COHAB has established its own definition of a family to cover various forms of union and dependency including cases of a married or unmarried couple with their own children, couples with children of one parent only who have lived together more than five years, individuals with dependent children, brothers or sisters or parents. The criterion which excludes those owning a house is similarly interpreted broadly to discount structurally inadequate buildings. In relation to income and age criteria, the receptionists are, with some variation, helpful to applicants suggesting for example that another member of the family may make the application or that a family member's wage may be discounted or included by the registration of employment. Documentary proof of dependency, residence and even identity may sometimes be made at this stage through secondary documents. The inflexible requirements are that work registration and income should be demonstrated.

The relative liberality of official tests at this stage is illusory; the submission of a proposal form offers no promise of success.

## Rules of eligibility for inscription

After the candidate has passed the first gate of formal eligibility conditions, he faces a second set of conditions which come into play as his suitability is assessed for inscription as an applicant for a particular housing scheme. The basic conditions are toughened or applied rigorously. At this stage, what is important is not that the candidate has the formally necessary income of twice the minimum salary but that he has enough to make the repayments on a unit in the housing scheme which is currently on offer.

In the case of the Borore estate, a family of up to five members would have to be earning at least four minimum monthly salaries for the cheapest house available; in the case of Guaianazes the lowest necessary income would have been three minimum salaries. Larger families would have to earn more. Yet of the proposals received for these estates, nearly one third showed earnings of less than three minimum salaries and two thirds of less than four. Certainly for all those earning less than three minimum salaries, their initial proposal was quite worthless. The president of COHAB defended their recruitment on the grounds that it was useful market research, although of course this was not revealed to the recruits.

Income entry conditions were, indeed, deliberately raised by COHAB so as to exclude more marginal cases. This was done

(i) by basing initial repayments on an artificially elevated estimate of the eventual price of the built units. The final price would be fixed by BNH after their allocation, but by then marginal cases would have been excluded;

(ii) by taking into account only the couple's salaries and not

138

(as COHAB purports publicly to do) whole family salaries;

(iii) by using the constant amortization system as a basis for spreading repayments over the twenty five year period. Chapter three showed that this has the effect of raising initial repayments.

As the president of COHAB said in interview, the raising of initial repayment also had the beneficial effect for COHAB of accustoming purchasers to high outgoings from the onset 'when they are more willing to find the money'.

At the stage of assessing proposals for inscription for a housing scheme, COHAB gives greatest importance to factors which favour candidates who represent less risk. This is ensured not only by selection of candidates with suitable income and registered work but also by the selection of those with a work location near the housing estate, those without debts and those with a clear and legal family situation. 'Consensual unions' can give rise to complexities not only for the candidate but also for COHAB where for example a deserted wife lays claim to a house allocated to a man and another woman. Clearly, the focus at this stage is on the security of repayment and not on the need of the applicant. The point is made clearly by a survey carried out by COHAB on 1000 inscriptions in 1969 (COHAB 1969). The survey found that 84 per cent of those inscribed were legally married, 92 per cent were literate, 40 per cent had been in their present employment over five years, and that they had higher salaries than the average of those who presented themselves to COHAB. All of this was seen as 'reassuring evidence' that the selection system was working properly to select more reliable families with a capacity to repay. The system worked even if indirectly to ensure 'the required economic and occupational stability'. The selection system was being found worthy precisely because it was excluding those in relatively greater need.

In spite of the basic eligibility conditions and of the elimination of candidates who appear to offer less security, there still exists many times more effective demand than supply. Even if inscriptions were reserved to candidates with an income of more than four minimum salaries, there would still have been twice as many eligible candidates as places before the books closed on the Carapicuiba project. Some other form of selection is apparently required. Moreover, the strict application of the formal criteria to each case requires exhaustive and time consuming attention from a small staff, and even after this detailed scrutiny there remain uncertainties about which candidates'incomes are more secure, which families are not going to split up and which will not incur future debts.

There have therefore emerged forms of which might be called 'procedural selection' which act without the need for administrative judgement about the merits of particular cases. Because they are not formally acknow-ledged, even within the administration, they appear not to exist; demand is in this way brought within manageable proportions without the organ-isation having to confront its overwhelming scale. Procedural selection applies at the two points that eligibility is considered (when proposals and inscriptions are made), at the point of prioritisation for allocation and at the point that new waiting lists are formed out of failed inscriptions.

## Procedures for limiting eligibility

The overt procedures already mentioned not only discriminate between applicants but also between applicants on the one hand and those who never reach the stage of application. Although there is considerable generalised publicity by the various levels of government and BNH about their plans for 'popular housing' no attempt is made to divulge the practical facts about how, where and what to apply for. From the point of view of COHAB with its low capacity to supply, there is no point in activating demand by advertising. For the same reason, the books are opened for the registration of applications for a particular estate only for a restricted period until applications reach about six times the number of available places. The procedural difficulties and long queues may be supposed to have a similar effect in dissuading applications.

Once the candidate has proved his basic eligibility by submitting a proposal form he 'awaits the call' for inscription. Most (80 per cent) of those who successfully submit their forms are in fact never called to the office. This reduction is not only achieved by the use of the criteria relating to income suitability etc; to many candidates these criteria are simply never administered. Their applications are diverted at the outset, without their knowledge, into lines for other 'counters'. Any candidate who owns or is buying land is automatically transferred from the queue for a completed house (for which he applied) to the queue for COHAB's new self-building scheme even if he does not fulfil any of the other basic criteria of this scheme. Similarly, any candidate whose work location is nearer to the next anticipated housing project at Itaquera (in the east of the city) than to Carapicuiba (in the south west) is transferred to the Itaquera queue.

The majority of candidates who do not reach inscription for the current housing scheme are not transferred to other queues but are simply passed out of the system. Since applicants are not told (unless they ask) that this has been their fate and that they must reapply if they wish to be reconsidered, most stay waiting in a non-existent queue for a call which never comes.

## Procedures for prioritisation

The examination of the applicants' experience showed that about half of the inscribed candidates are in fact successful in obtaining a house. All are considered eligible depending on their possession of required documentation and their freedom from debts. What is crucial to success is the order in which they are called to make their choice of the available housing.

COHAB's technical staff (in the public relations department) have elaborated a system which is designed to establish candidates' priority rating. According to this system first attention should be given to candidates from the waiting list for a housing project, that is mainly people whose candidature for other projects has been unsuccessful and who have transferred their inscription; then should be considered those who have more recently inscribed for that particular project.

Within these two categories, information would be taken from each candidate's inscription form to assess their merits against a points system. Highest priority would be given to those in a state of housing need (shared housing, badly constructed, overcrowded, illegally occupied, under threat of eviction), to larger (five to eight persons) but not the largest families, and to those whose employment and family situation was regular and legal.

This technical system based on length of waiting, need and legality has in fact never been used because of the urgency of each successive directorate to sell as many houses as possible during its administration and that of the ruling city prefect. The pressure (passed on down to the selectors from the directorate) is for quick action and evidence of results. A case by case re-examination and updating of the data on all candidates in the waiting list would introduce long delays. Instead the candidates selected have been those whose documents have most recently been shown to be in order and for whom there exists a current statement of income. Contrary to the technical staff's intention, this favours the most recently registered candidates and those candidates who have maintained their application in a live and current state by exerting insistent pressure on COHAB. Those 'who await the call' for allocation, as instructed, are the least likely to be successful; the head of the public relations department remarked that it was the most irritating who have the best chance.

The urgency for decision means that, at a certain point, the business of recalling waiting list candidates, of checking data off against the points system and of allowing candidates time to finalise documentation and clear debts is brought to a close. Uncalled and unprepared applicants are swept aside and the choice is made from those with 'everything in order', meaning their documents, income level and debts. In a situation where the choice is now narrow, the needs criteria become irrelevant.

*Passes for special cases*

This whole system of covert and overt procedures applies differently to some people, but their special status could not be recognised without the procedural complexity which applies to all others. The possibility for 'emergency' cases to be given more rapid treatment was frequently referred to in interviews with COHAB officials. The argument was that cases of ill health, extremely bad housing or eviction could be taken to the head of the queue, though they would still be expected to fulfil the basic eligibility criteria relating to documentation, the proper relation between income and house price, residence in Sao Paulo and possession of no other house.

It was clear from observation, however, that there was another category of applicant who could not be described as a priority case in that sense, although officials frequently continued to use the label 'emergency' case to describe them in official reports. Privately they were known as the *encaminhados* (the specially channelled). One applicant presented herself at the reception desk without queueing, was immediately handed a proposal form to fill in, then took this straight upstairs for inscription – this applicant's sister had already done the same for herself and grandparents. What made the approach unignorable for the receptionists was that the president of COHAB had already passed

141

a note of recommendation to the desk. He in turn had been recommended the case by the Director of BNH's regional office after an approach by the applicant's employwer, another state agency.

Such candidates are obliged to go through the same formal procedures of inscription and allocation, but the meaning of the procedures is different. They are not put into a queue with others; their inscription may take place before other proposals have been considered; the names of the *encaminhados* will then be held in a separate list to ensure that they are distinguished. The only conditions are that they should fulfil COHAB's basic criteria and that their case should receive the support of the COHAB president.

Most such cases are presented by the State or prefectural governments, by the BNH director, by a State deputy or municipal councillor, in something like the following terms:

> 'With my compliments, I am recommending to you my friend... who hopes to acquire one of the houses which COHAB is constructing... I would ask you to advise him as necessary...'[7]

The president of COHAB who also receives such recommendations by phone argued that such recommendations were a useful way for him to hear about cases of special 'social interest'.

An examination of the files on residents in the Borore estate showed that at least nine per cent of candidates had entered in this way. The numbers are not great, and of course could not be great without making it clear that a quite different selection scheme operated from the one that COHAB formally claims to operate. Such a special pass scheme depends on its insertion into some other more regular system. It also depends on the confusion (at least of the applicant and often of the official) that runs through that regular system in practice. If criteria of need or income and credit worthiness were rigorously, systematically and openly applied there would be no space for the *encaminhados* to pass discretely through.

### The waiting list

Inscribed candidates who are unsuccessful are called to the office to decide whether they will continue to wait for a place to become available in the housing estate for which they inscribed, or whether they will transfer to the waiting list for the next available estate. Those who do not respond to the call or who make neither choice are transferred to the 'dead file' where their applications are effectively discarded; this applied to half of the unsuccessful in the case of Borore.

Time also takes a toll on the waiting list as age and changes in income circumstances render a proportion of the inscriptions invalid for the next round of allocation. Nevertheless it would have been possible to have filled most of the places in the Carapicuiba project from the waiting list. It is a matter for conjecture why, in that case, it was necessary for COHAB to attract a further 20,000 applications in fresh proposals for the same estate. An official argued that the public relations department had been required by the president of COHAB to go through the new recruitment to demonstrate publicly (or at least to other authorities) that the organisation was still active in the business of providing houses to low income families.

POST ENTRY CONDITIONS

Applicants who do manage to enter COHAB housing apparently gain access
to fully legal house purchase, to repayments related to their income
capacity, to more or less dependable systems of water supply, electricity
and drainage, and to greater security of tenure than in rented
accommodation.  The question is how far these advantages are real.
Certainly, they also suffer disadvantages which become more apparent
after entry;  cheaply constructed housing, isolated peripheral locations
often very distant from work, transport and social and commercial
services, earth roads which are often impassable after rain, difficulties
in resale or transfer, and commitment to a repayment system whose demands
increase in money terms possibly at rates which exceed the growth of
family income.  However much COHAB tries to select low risk candidates
there are severe limits on its capacity to do so.  The result is the
unwillingness and inability of a large proportion of mortgagees to pay
for the COHAB service: in August 1975, fifty one per cent were behind
in their monthly payments.

## Costs of entry and repayment

Once the financial department has determined the likely costs of a
project, it calculates a sale price and the required minimum income
which the public relations department is to use in the selection of
candidates.  As has been shown, COHAB sets out to overestimate the price
so as to eliminate doubtful candidates;  moreover the tables which
have been developed for the fixing of required minimum incomes are
cautious in the proportion of a family's income which can be committed
to repayments.  The system permits a declining proportion of income
to be committed to repayments as family size increases and as family
income declines.  Only those families having five or less members and
an income over about six and a half minimum salaries can commit as
much as a quarter of their monthly income;  for families with eight
or more members and earning up to four minimum salaries, the most that
could be committed would be ten per cent.  Briefly, outgoings are not
permitted to exceed a cautious view of a family's capacity.

Included in total monthly outgoings are charges which are fixed
on the basis of the value of the mortgage repayment[8] - an additional
eight per cent for the insurance of the property, five per cent as
COHAB's 'collection and administration' charges and two per cent as
its 'community support' charge.  In addition to these charges paid
throughout the twenty five year period of the mortgage, COHAB requires
purchasers to pay five per cent of their gross monthly family income
as an inscription charge and one half per cent of the value of the
finance.  All these charges (except insurance) go to pay for COHAB's
services and also act as an incentive to the organisation to collect
repayments and return them to BNH as the latter's financial agent.

In these various ways - the selection of candidates by income, the
maximisation of the initial sale price, the minimisation of purchasers'
allowable income, and the incentives to collection by COHAB - the security
of the housing finance system is apparently guaranteed.  The repayment
habits of purchasers are then closely supervised.

Purchasers are required to make their monthly payments to the COHAB
central office or to the Bank of the State of Sao Paulo (BANESPA) or

to the State savings bank (Caixa Economica Estadual). The local administrator of the particular estate then checks the repayment records book of each resident each month and this information is confirmed against the monthly printouts of the collecting agencies. If a purchaser falls into more than three months' arrears he is required to make a new repayment plan and a one per cent additional charge is made for each month overdue. When it becomes clear that the purchaser cannot make his repayments he is asked to sell his house and repay COHAB out of the proceeds; if he does not, he can be evicted and COHAB sells the house collecting the back payments due. In the end, overriding its welfarist commitments, 'this is', as the president of COHAB said in interview, 'a programme for people who can buy'.

*Arrears*

In spite of the apparent security built into the system, about half of all purchasers were in arrears by more than three months in August 1975. In February 1976 in two estates, Ype and Guarulhos, only eight and thirteen per cent respectively were right up to date in their payments and more than half in Guarulhos were more than three months behind. The matter of non payment is of crucial importance to the effectiveness and philosophy not only of COHAB but also of the entire structure of the housing finance system as chapter three showed. Even if the system can support some non-payment, it has become central to its operating principles that no open subsidies are offered. COHAB officials were therefore anxious to achieve an improvement in levels of repayment whether resulting from improved services to estates, from incentives to early repayment or from threats of eviction. Indeed, almost the entire action of the community development department's social workers in the estates was related to the business of checking on payment and arranging new repayment plans with defaulting families. The social workers justified this involvement as a matter which was interlinked with their welfare concern with the employment and 'social responsibility' of families.

'Lack of education and shamelessness' was the main explanation for [9] non payment offered by COHAB's social workers and chief legal officer. The rationalisation of non payment as a matter of will underlay the treatment proposed by the social workers (rehabilitation) and by the legal department (eviction). Local social workers and the head of the community development section explained that the main problem of non payment occurred in the three first estates constructed by COHAB where later selection procedures had not been applied rigorously. In these cases the estates had been built as part of BNH's favela removal programme (see chapter three) to provide homes for people forcibly moved from the path of public works programmes (mainly road building between 1967 and 1969). Later problems were seen as springing from the forced and unselective nature of the rehousing which had introduced unwilling and uneducated (or 'marginal') people into the estates.

The implication in these explanations is that the problem of non payment was to do with earlier unselectiveness and individual failures. Yet, not only was the scale of non payment even higher in a more recent estate, Guarulhos, but also it is clear that, even with the best will, a large proportion of families was not in a position which would allow them easily to make their payments. A survey carried out by COHAB (1969) on incribed people showed that, after entry into a COHAB estate, twenty eight per cent would be paying more than the officially permitted one quarter of their income in mortgage repayments. Even with all the processes of selection described earlier in this chapter, there was no guarantee that after their occupation families would not slip into a precarious situation due to ill-health, unemployment or loss of wage earners.

A survey (SEBES 1973) by the municipal welfare department carried out by COHAB on its defaulters concluded that a large proportion simply could not pay:

'... the income of families is basically at a subsistence level, a situation which makes the payment of the monthly sums difficult if not impossible'.

The reasons for the delayed payments included:

| | |
|---|---|
| unemployment of family head | 48 |
| illness of family head | 43 |
| insufficient income | 24 |
| death of responsible person | 3 |
| abandonment by responsible person | 10 |
| other | 9 |
| | 137 |

Five or six years exposure to the social workers' community development in the older estates could hardly change the repayment record when more than one half of the surveyed defaulters were either in unregistered or irregular employment, or were unemployed or pensioned.

*Rights of ownership*

The purchaser is apparently entering into a state of ownership which will free him from the insecurity of renting and offer him access to services which are associated with the legal occupation of land. In fact there are limits on the services and rights he enjoys.

The land which COHAB uses is acquired because it is cheap, not because it is suitably located for the delivery of urban services. The two are unlikely to be correlated: cheap land on the periphery of the city is often damp or hilly and is usually beyond the planned extension of water and sewerage services. Moreover SABESP (the sanitation authority) is subject to the State government and not necessarily responsive to the needs of COHAB, a municipally owned agency. The result is that once an estate is established, public infrastructural services frequently fail to arrive. COHAB then has to make its own, often unreliable, provision of wells and sewers. At Guarulhos, COHAB's own wells were supplying one quarter of the amount of water required according to municipal standards. The Borore and Carapicuiba projects, once built, remained as 'phantom cities' for five years due to the unavailability of supplies.

In the case of communal services (such as health, education, trans- port and police), the provision of services depends on no initial planning but on the pressure coming from residents once the estate is established. Neighbourhood roads are gulleyed dirt tracks; rubbish at the Ype project was for seven years thrown out or burned until a public service was initiated in 1976; at Guarulhos the rubbish service

and the bus service in this isolated estate are unreliable - residents
frequently miss work when the road is impassable and the bus cannot
call; children have three hours free primary schooling per day, at
Ype in a wooden shack and at Guarulhos in a new building, in shifts
running up to 11 p.m.; secondary schools are distant from the estates
and not free.

It seems likely that without improvement many of the individual COHAB
houses will not last the 25 years of the mortgage repayment. At Borore
several of the houses collapsed in landslips before their sale; at Ype
after eight years the external plaster of many of the houses was falling
from the walls; at Guarulhos the corrugated iron roofs were blown off
by high winds in 1975 and had to be replaced by tiles. The small front
gardens in several estates had eroded to the point of threatening the
survival of the houses and even sites.

The question of the durability of houses puts one question over the
rights or sense of ownership which purchasers may feel. Another
question lies in the fact that residents do not acquire title to the
ownership of their house until they have paid off the mortgage entirely.
In the intervening twenty five years, there are severe restrictions
on their rights of sale. The new purchaser takes over the original
mortgage from BNH and must therefore be approved by COHAB; he will
often in fact be nominated by COHAB from the waiting list for that
housing project. Since the new purchaser takes over the outstanding debt,
the seller can only profit on the proportion of the mortgage which is
already paid off. This introduces a severe limitation on the
possibility of finding a second purchaser since he must fall within
COHAB's income limits and yet have sufficient savings (or access to
credit) to make payment to the seller.

Combined with the highly supervised system of repayment collection
and the forced removal of the residents of older estates, these
limitations on the real rights of ownership seem likely to contribute
to the low sense of ownership which social workers in the older estates
referred to in interview. Residents at Ype were said to refer to their
mortgage repayments as the 'rent', to the social workers as 'owners'
and to the inflationary correction of repayments as 'robbery'. A
survey (COHAB 1973) in the Carapicuiba estate found that only two thirds
of residents felt that their apartment was their property.

*Abandonment and eviction*

The high level of non payment and the physical decay of the houses on
the older estates leads to a discernible though not publicly stated
policy to move those residents who have failed out of the estates.
Pressure on the recalcitrants to pay serves the effect not only of
stimulating them to pay but also of encouragement them to move on.
Especially in the original estates, occupied by compulsorily rehoused
favelados , it was clear from interviews that it was considered a
measure of success for local COHAB workers to achieve a high level of
transference of ownership from the initial occupiers to higher income
people capable of improving and maintaining their houses as well as of
repaying. At Ype a fifty per cent turnover had been achieved.

Voluntary sale, that is the negotiated transfer of the owner's
contract with COHAB is relatively rare. In the one year until March

1976, the ownership of 178 housing units was formally transferred out
of a total of 3460 existing units. By comparison with this figure
more important, at least in some estates, is abandonment of his
property by the owner. In Guarulhos of 449 housing units, 80 had been
abandoned by owners who thus evaded further payments and penalties but
also gave up any claim to capital gains. In these cases, COHAB takes
court action to reclaim the property, but has to wait for approximately
three years before it can sell the property in case the original owner
returns.

Until 1976, COHAB's action to evict had been selective and exemplary:
the legal department had begun the process towards eviction in only one
hundred cases. At the beginning of 1976, the president of COHAB recently
appointed by the new city prefect, instigated a new programme of legal
action against all those residents who were more than three months in
debt. The action was to be pursued not only as a threat but to the
point of eviction. A new head of the legal department was appointed and
an official of the legal department was switched to manage the 'social
operations' department and in particular to harmonise the action of the
community development workers with the campaign to recoup payment or
to evict residents. By May 1976, 1250 households were involved in the
process towards eviction; of these 600 had been notified of a formal
legal action against them and in 300 cases (half of those notified)
legal action to evict had been initiated. At any stage in this process
before the sentence is arrived at, a household could enter into a new
commitment to repay according to a restaged and more compressed plan,
but only after paying off, in addition, COHAB's legal expenses. The
opportunity presented was to repay at a higher rate than the resident
had previously managed to maintain. Only one third of the 1250
households which had entered into the process had been able to make a
new repayment agreement. At that time (May 1976), therefore, fifteen
per cent of all COHAB residents (and nearly one quarter of those in
the five earlier housing estates) were due for eviction.

For the president of COHAB, the eviction campaign was a matter of
commitment to a fundamental principle of its operations.

> 'This is a programme for people who can buy. Up to now people
> expect public agencies to be easy but I want to prove that
> COHAB is not soft. If they can't pay there are many other
> people who want to'.

The other, welfare related, aspect of COHAB's operation, its commitment
to the housing of low income people, was respected in some limited
modifications in the process of eviction. In view of the 'social
aspects' the legal officer said that COHAB was prepared to give twenty
instead of the normal fifteen days delay between notification and the
initiation of action, to allow residents to stop action at any point
by making their back payments and to give 'non malingerers' the chance
to pay off their debts with a little further delay if it looked as
though their situation were about to improve. Thereafter in the logic
of an organisation which quite artificially claims a high degree of
comprehensiveness in the range of options it can present, the 'non
malingerers' who still fail to pay may have the opportunity to be
transferred to free temporary accommodation for a 'period of three or
four years education on the consequences of their action'. This
temporary or emergency shelter taken over by COHAB from the municipal
welfare department is of the most rudimentary sort. In 1976 it housed

a practically fixed population of 8000 in one room wooden huts.[10]

CONCLUSION: AN EXPLANATION

The official language of 'rehabilitation' and 're-education' like the division of the COHAB population between the 'recoverable' and the 'malingerers', clearly allocates the blame for failure to the people who enter the programme rather than to the programme itself. It is the adequacy of the people to meet the terms of popular housing which is put under question, not the suitability of the programme to its designated income groups. Even those officially responsible for the welfare component of COHAB's work, the social workers, come to rationalise their professional contribution in terms of its usefulness in promoting higher levels of repayment.

Moreover in their official context, all residents (whether defaulters or not) are obliged to participate in this view of themselves. Such contacts stress the dominance of official definitions and require the resident's conformity with them. Far from being clear owners of property, residents find themselves subject to the continuing and wide-ranging presence of the selling organisation in a series of authoritative roles whether as selector, social worker bent on training and rehabilitation, payments collector, the route through which appeal must be made for public services, the provider of water and sewerage, a source of reference and commendation to other public agencies, community developer, agent through which transfers must be negotiated, or as prosecutor. Residents are continuously and individually cast in the roles of applicant, potential malingerer or supplicant, dependent upon the benefits and protection of the organisation. What began as an opportunity for house purchase can, for many, quickly become an arrangement with many punitive consequences and with little defence in rights of ownership, of resale and of access to public services.

The ideology which is expressed in the structure of the relationship between COHAB and its beneficiaries is one which justifies the survival of the programme over the satisfaction of its clients. The implications are that action must be taken not only to promote the repayment habits of residents or to eject them but also to control selection more rigorously. However, ejection after failure is in some ways easier than selection before failure. The logic of COHAB's search for greater organisational security would be for the whole programme to shift upwards into the reach of more 'viable' income groups. Indeed the rules relating to credit-worthiness are, among formal criteria, those which are applied with most rigour. Prices and income and documentary require-ments have been raised; the whole COHAB programme has shifted from service of those earning between one and three to those earning between two and five minimum salaries; within this range, COHAB has sought to serve the upper brackets. However, there is a constraint (imposed by BNH requirements) on this upward movement, even though the upper limit on income is treated with a good deal of flexibility. COHAB is therefore left inextricably in a market of high risk and mass demand.

COHAB's more visible selection procedures suggest that housing is available to the lowest of its income range, that supply is large scale and that there is a serious chance of success. In the initial stages of selection quite artificially low minimum income 'eligibility' criteria are applied, qualifying rules are interpreted flexibly and the registration of new applicants is maintained permanently open; distribution is apparently based on a simple queue, standard procedures, and a waiting list in order of need and time inscribed. The consequence, however, is that these visible and orderly procedures pass on the problem of overwhelming demand to be dealt with at later stages of the administrative process. At these stages the formal criteria of selection are either insufficiently discriminating, as in the case of income requirements, or positively dysfunctional as in the case of (a) the application of need criteria (which would result in the choice of those applicants least able to pay) and (b) selection on the basis of time waiting (which would expose the length of the queue and the hopelessness of the wait).

COHAB, in this situation, has resorted to forms of 'procedural selection': the application of arbitrary cut-off points, diversionary queues , difficulties, confusions and limitations on the availability of information. The effect is to restrict effective demand, on the whole to select lower risk candidates, to reduce administrative time in processing, to defend the organisation against criticism that it is unable to respond to current demand, to disguise exclusion and, through the obfuscation, to permit the quick passage of selected groups.

COHAB faces two basic contradictions. The first is that while on the one hand it is required to demonstrate the mass availability of its product, on the other hand, given the low level of its production, it is required to limit the scale of effective demand. This contradiction is managed so that when it impinges on the candidate it is represented as his failure to meet rational and overt demands. The second contradiction is that while COHAB is required to maintain a programme for groups defined as unable to attain officially approved housing standards in the regular market, it is nevertheless also required to recoup the costs of the programme from its purchasers. This contradiction reaches the resident in a language which attributes failure to the inadequacy of his performance in the role of property-owning citizen, to the pathology of his poverty.

What is the force of the constraints which impose these contradictions on COHAB, on its officials and ultimately on its applicants and beneficiaries?

Most obviously, the agents of the popular housing programme have a clear place in BNH's scheme. While the finance accumulated through the housing finance system is invested in larger proportions in higher income housing, infrastructural works and industrial development (see chapter three), the rationale, the primary overt commitment of BNH, lies in the provision of 'a solution to the housing problem of low income families'. For the BNH as for the municipal prefecture, COHAB's programme[11] is the only sign (especially after the dismantling of rent controls) that government has a concern with mass housing conditions in cities such as Sao Paulo. Apparently large scale housing availability, apparently open and fair procedures of selection, criteria which seem to be based on need are the means through which COHAB demonstrates this concern. As agent of BNH and of the municipality, COHAB is not able to escape this role.

As financial agent of BNH, COHAB is also, on the other hand, obliged to recoup the finance loaned through it to mortgagees for the purchase of house and land. This is even more clearly a condition of its existence than its role as an apparent provider of low income housing. BNH anticipates a certain amount of non-payment in this programme, but ultimately a financial agent which consistently fails to collect loses access to credit from BNH. The prefecture has periodically covered COHAB's losses but only with a delay. COHAB's own return depends on its collection of the fees (listed earlier) associated with mortgage repayments. It is not able, as are the private financial agents of the BNH, to invest mortgagees' repayments for a period prior to their return to BNH. It therefore has a fixed income immediately dependent upon its performance in collecting its fees. In this way, it bears the risk of BNH's investments in relatively low income housing and is enmeshed in BNH's own need for a return on its investments.

By promising through COHAB a supply which cannot materialise, the responsibility for failure in provision and the collection of returns is reduced to a matter of COHAB's competence (see the introduction to this chapter). As a 'mixed economy' company, COHAB is required to support its operations out of its clients' payments as though it were a private company. Its failure to be self supporting is thus represented as a failure in its efficiency. New starts can be promised with new cheaper programmes (such as the self help project) or with a new more competent and aggressive administration (with each change in the prefecture). COHAB may fail, clients may fail but the myth of the existence of a 'social interest' housing programme is sustained.

COHAB is bound to fail because it shares the structural situation of its beneficiaries; their weakness in the property market is reflected in its own. The costs of construction, materials and land in Sao Paulo rise faster than their purchasing power. Periodically therefore, until the range of its income group and the maximum cost of its housing units are raised, COHAB has simply no capacity to build or sell. Even after the increase in the maximum cost of housing units to 500 standard capital units in 1974, COHAB could not afford within this limit to buy any land anywhere within the municipality of Sao Paulo. The maximum COHAB could offer in 1976 was twenty cruzeiros per square metre, while the lowest priced land in the municipality was then said to be eighty cruzeiros per square metre. Land therefore becomes available only on the periphery of the city in an entirely unplanned way depending on occasional offers from private landlords or public agencies.[12] Not only are these sources scarce, but also because the land is unwanted by the donor it usually involves high cost in reclamation or a good deal of waste due to steep slopes or boggy terrain.

The costs and the capacity of COHAB are increased by the action of other agencies which nevertheless are among those which blame COHAB for its inefficiency. Private construction companies, once they have started a project, have in most cases then held up work, demanding higher payment. This sort of action could simply be attributed to the pressure of rising construction costs which, for example, increased one hundred per cent in Sao Paulo during the two years until February 1976 (BNH 1976). But cost increases do not merely impinge upon but are also generated by the action of construction companies. COHAB finds it impossible to ensure against collaboration in tendering for its contracts. The State government found in 1976 that the Sao

Paulo Association of Public Works Contractors was indeed organising tenderers to force up contract prices by agreeing to make bids at the top end of the range of acceptable offers or even by boycotting contracts until prices had been raised by up to thirty five per cent. It is not far from this to the enforcement of higher prices by making completion conditional on increases.[13]

Public agencies also impose costs and delays, either through non-cooperation or through the imposition of standards which officially unapproved, self-built housing may escape. In principle any housing project requires the approval of the following agencies: BNH, the prefecture, the State sanitation agency (SABESP), the army, the air force, the fire brigade and the State metropolitan secretariat. In fact their approval usually arrives only after construction has begun (since COHAB has to seize its chances in land purchase); or it does not arrive at all, in which case the agency may refuse to cooperate with the opening of the estate. This has been the case several times with the water and sewerage services of SABESP. Since these services are financed by a State fund, SABESP can refuse to instal water and sewerage systems which do not conform to its own planning. In that case, COHAB has to provide the service from its own funds, as in Borore and Guaianazes. For its part, the prefecture imposes a charge equivalent to about US $ 120 (£60) on each housing unit for planning approval, and makes approval conditional on the achievement of minimum standards which are costly in their effect on land use: the inclination of a slope for housing may not be greater than one in ten, roads must be at least fourteen metres wide; forty per cent of the area of a site should be devoted to streets, open space and community services; individual sites should have a minimum ten metre frontage and 250 square metres area; a maximum of one third of each site may be devoted to construction.

It is these dependencies on other public agencies which provide the framework within which COHAB becomes permeated with obligations to service recommended applicants. They not only provide the framework of connections but also contribute to providing the conditions of scarcity within which special favours become important.

In summary, the interests which are deniable in the management of COHAB housing are those of the intended beneficiaries. The interests which are undeniable are those which are extraneous to the overt purposes of the programme. COHAB in no way challenges the structural conditions which give rise to the problems which its applicants face, that is the conditions of highly (socially and geographically) concentrated investment and income distribution, and the consequential exclusiveness of the land and housing markets. It is obliged to participate in BNH's role in the government's economic model, above all as an arm (though at this time a rather unsuccessful one) of its function as an investment bank. In fulfilling its own role, it is bound to respect the private financial interests of landowners, of constructors and of the hire purchase companies with which its applicants have debts; it is also indirectly bound to respect the orientation of the other public agencies on which it is dependent (such as SABESP, the prefecture, the BNH regional office) to higher income markets and to specially connected persons. Its function with regard to its intended beneficiaries is largely ideological: it helps to sustain the myth of availability over the reality of scarcity partly by attributing to itself and to its applicants the responsibility for failure.

NOTES

1. This chapter examines the performance of the Sao Paulo COHAB up until 1977. From 1978, COHAB clearly began to become a very much more productive organisation, in particular with a major scheme eventually involving up to 15000 units at Itaquera on the fringe of the city. This expansion of activity coincided with the slump in private building (see chapters two and three) which created both an opportunity and (from the point of view of construction firms and property speculators) a necessity for public housing agencies to expand their programmes. This later period of COHAB history requires a separate analysis (See Azevedo 1979).

2. Sao Paulo municipal prefect, Olavo Setubal, reported in Opiniao 19 September 1975.

3. In April 1976 500 UPCs were equivalent to about 150 minimum salaries or US $ 7884.

4. The author took from COHAB files a ten per cent sample of inscribed persons then resident in Borore and a one in three sample of those in the waiting list in 1976. This showed that after friends, relations, colleagues and personal knowledge, the next most significant source of information (accounting for only five per cent of cases) was the applicant's employer.

5. According to the prefecture's survey (Boletim Habi 1974 p.173) only thirty eight per cent of heads of family in favelas have registered work and only forty five per cent are insured with the social security system (INPS).

6. COHAB staff estimated that thirty per cent of candidate couples are not legally married. A survey by the municipal welfare department showed that in the favela population forty two per cent of unions were by consent rather than civil marriages (Boletim Habi 1974 p.75).

7. Text of a letter from a municipal councillor to the president of COHAB (8 January 1969).

8. The mortgage repayment itself includes an additional six per cent to cover COHAB's planning and administration costs.

9. The explanations of non-payment were offered in interviews by the author with the heads of COHAB's legal department and community development section and with social workers in the housing projects.

10. Valladares (1978b pp.72-76) recounts the process of eviction from COHAB projects into temporary shelter in Rio de Janeiro. This constituted an act by the administration to assert their control but she points out that this was only after those evicted had enjoyed a year's free housing. In Rio de Janeiro in 1974, 56 per cent of COHAB purchasers were in arrears by more than three months, a similar proportion to that found for Sao Paulo.

11. There are other programmes concerned with 'social interest' housing. In Sao Paulo there was the cooperative programme run by INOCOOP and the State wide housing scheme operated by CECAP. These were studied by the writer in equal detail as was COHAB. INOCOOP was only concerned with income groups (from about twelve minimum salaries) well beyond the limits of low income housing demand. CECAP focused its attention on cities outside Sao Paulo, and on one housing scheme in Sao Paulo where groups over about ten minimum salaries were housed.

12. The sites at Sapopemba, Guaianazes, Ype, Borore and Guarulhos were acquired from private landowners who thereby greatly increased the value of their remaining land which was thus connected to public services. Public land comes either from the prefecture or from BNH which obtains land acquired by the social security institute (INPS) from firms which have defaulted in payments into the security fund or from the providential institutes which were agglomerated to form INPS. Land is transferred by INPS to BNH at sub-commercial rates based on their value for property tax (Interview BNH 18 June 1976).

13. This paragraph is based on interviews with the head of COHAB's planning department and reports in O Estado de Sao Paulo 2 July 1976 and 6 August 1976. Similar cases can be cited from other countries (Cleaves 1974 pp. 260 272 on Chile, and Batley 1978 p.211 on Venezuela).

# 6 Urban renewal and expulsion in Bras

The experience of the mass of the population is not of contact with the services of the popular housing programmes but of exclusion without administrative contact.  Chapter four argued that much more typical of the experience of the poorer half of Sao Paulo's population than the administrative resolution of their housing problems was the continuous aggravation and redefinition of their housing situation in a sustained process of expulsion from the central city areas.

In the particular case of expulsion from the city core which this chapter examines, it will be clear that no simple distinction can be made between the private interests and the governmental actions which are responsible for urban development.  Public agencies involved in urban planning and resource allocation do not only operate within the context of the property and finance capital markets;  they also affect these markets. For example,  as chapter four showed, they allocate housing credit, promote investment in the construction and materials industries, instal infrastructure, zone land use for residential and industrial developments, and prohibit certain forms of housing settlement.  These kinds of controls and resource transfers create new opportunities in the urban property market, discriminating between economic sectors and differentiating between groups of the population. Benefits for some are penalties for others.  In the field of housing, some people, depending on their income or housing type, are more able to claim the administrative categorization which renders them eligible for cheap credit, public services, residential zoning, security of housing tenure and controlled rents. Similarly, some are more able than others to avoid punitive administrative action in the shape of penalties, insecurity, harrassment or eviction.  The practice of public agencies may thus be supportive to the very processes of speculation and concentration which they apparently intervene to resolve.  Chapter four showed that in Sao Paulo selective access to state benefits and protection tends to benefit those already favoured in the urban property market.

The particular case which is examined in this chapter relates to the building of an over- and underground mass transit railway and the effect which this had on a part of the city which previously accommodated a low income population and a wide range of small scale enterprises.

## THE SAO PAULO METRO COMPANY

The effects of the Metro Company's operations extend well beyond its
official remit - the construction and operations of a mass transit
railway system for Sao Paulo.  Because of its vast financial and
physical impact it is possibly the major urban agency in the city.
As one Metro official expressed it, in the absence of any other
effective official planning agency, the Metro seeks to take the
opportunities (which it creates) to direct the growth of Sao Paulo and
to integrate the plans of different authorities.[1]

The impact of Metro's work is concentrated along the two railway lines
of the mass transit system which were planned for construction during
the 1970s.  The North-South line was completed in 1975.  Work on the
East-West line began that year and was expected to be completed by 1981.
The construction cost of the first line was estimated at US $ 1000
million, and the cost of the second line was estimated in 1976 at US $
1500 million.  The National Housing Bank (BNH) was a major source of
finance;  in September 1976 it loaned the equivalent of US $ 80 million
to sustain the works for three months until the end of the year.  By
comparison, its budget for 'social interest' (PLANHAP) housing in the
entire country was less than US $ 130 million for the whole year.

The Metro Company is a 'mixed' enterprise in which the Sao Paulo State
government and the city prefecture have majority shareholdings.  The
prefecture of the municipality of Sao Paulo has direct responsibility
for receiving loans and finance and passing them on to the Metro
Company.  It therefore takes on responsibility for the repayment of
debts.  Since the Metro runs at a loss and is expected to continue to
do so, the prefecture has in fact to pay off these debts out of fresh
loans, State government grants and out of its own capital.  These
payments are converted into shares in the Metro Company;  the capital
so raised is used to pay off the loans contracted nationally and overseas.
In August 1976, the State was the largest shareholder, but the municipality by then had committed capital of approximately US $ 460 million.

The municipal budget for 1977 included the equivalent of US $ 45
million to cover the Metro's running costs and 65 million for the
continuing repayment of debts incurred on the North-South line.  For
the new East-West line in 1977, the State government budgeted US $ 55
million and the municipality allocated 73 million loaned by the BNH in
addition to its earlier 80 million.

What was new and beneficial to the prefecture in the BNH loan was that
(a) it carried an interest rate (about 20 per cent annually) which was
below the inflation rate (about 50 per cent) and below the rate for
borrowing on the money market (about 60 per cent);  and (b) it could be
made self-financing.  The terms of BNH's finance would allow it to be
used in the purchase from the Metro Company of swathes of land along the
line of the railway.  Housing would be built and the returns on sales
used to repay BNH's loan.  The Metro would be capitalised and the
prefecture would cover its costs through the purchase and resale of the
land.

In this chapter, I will examine the effects of these works on the
inhabitants of the areas along the route of the East-West line;  I will
give special attention to one particular area, Bras, which was being

directly affected by expropriation and demolition at the time that this
work was undertaken.  I am concerned not with the eventual effects of
the railway's operation but with those related to its construction.
The immediate consequences on the existing population receive less
attention in official statements than do the anticipated benefits
from the 'urban renewal' and more effective passenger transport.
However, several official agencies enter into contact with the resident
population in the administration of information, expropriation, eviction,
compensation, demolition and rehousing.  I will argue that, whatever
the official plan or intention, these processes have their own
differential effects on groups of the population, that in turn the
processes which touch the population are conditioned by organisational
relationships and that these relationships are themselves conditioned
by the terms of finance.

## BRAS

The transformation of Bras from a rural area on the edge of a small
town to an inner suburb of the largest city in Brazil (map 6.1) began
to occur from the middle of the nineteenth century.  The building of
the railways from the interior of the State to bring coffee and cotton
to the port at Santos signalled the development of the City of Sao
Paulo as a trading centre and eventually as a focus for the investment
of the new wealth in urban development and industrialisation.  Poorer
neighbourhoods like Bras grew up along the line of the railways as the
city's population increased from less than 30000 in 1872 to about
240000 in 1900 (IBGE, 1971).  A quarter of a million European migrants,
three quarters of them Italian, passed through the port of Santos
between 1832 and 1891.  Many of them stayed temporarily in a newly
established hostel for immigrants near Bras, and many did not move into
the coffee plantations as expected but stayed or returned to the city.
During the 1890s Italians were said to outnumber Brazilians in Sao Paulo,
and the particular focus of their settlement was Bras (Torres, 1969
p.119).

This period lays the basis for the present day reputation of Bras as
an Italian working class neighbourhood of small industries and mixed
housing ranging from slums to rooming houses, hostels and terraced
housing.  But, the development of new industries, the opening of new
streets and the growth of the population continued well after the end
of the century waves of European migration.  By 1920, Bras had reached
its maximum population of 67000.

Decay and decline is also part of the reputation of present day Bras.
On the one hand, there has been periodic municipal concern at the standard
of housing (and morals) in Bras and surrounding areas (Torres, 1969
pp. 168, 181, 212).  On the other hand, the municipality has itself
promoted radial and viaduct road improvements which have given impetus
to precisely the phenomena which attracted municipal attention, that is
the industrialisation and commercialisation of Bras and its decline as
a residential neighbourhood in favour of areas further to the east.
By 1966, Bras had 1106 manufacturing establishments, the highest number
among the districts of Sao Paulo.  They were small scale enterprises,
employing a total of 33000 workers, scattered throughout the area and
representing a wide variety of industries from textiles  and clothing,
to precision engineering, metal works, carpentry shops, motor spare
parts, jewellers and shoe shops.  The population had declined only

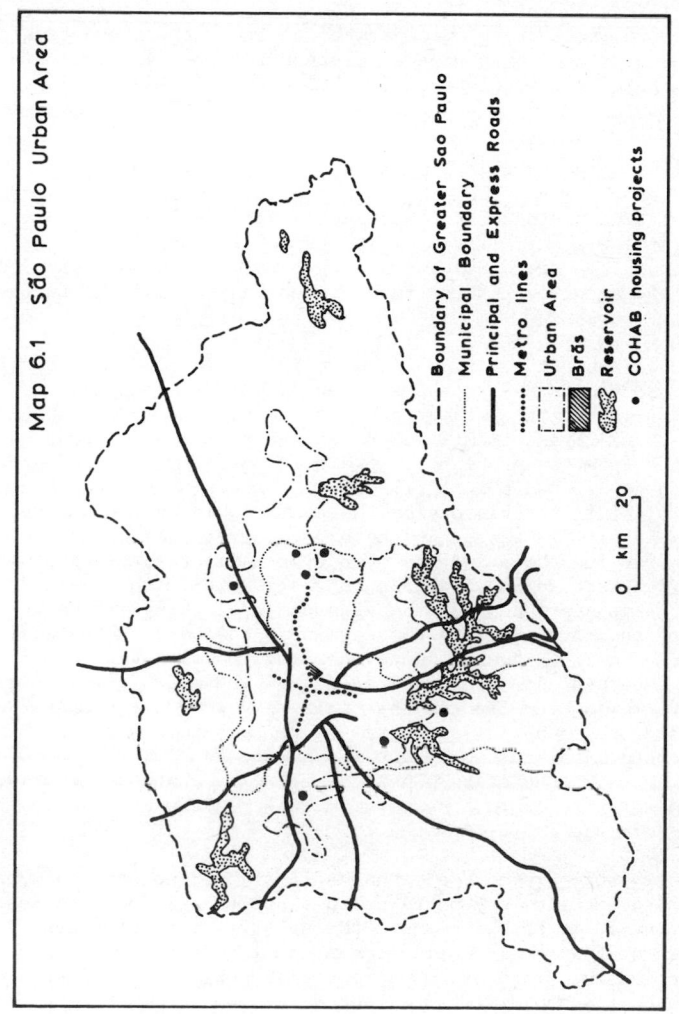

Map 6.1  São Paulo Urban Area

Boundary of Greater Sao Paulo
Municipal  Boundary
Principal and Express Roads
Metro lines
Urban Area
Brás
Reservoir
COHAB housing projects

0   km   20

fractionally to 62000 by 1967 but it was commonly supposed, often with pejorative implications, that the original Italian inhabitants had given way to migrants from the poor north eastern States of Brazil (PLANASA 1976).

In the view of the municipal authorities, the problem of Bras, was its inappropriate commercial activity, its obsolescent housing and its rundown infrastructure. The opportunity offered by the construction of the Metro line was to 'recuperate' an area of 7.5 square kilometres including Bras and parts of the neighbouring areas of Belenzinho and Mooca containing a population of 73000 people (PLANASA 1976).

THE PROPOSALS

Bras was affected by two interlinked plans - one for the construction of the Metro line and the other for the development of the area. In both cases the prefecture of Sao Paulo municipality had an important governmental responsibility, first through its participation in the ownership of the Metro company and then through the municipal urban development agency's (EMURB) involvement in planning the future of the area.

Prefect Olavo Setubal, appointed in 1975, regarded the construction of the East-West line as 'the work which will distinguish the administration of the present prefect' (O Estado de Sao Paulo 16 January 1976). Transport in Sao Paulo was a problem without solution but as the 'gravest problem... I gave it most time and resources' (O Estado de Sao Paulo 14 April 1976). It was to be 'the biggest urban project in the history of the city' (O Estado de Sao Paulo 28 February 1976); it was even 'the biggest ever project or urban intervention in Brazil and one of the most important in the whole world' (O Estado de Sao Paulo 28 February 1976). In the first, eastern stage, twelve stations and nine viaducts would be built between the centre of the city (Se) and the terminus (Itaquera); the station at Bras would be the biggest, being the junction with the North-South line and the suburban and main line railways. The metro line would run above ground following the line of the radial highway to the east (Radial Leste) and suburban railway system. The technicians of the Metro and the prefecture talked of a 'multi-modal corridor' which would mean that the residents of the eastern part of the city, hitherto deprived, 'would be privileged in transport, access roads and urban development' (O Estado de Sao Paulo 14 March 1976).

Initially, the prefecture announced that 3000 houses would be expropriated in a twenty metre strip along the line of the East-West route. Later, it was added that through Bras a further seventy metres each side of that strip would be cleared for development (map 6.2). This implied that in Bras, 600 properties would be demolished in addition to the 350 directly affected. It was to this wider area of 'urban recuperation' that the second loan of the National Housing Bank applied; indeed the loan depended on the inclusion of a sufficient area of land (a) to permit the construction of a significant housing project, and (b) to allow the municipal planning agency to make gains on the purchase and resale of the land.

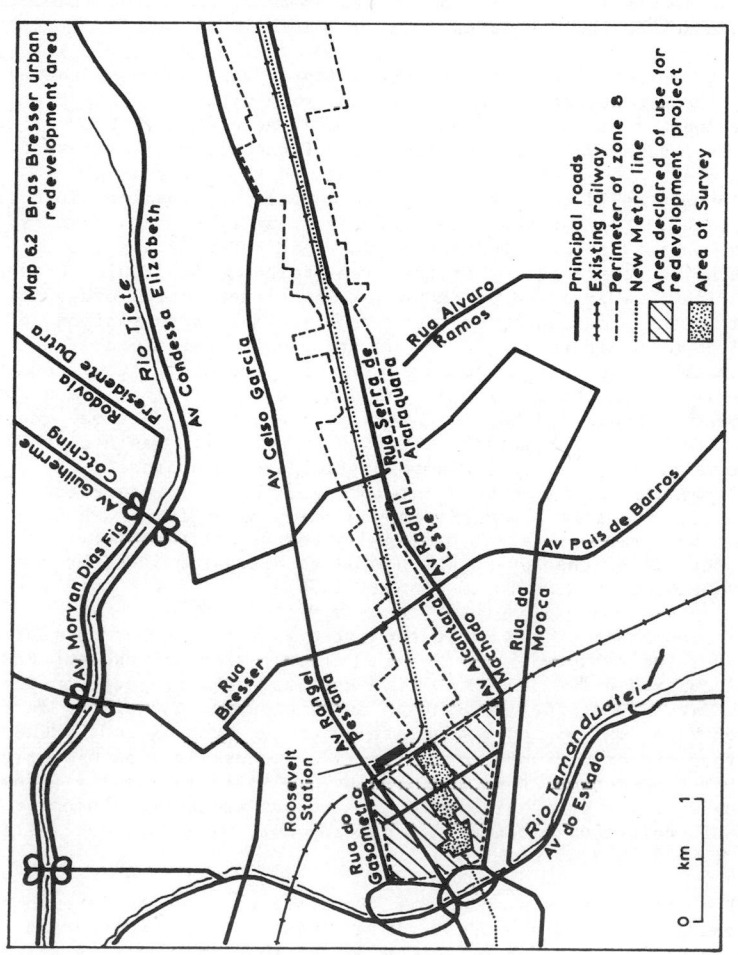

Map 6.2 Bras Bresser urban redevelopment area

Principal roads
Existing railway
Perimeter of zone 8
New Metro line
Area declared of use for redevelopment project
Area of Survey

Rio Tiete
Av Condessa Elizabeth
Rodovia Presidente Dutra
Av Guilherme Cotching
Av Morvan Dias Fig.
Av Celso Garcia
Rua Alvaro Ramos
Rua Serra de Araraquara
Av Radial Leste
Av Pais de Barros
Rua Bresser
Av Rangel Pestana
Av Alcantara Machado
Rua da Mooca
Roosevelt Station
Rua do Gasometro
Rio Tamanduatei
Av do Estado

km 0 1

The Metro's president argued that the local people would benefit from improved transport and services, from the removal of industries and from 'social and financial upward mobility' (O Estado de Sao Paulo 26 September 1976). Expropriation would be quick and cause the minimum of 'social traumas'; it was expected that in most cases 'friendly agreements' would be reached; in any case, according to the vice president of the Metro, an information office in the area would be able 'to guide people in the purchase of new property to replace the old' (O Estado de Sao Paulo 6 January and 11 March 1976).

From the moment of demolition, EMURB (an enterprise whose shares are held by the prefecture and which is concerned with the urban planning and development of the municipality) would, according to the official proposals, take over the redevelopment of the wider area cleared through Bras. The president of EMURB argued that,in general, redevelopment could be left to private initiative (as along most of the North-South route) but that due to the complexity of the street system in Bras, public sector intervention was required to achieve a comprehensive rearrangement of the area (Folha de Sao Paulo 10 January 1976). Diagrams produced by EMURB were published in the press to illustrate the president's argument that minimal expropriation and redevelopment would result in 'an urbanistically unacceptable solution', in 'problems of security' and in 'aesthetic problems'; comprehensive 'recuperation' on the other hand would allow car parking, green space, play areas, schools and health posts and a housing programme. Moreover, the president of EMURB argued that this intervention was necessary if the entire area around Bras was to participate in a process of redevelopment based on private enterprise: 'Private enterprise will thus have in the area a magnificent source of undertakings which normally it would only get with great difficulty because it would have to buy one by one all of the houses which will be disappropriated by the Metro works' (Folha de Sao Paulo 10 January 1976).

The framework of such a project existed in CURA ('urban communities of accelerated recuperation'), a line of credit established by BNH for special comprehensive projects. The case for CURA projects on the route of the North-South line (at Santana and Jabaquara) as well as on the East-West line was argued fundamentally on the grounds that EMURB was party to a process of universal historical necessity, 'an historical force which we cannot stop' (A Folha de Sao Paulo 10 January 1976): 'In Sao Paulo, as in other big centres, urban areas are subject to phases of evolution, a beginning, development, maturity, decline and death' (EMURB 1973 p.16).

EMURB's role in this process was therefore to renovate deteriorated areas and fit them to new uses. In a defence of its Santana and Jabaquara projects, EMURB officials argued that the function of the public sector intervention was to prevent private speculative gains in this historical process and to turn any advantages (of urban improvement and increased property values) to the benefit of present residents and owners (EMURB 1973 pp.19-20).

In the case of Bras, however, the president of EMURB's argument rested precisely on the possibility of stimulating the activity of private developers and on the need to introduce new middle class residents who would have the resources to finance the transformation of an industrial area into a commercial and residential neighbourhood just one kilometre from the city centre (O Estado de Sao Paulo 9 October 1976). This required the replacement of 'obsolescent' housing. The president argued that he could understand that there was a 'nostalgic attachment' to Bras but the fact that 'three generations may have lived in one house only went to show that they are obsolete and old dwellings'. The people may change but 'Bras will not die' (A Folha de Sao Paulo 10 January 1976).

By 1979, the idea of public sector intervention to renovate a larger area than that immediately affected by the metro line had been abandoned, but by that time the purchase and demolition of the scheduled areas of Bras had been undertaken on that pretext.

BRAS - OCCUPATIONAL AND HOUSING CONDITIONS

The 1976 redevelopment proposals referred to three areas (map 6.2):

   (i) the largest was the entire area of 7.5 square kilometres around Bras which it was hoped would be eventually affected by private redevelopment following the public intervention. The area was given a special zoning category (Zone 8) which could be used to prevent all physical change for three years until the phase of public intervention had been terminated;

  (ii) within the area of Zone 8, there was the wider strip of approximately seventy metres on each side of the metro line scheduled for demolition and redevelopment;

 (iii) lastly there was the priority area for immediate demolition to make way for the line itself.

A feasibility study commissioned by EMURB surveyed the population, its work and housing conditions in a sample of 677 households in the area of Zone 8. It also included a universal survey of public services, firms and the age of houses in the area. The study (PLANASA 1976) produced data which contradicted several of the assumptions expressed in official pronouncements on the redevelopment of the area.

Firstly, it was not true that a previously stable area was now characterised by a wave of recent migration from the poor north east of Brazil. Two thirds of family heads had been born in the city or in Sao Paulo State and 15 per cent had been born abroad; only 11 per cent were migrants from the north east. Secondly, it was not true that the housing was old and inadequate; 82 per cent of housing units had been built or fundamentally reconstructed since 1940; 96 per cent were in a 'good' or 'reasonable' state of conservation. The sample survey showed that two thirds of the housing was rented and one third owner occupied. Among owners the vast majority (93 per cent) had completed their purchase and only 16 per cent had required any sort of credit.

About half of the households were within the income range (from one to five minimum salaries) defined as the market of BNH's 'social interest' housing programme (table 6.1). But whereas COHAB, the agent of that programme in Sao Paulo, could only serve the top end of the income range, nearly a quarter of the families surveyed in Zone 8 earned less than three minimum salaries. Moreover COHAB, in its own struggle to equate its clients' spending power with market conditions, had managed to build only 6000 housing units in the ten years to 1976.

161

The area was not only able to shelter a population which COHAB could not reach,even in housing estates located on the periphery of the city, but also to do so in an area which:

(a) was entirely served by all public utility, transport and communications services (PLANASA 1976 p.20);

(b) offered education within their neighbourhood to 76 per cent of school-goers (PLANASA 1976: Anexo 11);

(c) offered employment in the same neighbourhood or in the nearby centre of the city to 69 per cent of employed people (PLANASA 1976: Anexo 11).

A more detailed survey was carried out by the writer,[2] This second survey applied to the area within Bras which was scheduled for immediate or eventual demolition (see area (ii) at the beginning of this section); it was based on a one in three sample of the approximately 780 addresses (household and business) within the area.

Table 6.1
Family incomes in the area of zone 8

| Family income range in minimum salaries | Per cent of families |
|---|---|
| Up to 1 | 2 |
| 1.01-2 | 8 |
| 2.01-3 | 13 |
| 3.01-4 | 16 |
| 4.01-6 | 15 |
| 6.01-8 | 19 |
| 8.01-10 | 8 |
| 10.01 + | 19 |
| | 100 |
| Base number | (593) |

Note: One minimum salary at end 1975 = Cr 532.8 (about US $ 60 or £30).
Source: PLANASA (1976).

Although the area covered was smaller, the characteristics of the population in terms of stability, housing conditions and employment were almost precisely the same as in the PLANASA study. The population was not only overwhelmingly from Sao Paulo State and city but also more than a quarter of the population was born in Bras itself. In a city of continuous destruction, expansion and rebuilding, Bras was characterised by a high degree of population stability; 62 per cent of survey respondents had lived there for more than eleven years.

Bras is part of a ring of inner urban areas which is primarily occupied by tenants. Two thirds of all houses and businesses are rented. Both surveys found that 80 per cent of households paid rents of under two minimum salaries (about US $ 120) per month - approximately the same proportion as applied to the city as a whole (Instituto Gallup 1971 p.44). Given these standard rent levels, the comparative distinction of Bras from many other areas is in the 'reasonable' or 'good' standards of maintenance of local buildings, access to public services and proximity to employment.

The importance of Bras in the employment situation of local people is indicated in two ways. Firstly, high proportions of employed residents find jobs in Bras (46 per cent) or in the surrounding areas (21 per cent) (table 6.2).

Table 6.2
Proximity of residents' employment to Bras (percentages)

| Location of work(b) | Employed heads(a) of households |
|---|---|
| Bras | 46 |
| Neighbouring districts | 6 |
| City centre | 15 |
| North and eastern districts | 4 |
| South and western districts | 13 |
| No information | 16 |
| | 100 |
| Base number | (128) |

Notes: (a) includes local business owners who are also resident.
(b) Areas are listed in descending order of proximity to Bras - 'neighbouring districts' are Mooca, Belenzinho, Pari and Parque Dom Pedro - 'city centre' are other areas within 3 km of Praca da Se.

Secondly, a large number of small firms are located in Bras. The PLANASA study identified 2183 industries and 3243 commercial establishments in Zone 8. My survey in the demolition area covered 72 enterprises employing 844 people (including the employer); the implication is that in this small area of demolition more than 216 enterprises (3 x 72) and 2532 jobs (3 x 844) are affected at least by disruption, if not elimination. A further 75 firms could be added to the total to account for the 25 where the owner could not be traced for interview.

Most of the Bras firms employ less than fifteen people (table 6.3); 47 per cent are family firms in the sense that they employ at least one other member of the owner's family; in 42 per cent of the cases, the owner of the firm lived in the Bras area. However, there is nothing uniform in the range of activities carried out by the firms, although there is an emphasis on the manufacture of mechanical parts (cogs, motor parts, metal pieces) for larger producers and on manufactured and trading services to other commercial and industrial enterprises. These enterprises are therefore often by their nature both inter-connected and dependent on a network of outside suppliers and entrepreneurial clients.

So the population's stability in the area seems likely to rest not only on nostalgia or sentiment, as the president of EMURB suggested, but also on the material facts of relatively favourable housing conditions, employment chances, public services and capital investment in firms.

Table 6.3
Size of local firms

| No. of workers (a) | Per cent of firms |
|---|---|
| 0-2 | 36 |
| 3-4 | 15 |
| 5-14 | 34 |
| 15+ | 15 |
| | 100 |
| Base Number | (72) |

Note: (a) Not including employer

THE PROCESS OF CONTACT BETWEEN THE POPULATION OF BRAS AND THE METRO COMPANY

Although the possibility of an East-West line to complement the North-South line had been spoken of at least since 1968, when an international consortium (Hocthief, Montreal, Deconsult) produced its proposals for both, it was only in November 1975 that the exact route of the first stage of the East-West line passing through Bras came to be known. The Metro Company then began to apply the procedure for expropriation to the owners of the 950 properties affected in Bras.

Once it begins, the process of expropriation is rapid. It starts with the visit of a surveyor to each of the affected properties. He confirms the identity of the owner, measures the building and assesses its state of conservation and material quality. In a large operation, such as that in Bras, a private firm is employed to do this work; the surveyors therefore know nothing officially about the Metro's plans and indeed are enjoined not to attempt to give information. On the basis of their reports and of complex formulae the Metro's disappropriation department calculates each property's value and then calls the owner to appear within three days at the Metro's headquarters office to hear the offer price. This is not negotiable, unless the owner can demonstrate that the data on which the valuation is based is false. If the owner disputes the valuation itself, he must take court action.

Within three to five days of the first meeting, the owner must return to indicate his acceptance or rejection of the offer, to produce documentary proof of ownership and to sign a sale agreement. In the case of a tenanted property, the Metro then (as owner) takes court action to require the original owner to evict tenants. If the owner accepts the offer, he receives the full purchase price within the following 30 days. He then has normally up to 20 or 30 days to leave the house unless he can argue an 'exceptional' case for extension. When the owner has tenants he is allowed a further 20 days and they must be given at least 10 days to leave.

From the moment that the letter is received by the owner informing him of his disappropriation, the whole process takes between 56 and 68 days (plus 20 days in the case of rented property). Legal action, which would delay that process was rarely taken by owners; three quarters of them entered into what the Metro described as 'friendly agreements' (O Estado de Sao Paulo 28 February 1976). However

'friendly' these agreements were, it was certainly true that they
were negotiated under pressure of time. Demolition of the approximately
350 properties in the direct line of the railway through Bras was begun
on 22 January 1976 and scheduled to be completed by 15 February.

At the time of my survey (6-20 March 1976), some demolition had taken
place. The area was divided by a strip of half demolished, half empty
houses. Life outside the immediate area of rubble, dust and cranes
seemed to proceed routinely, but what was striking was the residents'
uncertainty about what was happening and about what they should do in
the face of a threat which was both certain and imminent.

Authoritative information was not easily available to residents.
Practically all respondents to the survey had known that there were
some plans for the construction of the metro railway line through Bras,
even before the expropriations began to be announced. However, the
sources of information on the plans and their effects were largely
unofficial (table 6.4). Residents (and especially tenants) largely
depended on the press and on local people or rumour for their
information. Among the more official sources, only the visiting
surveyors and the Metro's local information centre had any importance.
But as was noted earlier, the surveyors were themselves not acquainted
with the plans and had been ordered not to give advice.

Table 6.4
Main sources of information on the metro plans (percentages)

| Source | House owners | House tenants | Business owners | Business tenants | All Respondents |
|---|---|---|---|---|---|
| Newspapers | 63 | 36 | 65 | 55 | 48 |
| TV/Radio | 29 | 16 | 13 | 31 | 21 |
| Local population | 32 | 41 | 26 | 31 | 35 |
| Rumour | 29 | 38 | 30 | 31 | 32 |
| Evaluator | 14 | 11 | 13 | 18 | 12 |
| Information centre | 20 | 8 | 17 | 10 | 12 |
| Official letter | 5 | 1 | 4 | 0 | 2 |
| Other sources | 7 | 4 | 0 | 12 | 6 |
| Base number | (59) | (114) | (23) | (49) | (215) |

Note:   The question allowed several responses. The columns do not
        therefore add up to 100 per cent.

Officials of the information centre could respond to requests for
advice only in the most general terms. Although it received 8000 calls
in the seven months up to August 1976, the only information the centre
could give was (a) to confirm whether a house was included in the area
to be demolished, (b) to recommend a list of estate agents, (c) to
indicate the documents needed to prove ownership and (d) to advise
people not to sell to speculators. As the head of the centre argued,
it was to 'improve the Metro's image and to calm people'. At no time
was any information given on occupants' rights to compensation, to
legal representation, to refuse the first offer, or to appeal, nor was
the basis of valuation disclosed. Firm advice on the level of valuation
and on dates for leaving was only available as individual cases came to
be treated by the disappropriation department. Tenants (two thirds of
the population of Bras) were entirely outside even this limited

information system since official agencies had no need to contact them; they were due no compensation and they were to be evicted by the ex-landlord and not the Metro. The receipt of information largely depended on the subject's involvement (or not) in these two other processes of compensation and eviction.

Certain information on dates for leaving present accommodation was thus limited to little more than a quarter of the population, that is to those 29 per cent who had been offered a price for their property and to their tenants. Even the transmission of information from landlords to tenants was uncertain; as a study by the Metro company showed , proprietors sometimes '... do not advise the tenant, or encourage him to stay on so as to continue receiving rent' (Metro 1976 p.4).

So the requirement to leave came on the whole without official warning, either in the shape of a letter from the Metro which would normally allow the owner between two and three months to find alternative accommodation, or in the shape of a court order for the eviction of tenants within ten days. At the time of the survey, of those 79 respondents who could give dates half had to leave within one month and a quarter in less than ten days.

COMPENSATION

Most residents were tenants who do not qualify for any right to compensation for removal although a few were offered certain discretionary help. In law, tenants of buildings used for business, like the owners of business premises, can claim for 'lost profits', that is profits remaining after payment for the use of the premises. In practice, they were not informed of this right. Owners of property are the only group called by the Metro company to discuss compensation for the loss of their property. Even in their case, however, there was considerable variation in the way this standard principle worked out in practice.

The valuation is based on the measurements and qualitative assessments made by the surveyors and on a complex series of adjustments to take into account local land and building prices. A standard basis of assessment exists in the fixed replacement cost per square metre of construction which is used by public authorities throughout Brazil (though the fixed cost varies by State and city). A standard land value per square metre is also established by a survey of current land prices in other parts of the city and their transfer to the particular area (Bras) according to a relative weighting based on planning zones of the city. This acts as part of a cycle of cumulative causation - zoning decisions attribute low value to an area and this is confirmed by public purchasing policy.

On the basis of these standard land values and construction costs, adjustments are then made for particular properties. This is partly by comparison with property of similar size and condition in other parts of the city and the use of valuations for property tax *(valor venal)* as a basis for transferring prices from one area to the other. It is also by attributing particular advantages to plots depending on their location, shape and size. Thus corner sites, are given a higher valuation while plots which are narrow and deep or which fall below the municipally permitted minimum (of ten metres frontage by twenty five metres depth) lose value.

Metro officials consider that they are offering a fair market price
and that this is demonstrated by the fact that threequarters of owners
accept the first offer in a 'friendly agreement': 'we would consider
that we were offering too much if for example ninety per cent of people
accepted'. Clearly however, the assessment relies a good deal on
nonmarket factors both in respect of the administrative judgement of
relative worth and in the exclusion from consideration of the higher
values likely to result from the introduction of the metro line.
Property is assessed at existing zoning and use values.

Whether or not the price is a fair estimate of market value, negotiation
about property values is limited in various ways. Firstly, the
complexity and covert nature of the evaluation formula put it beyond
simple challenge; secondly, owners are called for consultation
individually as the valuations are produced, thereby limiting the
chances for comparison and organizing a local response; thirdly, the
immediate onus is on the owner to prove his possession (a considerable
problem for people lacking ownership certificates and title deeds on
old and inherited buildings) and to react to the offer within days;
fourthly, if he does not accept the offer he forfeits the opportunity
of a certain cash payment for an uncertain and very delayed increase.

The first offer by the Metro is indeed formally non-negotiable except
by resort to court action. Nevertheless, officials of the disappropriation department agreed that representation of the owner by a lawyer
could often result in an increased offer, since the lawyer was likely
to be informed of the valuation procedure and able to question the
particular outcome. However, only about five per cent of owners were
represented in this way. 'Everybody', said a local lawyer in Bras,
'could improve their compensation but most people distrust the
authorities and don't know how to do it'.

Court action on the question of compensation occurs in about thirty
per cent of cases, that is where no 'friendly agreement' is arrived at.
This is either where title to ownership is disputed, or where an owner
claims an increased valuation or where owners of business claim for 'lost
profits'. Claims by owners are indeed risky undertakings. The court
action will take eighteen months to two years to be heard; in the
meantime the property is demolished (the Metro demolishes first and
negotiates afterwards) and the owner receives temporarily only eighty
per cent of the valuation for property tax purposes (about ten per cent
of the market value); the owner who brings an action has to pay at
least for his lawyer and for the court expenses if he loses. Moreover,
a case based on 'lost profits' has to present accounting evidence that
the profits were earned and that the due tax was paid on them. Even
then the chances of an increased valuation are small. Of seven cases
relating to expropriation on the North-South line, the writer noted only
two where, after two years the court awarded an increase which exceeded
inflation over that period.

Except where the owner has recourse to good legal advice and
representation and has the capacity to await an eventual improved offer
or withstand a loss, the logic of the procedure of compensation and
expropriation clearly moves the owner in favour of quick acceptance
of the first offer. 'Friendly agreements' have to be viewed in this
context: the small owner is isolated, under pressure and uninformed.

THE DIFFERENTIAL EFFECTS OF EXPROPRIATION AND EVICTION

Most official statements about the plans for Bras justified them in terms of the physical improvement or re-equipment of the area. Where local people were mentioned it was to suggest either that they would benefit from these changes or that at least they would be protected in the process of transformation. Complaints in that case were to be attributed to 'nostalgia'.

The survey results, however, indicate a high level of antipathy to the impending changes and suggest that this was based on adversely affected material interests, even if also on sentiment. The data allowed some distinction between the effects on and interests of groups according to their position as owners or tenants of housing and business premises.

Local people's assessments of the plans for the demolition and redevelopment of the area were discriminating. Unlike officials in public statements, respondents to the survey made a clear distinction between the advantages which the city population and remaining local people might gain from the development and the installation of the metro line, and the losses which those directly affected by demolition would incur (table 6.5). Overwhelmingly, 79 per cent of respondents

Table 6.5
Assessment of plans (percentages)

|  | Good | Bad | Depends | Don't care Don't know | Total |
|---|---|---|---|---|---|
| For the city | 82 | 11 | 1 | 6 | 100 (215) |
| For Bras people whose house or business will be demolished | 12 | 66 | 15 | 6 | 99 (215) |
| For Bras people whose house or business won't be demolished | 55 | 27 | 9 | 9 | 100 (215) |
| For self | 26 | 55 | 7 | 12 | 100 (215) |

would have wished to remain in Bras had it not been affected. Even if it were true that 'time will break their emotional links with the neighbourhood' (President of EMURB, O Estado de Sao Paulo 10 January 1976), it was apparently not true that time alone had been responsible for building links up. Younger and more recent residents manifested slightly less but still an easily predominant wish to stay in the area; even among residents of less than two years, 68 per cent would have wished to stay. Nor was the commitment less among owners of property and businessmen in general, although these, by comparison with tenants, had access to compensation (table 6.6).

Most respondents expected to lose by the change; 56 per cent of owners thought the Metro's offer for their property was low and only 14 per cent thought that it was at a reasonable level: 'We are not selling, we are being imposed upon'; 'I want to make a friendly agreement. They are very strong, it doesn't help to fight'. Most tenants of housing (74 per cent) and of businesses (86 per cent) expected to pay much larger rents in their future tenancies (table 6.7). Of the 74 in the sample who knew their future rent, it would be more than double for three quarters of them and more than four times as much for one quarter.

168

### Table 6.6
#### Preference for staying or leaving Bras (percentages)

| Preference | Residential tenure(a) | | Period in Bras(a) | | Age(b) | | All businesses(c) | All respondents(d) |
|---|---|---|---|---|---|---|---|---|
| | Owner | Tenant | 0-20 years | 21 years + | Under 39 | 40+ | | |
| Stay | 78 | 78 | 72 | 86 | 64 | 87 | 84 | 79 |
| Depends | 0 | 2 | 3 | 0 | 4 | 0 | 0 | 1 |
| Leave | 22 | 19 | 25 | 14 | 31 | 12 | 0 | 19 |
| Don't know | 0 | 1 | 0 | 0 | 0 | 1 | 16 | 1 |
| | 100 | 100 | 100 | 100 | 99 | 100 | 100 | 100 |
| Base No. | (59) | (114) | (94) | (79) | (70) | (144) | (72) | (215) |

Notes: (a) Total 173 = all residents
(b) Total 214 = all respondents less one who gave no age
(c) Total 72 = all owners of business (including tenants of property)
(d) Total 215 = all respondents

### Table 6.7
#### Expectation of future rent – tenants of property (residential and business)(Percentages)

| Expected future rent by comparison with present rent | House tenants | Business tenants |
|---|---|---|
| Much more expensive | 74 | 86 |
| Slightly more expensive | 8 | 5 |
| The same | 2 | 2 |
| Cheaper | 3 | 0 |
| Don't know | 3 | 0 |
| Not applicable(a) | 11 | 7 |
| | 101 | 100 |
| Base Number | (104)(b) | (43)(b) |

Notes: (a) Present tenants who in the future would buy or share or return to owned property
(b) Totals are of those tenants who knew that their property would be affected

In spite of the immediacy of the move, 66 per cent of residents had not yet arranged a place to live. About one third had found or were looking for accommodation in the areas near Bras and around the centre of the city, but respondents frequently said that they had begun looking near Bras and then found that house prices and rents had forced them further out of the city. One third of those who had already arranged accommodation had moved out to more distant areas with lower levels of public services provision. The obtaining of a place to live was a product of income and chances rather than choice: 'We have to move. It doesn't help to think whether it will be good or not'.

Most local businessmen, like residents, expected to lose from the move in a direct financial sense, whether from low levels of compensation or from drastically increased rents for premises (table 6.7). Nevertheless 78 per cent expected to, and presumably indeed had to, continue in business. The enterprises which were most likely to fail were the bars and small stores on rented premises, which depended most on a local network of clients.

Besides the question of the level of compensation, most businessmen had to bear high costs of new premises and the trading losses and expense incurred in the period when the business was being moved. A third cost, the loss of a known location (*ponto*), could be reduced as far as possible by moving within the area. But, this locational cost was what local businessmen seemed most to fear. For small businesses it implied the loss of a local network of suppliers, trading outlets and workers and the loss of clients who could not easily be recaptured by advertising: 'I will have to close the firm for at least a month. I will lose the location and all my goods. I will lose 80 per cent of my clients and the telephone which is essential to the business. It will ruin my life'.

The Metro company was apparently concerned to ease these outcomes (a) by paying the market price which would encourage owners into a 'friendly agreement' with immediate cash payments which would allow the purchase of new accommodation, and (b) by offering advice and guidance to tenants as well as owners. The difficulties of local people were then treated (or ignored) as though they were the residual problems of special 'social cases' whose responses were 'inadequate' or who for perverse reasons failed to accept the valuation offered.

The personnel department of the Metro carried out a survey of disappropriated people which showed that problems were felt more generally (Metro 1976): 68 per cent of owners were found to have too low an income to sustain mortgage repayments on a new house; 63 per cent of tenants had insufficient income to pay the rent on housing equivalent to their existing accommodation, and frequently could not pay a three-month deposit in advance nor find an owner occupier to act as guarantor of the rent repayments. Owners had only the few weeks after they had received the Metro's offer to look for accommodation; tenants had even less warning. Pressure of time and the wish to stay in the area had led to an inflationary increase in local rents and prices. The personnel department proposed that the Metro should be prepared to arrange transport for people moving, to pay deposits and to make special connections with the municipal housing agency, COHAB, so as to secure places in its next round of house allocations. By August 1976, when most of the removals in Bras had taken place, the Metro had paid deposits in only twenty cases.

The outcome of the Metro's intervention was not universally catastrophic for the people of Bras. For some people it represented an opportunity to sell property in an area blighted by industrial activity, busy roads and the uncertainty of the redevelopment proposals, and to use their gains as a down payment on a new house. Though seen by most people as detrimental, the effects of the intervention were variable.

The variability was partly a product of the Metro's own procedures.

Some local people (notably residential tenants) were not eligible for compensation; they were thus effectively disqualified from the receipt of official information and therefore they were less able to prepare for their removal. Businessmen who were tenants of premises were formally qualified to receive compensation for the loss of profits but were not informed of this right.

The ordering and processing of cases had the general effect of imposing conditions of urgency, confusion and isolation on the owners dealt with; it also had the particular effect of relatively favouring those who understood and who could withstand the processes to which they were subject. The basis of the valuation was a mystery beyond dispute except to those who could afford legal representation. The disputing of claims was virtually impossible except for those who could manage without their present accommodation or who could withstand a two year delay in the receipt of compensation. The registration of a claim for lost profits itself depended on previous conformity with tax and accounting standards which were unlikely to have been respected by small businesses. Moreover, the valuation of, and negotiation with, large firms is not managed through the normal procedures but negotiated personally by the head of the Metro's disappropriation department.

The outcome for individuals therefore depended on:

(a) their belonging to broad categories (house owners and tenants, business owners and tenants, large and small businesses) for which eligibility for information and compensation differed;

(b) their capacity to deal with the complexity and urgency of procedures and to withstand the costs and delays implied by interrupting the procedures;

(c) their dependence on local housing and employment markets. A move away from the area implied greater costs (in lost access to clients, suppliers, work, schools, services and city facilities) for some than for others. Similarly, compensation which for the young might be sufficient to make a down payment on a new house bought through credit, for the old had no such significance since long term credit could not be obtained by them. The basis of compensation could not allow for those particular dependencies on local markets. At the same time the intervention in the area itself inflated local property prices (but did not compensate for them) and made it less likely that people who depended on the locality would be able to find accommodation or premises there.

(d) the official standards used to assess the expropriation value of property, which had no relation either to the use value of the accommodation to the occupant or to his capacity to find smaller property at the same price. Thus valuations were downgraded according to the age of the building and according to their nonconformity with space standards introduced after their construction. The effect of this administrative reduction in local values was to increase the costs and losses involved in moving house or business.

WHY NO RESISTANCE?

The extension of the metro line through Bras clearly did not present itself as a universal benefit. The interests of many people seemed

171

likely to be damaged profoundly.  In the survey interviews and in press
reports local people expressed their distress openly.  Yet there was a
complete absence of organised or individual resistance, or refusal to
cooperate.  The fact that most owners fell in with 'friendly agreements'
on their expropriation was itself taken by Metro officials to bear out
their view that demolition was proceeding with the goodwill of all but
the old, nostalgic and special 'social cases' who presented themselves
as 'problems' to the social workers at the information centre.

Distress was very much more general than the official view allowed.
There was apparently a common interest in collective action to hold up
or postpone the Metro's plans, to make demands or seek information, to
seek joint legal representation or to campaign through the press or the
municipal council.  All of the 'stakes' in the local neighbourhood,
which North American political sociologists (Clarence-Davies, 1966;
Kaplan, 1963;  Rossi and Dentler, 1961) have found to be associated with
an active local response to urban renewal programmes, were present in
Bras:  economic stakes in business and home ownership, affective stakes
in tenancy, social stakes in the 'community', status preservation and
'community consciousness'.

At one level, the absence of organised and overt resistance could be
simply explained in terms of the consequences of such action.  It would
almost certainly have been suppressed by police or military force.  It
would also have been easily avoided by the authorities.  As has been
noted in the case of British and American studies of demolition and
slum clearance programmes, where the authorities have legal powers to
achieve their ends the cooperation of the public is simply not required
(Kaplan, 1963;  Dennis, 1970;  Batley, 1972).  This was even more
clearly the case in Bras;  whatever the public response, demolition was
going ahead as a quite self contained activity.

What is more surprising is that there was scarcely any dispute about
compensation or dates of leaving, no objection to eviction, little
employment of legal representation, no joint approach to the Metro to
negotiate more favourable terms nor to claim compensation for lost
business profits and locations.  Several sorts of explanation can be
offered.

Firstly, there was the overpowering nature of what was happening.
Dennis (1970 pp.350-2) has identified the disincentives to 'public
participation' in British slum clearance situations:  the threat at the
stage that demolition is announced 'is not immediate enough to form a
basis for organised opposition...';  the sheer magnitude of the change
'... the possible ramifications of which may be too complex to grasp
and too obscure to be contemplated';  the 'sense of helplessness'
engendered by 'the planning machinery and the behaviour and attitudes
of the planning personnel'.  Any sense of shock or helplessness can be
imagined to be the greater in a situation, as in Bras, where the threat
was immediate rather than delayed.

Secondly, as Dennis argues for the British case, the expression of
official plans and justifications itself promotes the view that the
demolition and urban renewal are inevitable, beyond sectional interests
and too big to make adjustments to the people of a particular locality.
Earlier, I indicated that the Metro and EMURB saw themselves engaged

in a historical process of evolution, acting in favour of progress over decline. The work was massive so that what was happening in Bras was merely an aspect of a general improvement for the city. What was striking was that on the whole residents of Bras, in spite of their personal grievances, appeared to share the view that what was happening was not only inevitable but also that it should not be resisted, because it represented progress against which no man could be seen to stand. Atlhough they were aware of the gap between the interests of those who would be expelled and those who would remain to use the line, they behaved as if it were the assumed benefit to the city population as a whole which was paramount (table 6.5). The association of 'progress' with the construction of the metro implied that those who claimed that their interests were damaged would be assigned the unattractive role of 'obstacle to progress'.

Thirdly, and underlying also the first two explanations, is the force of the organisational procedures within which officials and subjects are locked. 'Demolition' and 'redevelopment' may carry general connotations but the programme in Bras only acquired its particular significance as it came to be implemented. The inevitability, urgency, complexity and obscurity which events assumed was a product of the way in which official agencies dealt with the people being affected: the propagation of late and partial information forced people back on reliance on rumour; the mystery of the evaluation procedure and the relentless independence of the process of demolition made people in fact helpless. Similarly, the procedures ensured that the primary concern of those affected was (a) with their individual circumstances and (b) with what would happen next rather than with what was happening now. They might have a common interest in staying in Bras, but any consensus was fragmented by the way that the processes of information, compensation and removal treated them separately and even required some (landlords) to act for the Metro in dealing with others (tenants). The crucial issue of expropriation was conducted case by case (but in no predictable order) on the terms (and on the territory) of the expropriating organisation. Attempts to negotiate implied sure delays and, therefore, certain losses for uncertain gains. The abruptness of the procedures meant that people must be more concerned with finding their next accommodation than with negotiating over their lost property: 'to get mixed up with lawyers at this stage only wastes time'; 'we can't say anything in case they pull the house down with us in it'; 'I went to Rua Augusta (the Metro HQ) and they said that when the notification came we would have to get out – end of conversation'.

## CONSTRAINTS ON OFFICIAL AGENCIES

The adverse effects of local people did not pass unnoticed by Metro officials. The head of the disappropriation department was aware that the urgency of their removal did not allow people to find alternative accommodation nor to register their children for new schools; he knew that people were 'often temporarily shocked'; officials in his department knew that owners of large businesses with legal representation got a better deal than small businessmen without assistance. Social workers in the personnel department were aware from their survey that a large population of the population could not find alternative accommodation; they appealed for resources to allow them to meet 'the basic needs of the expropriated population' (Metro 1976 p.16). EMURB officials often privately expressed a commitment to the idea of turning the advantages of public sector investment to the benefit of affected residents; indeed this was stated policy in the case of the redevelopment of Jabaquara and Santana through which the North-South metro line was constructed.

It was, however, the process of implementation, not good intentions, which determined the outcomes for affected people. It was the Metro's own procedures which helped to generate local helplessness and confusion. Officials themselves were not independent of nor wholly able to control these procedures. There were limits to change. The procedures broadly conformed with the requirements placed on the Metro company by its relationship with other organisations, including the municipal, State and federal governments, and internal and external creditors. These relations were all thoroughly interpenetrated so that for example the Metro's relationship with the federal government was through the municipal government (the prefecture) and the point which underlay this relationship was, on the whole, the question of access to credit.

The Metro's relationship with the prefecture was especially direct, first because, after the State government, it was the largest shareholder and second because all credit allocated to the Metro was channelled through the prefecture as guarantor of the repayment of the finance. It was precisely this guarantor role which had forced the prefecture into its significant shareholding; periodically it has repaid the Metro's debts by purchasing shares, the capital so raised being used to pay off arrears. On the one hand, the construction of the city's metro railway system was a considerable liability of which the prefect as much as local councillors complained; on the other hand, it was a matter of prefectural pride and achievement and a matter in which the prefect could be obviously influential on the development of the city.

The question of prefectural commitment to, and influence on, the Metro has several contradictory implications. The works offered a rare opportunity for prestige and effectiveness to the prefect; they gave access to large scale credit in contrast to the usual requirement on the municipality to undertake its commitments out of its own funds; long term funding, the scale of the works, and the consequent association of the prefect's reputation with the success of the project gave the Metro a certain promise of continuity. However, the continuity, scale and sophistication of the works and the wider ranging sources of finance in their turn gave the Metro administration a greater degree of independence from the prefect's control than other 'mixed economy' municipally financed enterprises could claim. For example, EMURB, the municipal urban development agency, was subject to continuous alterations in its directorship and its plans with each change in the prefect (there were three changes between 1972 and 1976). The Metro, on the other hand, had had one president in its seven year life, although he was formally subject to appointment by the shareholders. A slow down in the works, a decline in future levels of finance threatened the loss of the technical team which he had built up; this was a possibility which he was able to employ in budgetary negotiations with government and which worried the federal as much as the local authorities.

The Metro therefore had a particular power to negotiate its survival and the continuity of its works. On the other hand, the factors (the scale, sophistication and wide ranging organisational connections) which gave it this power, also made the Metro particularly vulnerable to change

174

- this was precisely its negotiating point. Thus, a new prefect
(Miguel Colasuonno) could require the abandonment of detailed plans
and already initiated works for the construction of a line under a
principal avenue (Paulista), for these plans only to be revived and
considered four years later under a later prefect (Olavo Setubal).
Financially, the indebtedness of the metro project made it extremely
vulnerable to changes in prefectural, State or federal government
priorities.

All these factors gave an urgency to the works. The nature of the
undertaking carried its own logic in favour of continuity, which the
Metro company was able further to exploit so as to maintain the
commitment to and the pace of the undertaking. The uncertainty which
nevertheless hung over the works made it that much more imperative
to carry out each stage of the programme quickly while funds and
government commitment were there. Once that stage had been initiated,
the prefect and his administration had an interest in pressing for its
conclusion during their term of office, and the Metro company had an
interest in maintaining prefectural support by promising success in
achieving that objective.

There were other more directly financial reasons for haste. These
related partly to the sources and terms of finance and partly to the
piecemeal nature of financing; ultimately, these factors required the
Metro company to act quickly and without much regard to local interests
in Bras.

The financing of the metro work was undertaken entirely through the
prefecture which received the finance, guaranteed it and took on
responsibility for repayment. It was, however, the federal government
which organised internal loans and which contracted foreign loans
through the central bank; the State government's authorisation to
raise external credit was withdrawn by the federal government in August
1976, six months after the State had contracted a loan of US $ 175
million on the London money market for investment in the construction
of the East-West line. The prefecture was, dependent, therefore,
primarily on the federal government for raising finance, but also on
the State government for obtaining a proportion of the loans and for
contributing to their repayment.

Finance raised abroad accounted for more than half the cost of the
construction of the North-South line, split almost equally between loans
tied to particular purchases and untied credit. The principal creditors
were British, North American, German, Italian and Japanese banks, the
International Bank for Reconstruction and Development and the Inter-
American Development Bank.

The advantage of foreign loans was that they were relatively long
term (between five and twelve years). They were also relatively cheap
in terms of foreign currency: interest was between 8 per cent and 12
per cent per annum (according to the London Interbank Offered Rate -
LIBOR) with an additional 'spread' of 1.76 to 2 per cent for the
Brazilian risk and of a Brazilian central bank rate of 3 per cent.
Against this, repayment of national loans raised through federal
agencies was indexed for inflation. However, overseas debts had to be
repaid in foreign currency which meant that they also were effectively

indexed; in this case the adjustment followed from the devaluation of the cruzeiro on international money markets (which turned out to be a more severe correction than the internal inflationary index calculated by the federal government).

The passage of time was thus crucial to the scale of the debt incurred through loans : with time, the costs of credit, materials and works increased. As the president of the Metro expressed it: 'productivity increases with speed' (O Estado de Sao Paulo 9 October 1976). The figures on the outgoings involved in meeting the Metro debts are confusing but illustrative. According to a statement by the city prefect, the municipality was committed between 1976 and 1982 to yearly outgoings of about US $ 150 million in repayment of loans and running costs (O Estado de Sao Paulo 24 August 1976). Another statement by the prefect claimed that the metro had absorbed thirty eight per cent of municipal investment between 1968 and 1976 (O Estado de Sao Paulo 14 April 1976). Yet another report suggested that the total debt remaining to be paid on the North-South line in 1976 was US $ 250 million, before any further debts on the East-West line were assumed (O Estado de Sao Paulo 6 September 1976).

Ultimately this repayment could only come from the capital contribution of the prefectural and State governments. The metro itself, it was agreed, would offer no return; indeed it was running at a loss which was being subsidised out of new loans and State and municipal grants, as well as by the rundown of the fund intended in the long term for maintenance. The construction of the East-West line was crucial in that respect because it offered the prospect of increasing the traffic on the system as a whole, in a situation where the North-South line on its own had turned out to be running below a viable passenger capacity.

The need to maximise the use of expensive credit and the need to bring the second line into service to help reduce the net running costs of the whole were two important reasons for haste. They were also reasons for minimising the costs of expropriation and construction.

There was a further factor; the piecemeal and uncertain nature of the funding favoured the elimination of all costs which were easily dispensable and the continuous demonstration of cost effectiveness to would-be creditors. During 1976 there was a series of threats and counterthreats by the prefecture , State and federal governments addressed to each other to the effect that they could not be counted upon to bear the costs of the East-West line's construction. The prefect said that he would contribute 'not a penny more' (O Estado de Sao Paulo 27 August 1976); the State government reserved its position until the second half of the year saying that its budget was extremely tight; the federal urban transport company (EBTU), which was responsible for organising finance for allocation throughout the nation, argued that the local authorities should take the initiative and that until then even those funds already assigned to Sao Paulo would be withheld (O Estado de Sao Paulo 9 October 1976). Into this breach stepped the president of the Metro arguing that the 'accelerated execution' (and therefore reduced cost) of the works was contingent upon a commitment from all three parties (O Estado de Sao Paulo 9 October 1976). Respite came with the second loan from BNH negotiated by the prefecture; this would be used to purchase land from the Metro company for use in a

176

housing programme.

The product of this uncertain and piecemeal financing was a continuous
need for the Metro to conduct its work urgently as funds became
available and while they retained their value, and to demonstrate that
it could act as quickly as it had promised to government fund raisers.
Indeed, an official suggested that the wide variety of sources and
terms of finance itself led the Metro administration to spend credit
as quickly as it became available so as to reduce confusion with later
packages of credit on other terms from other sources.

WHO LOSES?

Under these constraints, protracted negotiations with local people
about compensation and dates for removal could only stand in the way
of quick action; what was needed was a clear field of expropriated
and razed land ready for immediate construction work.

Secondly, what was needed by the Metro and those who paid for its
finance was the minimisation of its costs; partly this could be
achieved by reducing inflationary increases through speedy action but
there was also every reason why the Metro should attempt to avoid
dispensable costs. These included compensation in excess of that
needed to remove owners, and compensation for lost commercial profits
and sites on which business tenants were ill informed. More fundamentally, the very decision to build the railway overground through
Bras and beyond, but underground in more central areas, was based on
calculations relating to the cost of land purchase to the Metro by
comparison with the costs of underground construction. The result
was that businessmen and residents of the most central, highly valued
areas of the city gained twice: first from nonremoval and second from
the further increased values consequent upon the improvement of
transport. Removed people in other areas lost three times: first by
their removal, second by their non participation in enhanced values,
and third by the inadequacy (or non existence) of the compensation
in relation to the cost of purchasing property at standards similar to
those they originally enjoyed.

Thirdly, the Metro and those who organised its finance were interested
as far as possible in the recovery of its costs. The special opportunity which the Bras project provided was in the opportunity to recoup
costs by the resale of land at prices which reflected its improved value.
This was made possible by the special terms of the loans from the
national housing bank (BNH) which, under a special line of credit for
'urban recuperation', allowed the purchase of the swathes of land on
either side of the metro line for their eventual redevelopment for
commerce and middle class housing, both privately and through the
cooperative housing institute (INOCOOP). Metro and EMURB would gain
on the resale of the land.

The BNH was the only financing organisation through which such a
transfer of mutual benefit to public authorities could be arranged.
It carried with it the requirements that sufficient land should be
available to make 'recuperation' possible and that sufficiently well off
occupants should be introduced into the housing and commerce to pay off
the increased values which the metro's arrival would generate. Ironically, the BNH had come to participate in a process which was not only

extraneous to its original purpose of housing provision but one which was responsible for the destruction of the low income housing which was supposed above all to benefit from the bank's finance. The demolition in Bras alone was equal to one sixth of the units sold between 1966 and 1975 by COHAB, the Sao Paulo arm of BNH's 'social interest' housing programme.

Moreover, whatever else the advantages of the metro to the city and remaining local population, experience suggested that the process of expulsion did not stop with the direct impact of demolition. As the president of EMURB had made clear, the objective was to initiate a process of private redevelopment. In the area of Vila Mariana and Santana, served by the North-South line, the increase in property values had continued to displace business and residential tenants; after one year, high rise flats were replacing houses, commercial sites were being bought by large stores at prices five times higher, small businesses which sold 'on tick' to known customers were giving way to firms selling on hire purchase (O Estado de Sao Paulo 26 September 1976).

One effect of urban redevelopment was thus to further incorporate these areas with their surviving and new populations into the credit-based housing and consumer goods markets. The new opportunity presented to creditors was marked by the campaign by the Commercial Association of Sao Paulo to promote hire purchase in the newly 'opened up' areas with the slogan 'credit is the solution'. Through its constraints on the Metro's operation, credit had already played its part in removing those for whom credit was not available as a solution to the new patterns of consumption imposed in the 'recuperated' areas.

The longer term expulsive effect of the process of redevelopment was recognised to various degrees by the members of a working party (including the presidents of Metro and EMURB, the municipal planning coordinator and the municipal secretary of public roads) set up by the prefect to consider the future of the area along the East-West line. The president of the Metro was least convinced; in his view the redevelopment presented the east zone population with the possibility of 'social ascent'. The planning coordinator pointed out that: 'for owners it will be a good business (but) for those who live in rented accommodation, prices will rise and probably they will have to move. I see no solution for this' (A Construcao 3 May 1976).

The president of EMURB attributed the outcome to the same sort of historical necessity as he had earlier attributed to the life cycle of urban areas: 'To wish to avoid this process /of expulsion/ is more or less like attempting to revoke the law of supply and demand. Besides if we reasoned like that we would arrive at the absurdity of proving that the process of development is itself bad... We have to be realistic because this is the process of development' (A Construcao 3 May 1976).

CONCLUSION

However impersonal, objective, external and inevitable this development and its effects appeared to the active participant (whether official or member of the public), they were nevertheless the product of social forces or interests operating through organisational procedures. I have

argued that the terms of finance are a principal constraint on the
action of the public agencies examined, underlying the relationship
between these agencies and the public. The constraint, however, does
not appear as an external obstacle. In setting the terms on which
organisations operate and survive, the logic of capital accumulation
through credit comes to be internalised in the action of public agencies
and officials. There develops a mutuality between the terms of capital
and the operation of official organisations: on the one hand, agencies
are able to turn the terms to their advantage, on the other, public
procedures become functional to accumulation. The outcome is that
redevelopment shifts gains from tenants and small owners back to
creditors, to the recipients of large scale reorganised land and to
those who are able to meet the conditions of the extended credit-based
land, housing and consumer goods markets. Expulsion is thus related
to accumulation.

NOTES

1. Where statements by officials are not attributed they are from
   interviews by the writer. Interviews were conducted with officials
   of the Metro's planning and disappropriation departments, its
   information office and its financial adviser and with officials
   of EMURB's planning and disappropriation departments.

2. The survey was carried out with the help of Dr Zilton Luis Macedo
   and Professor Gabriel Bolaffi.

3. There are clear connections between what I have argued here and
   Castell's analysis of urban renewal in Paris; he identifies its
   effects in accentuating 'spontaneous' trends towards spatial
   segregation, in demobilising demands and in reinforcing the
   'consumption dynamic' in renewal areas (Castells 1978a, Chapter 5).
   I hope to have added an understanding of the way in which interests
   act through organisational processes.

# 7 Conclusion: urban politics and bureaucracy

It was argued at the outset that an analysis of administrative practice in the implementation of policy was essential to an understanding of the interests which were expressed in policy and of the means by which some were favoured over others.  In this I was seeking to redress or to contribute to the development of two trends of thought.  On the one hand, there has been a growing interest in British studies in moving away from purely local explanations of urban policy into a consideration of wider structural constraints on administrative action.  On the other hand, there has been a somewhat contrary tendency in some Latin American attempts to move towards explanations of specific forms of state administration starting from a wide concern with the political economy of national development.

This chapter will briefly re-examine the argument that while these two strands of thought need organisational analysis, organisational analysis can itself best be interpreted in the light of a more general understanding of class relations and the formation of the state.  It will then summarise and interpret the findings, terminating with some theoretical propositions which emerge from the analysis.

THE PLACE OF ORGANISATIONAL ANALYSIS

A concern with the administrative allocation of benefits and penalties is hardly new.  As the scale of urban planning and social policy 'interventions' has grown so has the body of research which has traced the effects of policy, the distortions from stated objectives, the unintended consequences and the response of those affected.  Policy could either be treated as an intervention from outside on the social organisation (e.g. the 'community') of the city or it could itself be seen as part of that social organisation.  In that latter case, the action or urban managers could not be regarded as neutral and therefore 'arbitrary or random' (Rex 1973);  managers were instead social actors who had the power to 'impose their goals and values on the lower participants in the urban system' (Pahl 1975 p.207).  The questions then arise - what are the factors which underlie officials' definitions, solutions and means?  To what interests are they responsive in decisions

about constituting policies, about distribution and about the
maintenance and evolution of programmes?

The research which attempted to respond to this sort of question in
the 1960s and 1970s in Britain and the USA accompanied the waves of
governmental intervention in slum clearance, urban renewal, local
government reform and urban poverty programmes. It devoted close
attention to the organisational processes through which these interventions took place and through which the interaction between officials
and the public was managed. It showed how outcomes were influenced by
a range of factors including professional ideologies, constraints
imposed on local official policy by private urban managers and central
government, the differential capacity of affected groups to organise
and express their interests, and the effect of complex bureaucratic
procedures in setting up barriers and allocating resources unequally.
Administrative action was apparently not the neutral product of a free
and equal interaction between interest groups; it, consciously or not,
injected biases which favoured some interests over others. The criticism
of much of this policy oriented research was that it was purely
'managerialist', meaning that there was an underlying presumption that
official managers were autonomous or an 'independent variable' (Pahl
1970 p.215) rather than subject to wider economic and political forces.
What was unclear was whether there was anything systematic in this
administrative bias or whether it was a matter of particular influences
producing particular biases in particular circumstances.

The structuralist view associated with Castells changed the nature of
the discussion by claiming to answer these questions on the basis of
theory. In this view, the limits on state intervention are set (a) by
the class formation of the state and the balance of interests which it
therefore represents, and (b) by the role of urban planning institutions
as part of the state's regulatory apparatus. Within these 'structural
limits', planning institutions act in the particular and concrete case
as a biased 'context for conditioned and institutionalised social
negotiation' (Castells 1978a p.87). The particular intervention is
then to be explained as an outcome, on the one hand, of structural
limits and, on the other, of the subordinate exercise of specific local
demands and circumstances. Castells therefore draws attention to the
interrelationship between the global, the historical development of
states and the formation of policies, and the specific, the interests
realised in the outcome of policies. However, he gives little attention
to the organisational processes of implementation and interaction
between agencies and the public.

A renewed concern with organisational (or institutional) analysis
is compatible with Castell's approach, although he does not explore
such matters. I am not seeking to resurrect the case for local
autonomy but rather the opposite, to show how the local case is itself
permeated by the social structure. This is based on four main arguments.
The first, the most basic, point is that the wider social processes
which condition and constrain policy interventions are not simply ' a
whole range of factors outside the state apparatus' (Dunleavy 1980 p.51).
Rather, the interests and ideologies which have a continuous effect are
those which cease to be 'outside the state apparatus' and are internalised
in the routine practice. Dunleavy (1980 p.126) provides a good example
of this in the internalisation of the requirements of the money market

into the operations of local government in Britain. The analysis of
organisational practice is therefore a beginning point (as Dunleavy
1980 p.48, also seems to argue) for the identification of all effective
interests - that is, all those which affect outcomes. The focus on the
organisation does not restrict the analysis to the 'internal' interests
of the bureaucracy. Second, such particular and local interests have
also to be identified as factors influencing the nature of specific
interventions, even though their expression is restricted by broader
structural interests.

Third, it is not simply in the outcomes of policy but also in the
process of implementation that the 'interests catered to by various
agencies' (Castells 1978a p.95) may be revealed. It is there that the
constraints and requirements on the administration are constructed into
rules of procedure whose development and application may be more or less
observable to the researcher. The production of differential outcomes
can itself be observed not only as a final distribution but also as a
process of discrimination between groups of applicants with a varying
capacity to manipulate or conform with organisational requirements. It
is in this process that the requirements of policy are brought into
direct contact and sharpened contrast with the requirements of the
social groups affected by policy. Fourth, administrative procedures
produce effects in their own right and not just in the sense that they
eventually produce concrete outcomes (houses, collective services,
the organisation of space). It is difficult to see how the state's
regulatory function can be understood without reference to the procedure
of administrative action, their ideological effects and the relationship which they establish between individuals or groups and the state.

In sum, there are some social effects of state interventions which
can only be understood by a detailed analysis of the interaction of
administrative organisations with subjects. A conception of state
administration as structured to reflect interests is the basis of the
case for using organisational analysis as a beginning point for tracing
back to the wider origin of policy, provided that such tracing back
is guided by some previous conception of the social structure within
which administrative organisations and their public are located. This
wider context cannot, however, be derived for all time and all places
from an abstract and mechanistic model of a sort of universal capitalist
state. It requires what Castells (1978a p.181) calls a 'theorised
history' of the particular state. Thus, in the case of Brazil, chapters
two and three surveyed the historical development of class relations
and the formation of the state, progressively specifying the analysis
to the conditions and demands which led to the generation and
structuring of an urban policy based on the national housing bank.
From this point, the case study could seek to understand the way in
which class and group interests, the form of the state, the forces
which have generated national policy and the organisational arrangements which have sustained it are manifest in the particular case.

The condition of this matching of global with more specific analysis
is that each is regarded as inadequate on its own - general theory
cannot predict the political arrangements, administrative actions and
social effects which may arise; case studies cannot on their own
define the structural limits on local actors. The tendency in some
French Marxist urban research to the mechanistic application of general

theoretical labels to events had been criticised by Castells himself (Castells 1978a pp.11-12) as well as by other writers (Saunders 1979 pp.184-185, and Dunleavy 1980 p.54). Of course such a mechanistic approach makes detailed and exploratory case studies superfluous - it knows the answers in advance.

Cardoso rejects precisely this determinism and its imposition of pre-established generalised explanations on specific events (for example Cardoso 1973 pp.104-122). The essential point is that while, according to this view, the historical development of the mode of production determines the emergence of classes and defines their broad interests, it cannot specify how the political relationships between classes will work out in practice. Particular concrete political forms, such as 'authoritarian bureaucracy' can be explained in terms of the relations between classes which they express; but political forms cannot be predicted from an abstract reading of class relations.[1] There is a 'loose fit' between the interests of dominant classes and the forms and practices of the state; other interests may insert themselves (as in the particular case of the 'technobureaucracy', the 'state bourgeoisie') to modify the form of the state while also maintaining the conditions for capital accumulation. In brief, this is an explanatory methodology - it is a matter of searching for explanations of political institutions, ideologies and actions through an analysis of the interests which they contain.

This open ended and nondeterministic view is compatible with a methodology which combines global analysis of the political economy with the analysis of organisational practice. Although Cardoso and O'Donnell pursue their analysis at a general level, their approach invites and even requires to be met by a form of analysis which examines the practice of specific state agencies. The bureaucratic regimes which they consider are not seen by them as an inevitable consequence of a particular pattern of economic development and social formation. There is a historical context in the development of a mode of production which defines the structural situation and interests of classes, but what is instrumental in their analysis is the capacity of classes and groups actively to seize opportunities, to structure institutions, influence policies and maintain ideologies in their interests.

What I have taken from Cardoso, O'Donnell and the other Latin American writers to whom I referred in chapter two is the historical analysis of changes in productive relations and of the development of classes. This is the context within which particular interests and values then come to be represented in and excluded from organisations and policies. What I have tried to contribute in chapters three, four, five and six, by an examination of particular organisations and policies, is an exploration of the interests which are incorporated as constraints on administrative action. The particular combination of interests will vary between organisations; the question is whether it is possible to show how these variations are nevertheless limited by the conditioning of the political economy.

The focus on the organisation does not restrict the analysis to the study of the 'internal' interests of the bureaucracy. My argument is that 'external' constraints do not simply act upon organisations;

they are only effective if they are internalised in structure and process. Organisational practice is therefore a beginning point for the identification of all effective interests - that is, all those which affect outcomes.

In this study I have attempted to trace explanations for the rules of procedure which affect the subjected public. Briefly stated, the objective has been to examine how organisational procedures exclude and include subjects, to trace the origins of those procedures to the interests which act as constraints on organisational action, and to examine how in this access relation between officials and the public the response of those affected is managed. The approach adopted has been essentially two fold: first to explore the context in economic change, the emergence of classes and their representation in the state; second, to examine the structure and procedures of operation of particular policies. In this second and main aspect of the research there were two 'points of entry': one was to begin from the setting up of a structure (the housing finance system) for the implementation of policy, and to examine how this evolved over time under pressure of the interests which it contained; the other was to begin from the point at which agency and subject come into contact in a relation of access and allocation.

THE FINDINGS

At one level, the four studies of policy implementation were about the working out of the contradictions within policies which were apparently designed to compensate for market deficiencies but which were at the same time expected to conform to market principles and pressures. The organisation which linked the four studies was the National Housing Bank (BNH). This is not to suggest that the contradictions emanated wholly from that source; in each study administrative action was accounted for by numerous constraints besides those directly traceable to BNH. For each case, identifying the effective procedures and showing how they were derived was a complex and detailed matter. The complexity of the explanation was enhanced by the fact that explanations of the effect of procedures were sought both at the level of the ideology which they expressed and at the level of the distribution which they decided. Distillation from this complexity risks gross simplification 'because neither the operations of bureaucracies, nor the institutional encounters experienced by the applicant and his reactions can be neatly categorised and pigeon-holed' (Schaffer and O'Keeffe 1978 p.4). However, abbreviation allows examination of the interrelationships between parts of an organisational structure which operates nationally, locally, in different sectors and between market and administrative forces.

The housing finance system and BNH were the product of their time; government agencies had not previously intervened so directly or massively in the housing market. There were peculiar reasons why they should do so in the 1960s when the state was apparently involved in a withdrawal from social expenditure. Chapter two showed how at least since the 1930s the participation of the government in the management of the economy had grown in response partly to external conditions (the breakdown of trading patterns which resulted from slump and war) and partly to internal demands for compensation and

protection.  The government's role in promoting the transfer of surplus
from agriculture to industry and from consumers to producers can be seen
initially as the consequence of response to crises but eventually as a
more deliberate attempt to direct investment through differential
tariffs, exchange rates, import permissions and foreign currency access.
State involvement grew specifically in the development of infrastructural
industries, in the organisation of the capital market, and in the
direction of investment above all through the national bank for economic
development.

The process of industrialisation created its own constituency of
support not only among industrialists but also among urban workers.
The growing urban population was both the market which sustained the
dynamic of import substitution and an important (though highly
dependent) part of the political support for governments which maintained
that dynamic.  The argument is, however, that the process was economically
and politically constrained by the gulf between, on the one hand, the
terms on which capital was available to sustain new waves of large scale,
technologically advanced industrial investment and, on the other, its
dissipation in the satisfaction of demands inherent to the existing
pattern of development.  The route out of the impasse was negotiated by
the installation of the military regime in 1964.  This was able both to
suppress the organised demands of the urban working class and to create
the internal financial stability and institutional framework necessary
to the attraction of foreign capital and to the accumulation of national
capital.

One condition for this rearrangement was 'a state which enormously
increases its capacity for control over civil society' (O'Donnell 1978
p.15).  But the state does not rest simply on overt suppression;  it
also creates its own constituency of support (a) in particular, among
those who benefit from concentrated income distribution, those who form
a market for newly available goods and those who can find new employment
and investment opportunities, and (b) in general, through the very
exercise of control and hence the construction of an institutional
framework and practices which can claim to represent normality, the
general interest, or even the particular interests of excluded groups
(O'Donnell 1978 p.20, Cardoso 1975 p.195).

The National Housing Bank, set up in 1964 as one of the first acts of
the new regime, represented all sides of this argument.  It was part of
the attempt to construct a new economic model in the sense that it was
designed to stimulate economic activity, to accumulate savings and to
apply them on strict financial terms.  It also served as demonstration
of the government's sensitivity to the housing and employment needs of
the masses who stood to lose most from the unfolding of the new economic
policies and whose political voice had been most immediately stifled.
In fact, its output responded primarily to the new model's constituency
of beneficiaries.

The bank was at the heart of a housing finance system of public and
private agencies concerned with the accumulation of forced and
voluntary savings and with their application to the whole range of the
housing market.  The stated policy was to serve above all the low income
sector.  The BNH was bound into a financial system whose condition of
existence was that it promised a rate of return above the level of

inflation to its small investors and which therefore had to recoup on average at least this rate from its borrowers. Chapter three showed that it was soon faced with the paradox of rapidly increasing resources (by its fifth year BNH was Brazil's second largest bank) and growing difficulty in applying them to the housing of the mass of the population. Increasingly resources were oriented to higher income groups and to non-housing investments. Indeed the only programme which really applied to the majority of the population - that run principally by the COHABs - had received less than ten per cent of BNH's total funds by 1979.

What was striking was the institutional impetus behind this shift of resources. The organisational structure, once established, led the housing finance system in a logical (which is not to say determined or necessary)movement to respect the financial and real estate interests which it contained. In 1972, the BNH moved back from its position as direct creditor to adopt a role as a second line reserve bank in order to protect its own financial position; private financial agents (mainly savings and loans associations, real estate companies and commercial banks) were brought further into the system to manage the application and recuperation of BNH's own funds. The protection of BNH's banking role and the involvement of the financial agents depended on the viability of their investments and on the preservation of their capital from risk. Upper income limits for borrowers were abolished, loan levels were raised, and selection of candidates for credit worthiness was made more rigorous. Although the State and municipal housing companies were the only part of the system to remain free of the intervention of the private financial agents, they were affected by the shift of resources into the more financially attractive programmes.

The dispensable part of the housing policy was its orientation to low income groups as the understandings and constraints built into and surrounding the structure of the housing finance system asserted themselves. Since housing built through the system, with its strict respect for the market price of credit, of land and of construction, became progressively expensive it faced crises of non-payment. Existing occupants therefore had to be subsidised, not by price subsidies (which would bring in more purchasers unable to cope with repayments) but by reductions in the interest return to the forced contributors of savings to the system - that is, the social security (FGTS) investors and taxpayers. Private, voluntary investors had of course to continue to earn a market rate on their savings. Those who lost out were people who could not face the terms of entry to house purchase and those who had no voice about whether and where their funds were invested.

Given the absence of a'viable' mass housing market the finance system had to find other ways of investing its funds and ensuring a return - in higher income housing and infrastructural and industrial works. Because the changes were piecemeal, they could at each stage be justified as part of a new search to satisfy the housing needs of the poor by putting the total system on a stronger financial footing. This was not a conspiracy but a series of responses to constraints and pressures contained within the housing finance system itself.

Chapter four showed, in relation to the Sao Paulo housing market, that the interpenetration of administrative and market forces has a further dimension. It is not only that the housing finance system is structured so as to give primacy to governmental and private financial interests in capital accumulation. It is not only that BNH and its housing agencies confront the conditions of the market in the sense that (a) they compete for credit, land, labour and materials, and (b) they seek to respond to the needs of purchasers unable to compete in the formal housing market. It is also that state agencies, including very powerfully the BNH, themselves create the conditions of the market to which they then in turn have to respond. State allocations, permissions, benefits, standards and recognition enhance and create differentiation in the housing market, contributing to the process of urban concentration and expulsion which both the poor and state agencies face.

No part of the housing market is free of administrative influence on the conditions of its existence (whether by zoning, service distribution, rent control, tax rebates or harassment). In most cases, administrative action reinforces market inequality: selective access to state benefits and protection, for example, acts to increase the significance of market success and failure. It is true that at some level the market satisfies even the poorest, even if this requires the avoidance or waiving of administrative controls (for example on illegal occupation, building regulations and tax payments), but these sectors are always subject to the possibility of costly and sometimes punitive administrative interventions as well as to uncontrolled market exploitation. In a situation of great inequality, of rapid urban expansion, of speculative property investment and of insecurity of tenure (whether due to the conditions of rental or of illegality of occupancy), even the extension of public services implies increased property valuation and direct administrative or market enforced expulsion. Since the market is continuous, intervention in one part of it affects all others whether by raising costs of land, property and materials, or by expelling populations and shifting demand.

The people who seek publicly provided housing therefore have options but these are constrained by administrative action as much as by the market. They are dependent upon administered solutions partly because their incapacity in the market has been exacerbated by exclusive administrative action.

Chapter five showed that agencies which seek to satisfy this demand are then faced not only with overwhelming need but also with the same circumstances (very unequal market conditions) which have driven people to seek their help. Paradoxically, they have also to represent the government's claim that it is able to satisfy 'sub-market' need, that there is a programmed solution for each income group. The Sao Paulo COHAB has to manage the contradiction between its promotion of an ideal possibility - a mass programme for sub market groups - and the require- ment to do so within a framework of respect for the credit and property markets. Organisational survival depends on the management of the contradiction. Bridging this gap means that, while there is pressure on the organisation to include those most likely to repay, it has a limited freedom to apply clear criteria to achieve this. It is necessarily trapped in a high risk and mass demand market where selection cannot be clearly on either a market or a welfare basis.

Given overwhelming demand, COHAB resorts to 'procedural selection' a slow elimination of candidates through processes which are complex and

diversionary and outcomes which are unexpected and to a great extent
arbitrary. These include long queues, repeat visits, lack of information
on availability and procedures, passing applicants to other queues or out
of the system without informing them and complex documentary requirements.
The most systematic feature of the selection process was that through the
confusion it favoured those who broke the formal rules - those capable
of persistence and those who had access to special passes through
interorganisational dependencies.[2] It is through its dependence on other
public agencies (such as the State water company and the regional office
of BNH) that COHAB is subjected to obligations to service recommended
applicants.

The rules serve other functions which may be described as ideological.
They maintain the 'myth of availability' in the sense that they suggest
that there is something at the end of the queue and that it is to be
allocated in a rational and orderly way. They also disguise exclusion
by leaving cases in the waiting list or in the *arquivo morte* (the dead
file) rather than rejecting them. The procedures which act to select
thus also act to disguise their own exclusiveness.

In conditions of massive demand and minimal supply, the necessity for
selection is clear. Failure, however, comes to appear not as the
necessary outcome of a programme which cannot combine the terms of the
formal property market with the capacity of its applicants, but as the
failure of the COHAB organisation to produce an adequate output, of the
candidates to make an adequate application, and of both to fulfil their
obligation to offer a return on credit. A new start with a better
administration, cheaper programmes, better selected candidates or the
eviction of 'malingerers' is always held out as a possibility.

This was not the response either of an inefficient or of a ruthlessly
efficient (technocratic) administration, but of officials struggling to
maintain or construct a set of rules in the face of contradictory
requirements on the organisation. The conditions of COHAB's existence
were that it was presented with overwhelming demand but could not close
its books, that it should serve 'sub market' groups but ensure a market
return on investments, that it should select bureaucratically but let well
connected people through. Among these contradictory demands, the most
ignorable, because least organised, were those of COHAB's applicants.

In the metro case (chapter six), the people affected by the works
appeared less in the role of applicant than of subject: they were in
no sense voluntary participants in their interaction with public
authorities and to a great extent were not even brought into direct
contact with the authorities. This was one example of the continuous
process of redefinition of the housing situation of the mass of the
population which results from the joint and overlapping effects of
market and administrative action. Through its history Bras has been
continuously exposed to public concern at developments which have,
however, themselves been to a great extent consequential on the action
of public authorities. Governmentally promoted migration into the
country at the turn of the century contributed to the rapid development
and densification of Bras as a central working class neighbourhood of
the city. The construction of main through roads and viaducts
contributed to its eventual commercial mix, residential decay and
congestion. Public concern at this decline is taken to justify further

action which in turn produces its own unforeseen problems.

The metro development was the latest in this wave of public projects which found part of their official justification in the capacity for the improvement of the area. The survey findings indicated, however, that in terms of the housing and employment alternatives of residents and businessmen (a) their existing conditions were relatively good and (b) conditions were likely to worsen for the removed population. The official myth of improvement nevertheless allowed complaints and reluctance to leave the area to be discounted as residual and special cases.

The eventual outcome for some people was a windfall opportunity to leave the area, but for most businessmen and residents the removal meant serious losses in terms of accommodation costs, access to public services, and proximity to clients, suppliers and jobs. The processing of cases also had the general effect of imposing urgency, confusion, and helplessness on most people. But beyond this general experience there were important variations in treatment depending upon the particular case's place in administrative definitions and upon the fit between particular needs and the outcomes assigned to categories. Thus, eligibility for compensation, and therefore information, depended on belonging to formal or informal adminsistrative categories (owners, tenants, large and small businesses); standard outcomes (in removal and levels of compensation) had different significance for different groups varying largely with their dependence on local housing and employment markets; apparently standard procedures (for eviction, evaluation and disputation) contained their own distinctions according to the capacity of subjects to confront their complexity and withstand the costs and delays of negotiation.

The effect of administrative procedures was certainly to limit the scale of necessary compensation (by limiting eligibility and access) and to negotiate the expulsion of the population speedily. They additionally limited the possibility of public response by the very urgency which they imposed, by the individual nature of the negotiations, by the fragmentation between categories and individuals as cases, and by the inevitability and institutional weight which procedures assumed. The dominance in practice of official definitions required the subject's conformity with them.

The origin of this approach was not in official malice but in the major requirements on official agencies. Organisations at different levels (the Metro company, the prefecture, the State and federal governments) were bound together in the need for rapid implementation and for minimising dispensable costs. This pressure emanated from the terms on which national and international credit were available, but within this general constraint different organisations had their particular interests: the prefecture with its massive investment in the metro, its need to hasten operation of the new line, and the interest in achieving visible outputs within the electoral term; the Metro company with the survival of its team and future works dependent on present prefectural and government commitments. The passage of time was crucial to the scale of the debt and the usefulness of available funds. The involvement of BNH offered a particular opportunity to recoup investment costs but at the cost to local residents of adding to the case for large scale redevelopment. The BNH was not only investing funds in a project with no relation to the needs of 'social interest' populations, but was participating in the development of pressures for their expulsion from existing housing.

In this case, the intention as well as the consequence of administrative action was to extend the credit based housing and consumer markets through the valorisation and regrouping of urban land and the displacement of non credit worthy populations.

## CORPORATE INTERESTS AND INCORPORATED APPLICANTS

Two main factors set the conditions of the operation of BNH, COHAB and the Metro company.

i) The terms of financial capital which determined the rate of return required, the volume of capital available, the period of return, and the guarantees and tests of credit worthiness required for the application of funds. These requirements were operationalised through the direct participation of credit institutions in public programmes and through the action of state agencies as mobilizers, guarantors, distributors and recuperators of credit. Private creditors and intermediaries gained in three ways from these programmes: from the establishment of guaranteed institutional structures for the mobilisation and allocation of finance, from the return on investment and from the extension of credit based housing and consumer markets. The elements of subsidy and guarantee which existed in some of these programmes were paid out of forced savings – the social security fund (FGTS) and tax. The requirement on public authorities was to privatise the profitable parts of their operation (chapter three).

ii) The conditions of the urban property market, itself inflated by the concentrated distribution of capital and of access to credit, set the terms on which applicants or subjects confronted public agencies and on which agencies were able to respond. People living at the margins of the formal housing market approached agencies in a state of need and dependence whether they were exposed to selective inclusion or expulsion. Agencies were then confronted with overwhelming need. In the case of COHAB, the property market limited the capacity of the organisation to respond in terms of the number, location, servicing and cost of housing units, and in terms of the possibility of attracting builders from more lucrative opportunities. In the case of the Metro company's operation in Bras the terms of the intervention were equally conditioned by the property market – for example in the decision to run the line overground and the need to pay for the project by creating the conditions for profitable private redevelopment (chapter six).

The identification of financial capital and the urban property market as the fundamental constraints on these public programmes does not mean that they were external to public agencies.[3] They were effective partly through these agencies; indeed, the significance of property and the terms of credit were to a considerable extent defined and defended by administrative means (chapters three and four). In intervening to solve problems arising from the market, state administration is also a part of the context which creates the problems: this is particularly and ironically clear in the double role of BNH. There are, then, those constraints which set the conditions for the operation of policies and within which the interests of particular creditors, developers, property owners and contractors will be served.

Within these conditioning constraints which have to be respected, others find their place. The credit and property markets are not so constraining as on their own to determine the outcome of programmes. There apparently remains some 'room for manoeuvre'. However, this is not a space for the exercise of free administrative discretion. Other interests, which are or make themselves compatible with the overriding constraints, insert themselves and in so doing form the particular policy. The 'room for manoeuvre' is occupied by interests which have a greater or lesser degree of incorporation in the administration of the policy.

In the BNH example, this incorporation was achieved partly by the direct representation in the administrative structure of agencies with a primary responsibility for the management of the credit and property markets - for example, the private financial agents of BNH and the BNH itself as a bank. But, more widely, all bodies involved in the administration of the housing finance system adjusted their performance to the conditions of organisational survival and were even able to benefit from these conditions. Successful adjustment, as the BNH's expansion testifies, meant organisational (and career) development both in response to the demands which could be expressed and satisfied through existing programmes and in response to the continuously exposed need to develop new programmes to reach as yet excluded populations. In the COHAB case, administrators, lawyers and, most strikingly, social workers were able to redefine and justify their role in terms of its effectiveness as a contribution to the collection of credit repayments. In the Bras case, the terms and uncertainty of credit set conditions for the prefecture and the Metro company which these agencies were able to turn to their advantage. The company was able to use these conditions to gain an increased commitment to the rapid execution of works, thereby transferring costs to the population; for the prefecture the pressure for speedy implementation was wholly desirable since both reputation and the reduction of future expenditure depended upon it.

Moreover, the major constraints on programmes provided opportunities for what might be described as 'entrant interests', extraneous to the formal structure of the administration, to make a claim on programme resources. Thus, in the COHAB case, the scarcity of supply was the necessary condition for the entry of connected organisations into the business of allocating housing through patronage networks. The pay off was mutual: without scarcity, there was no case for people to seek special channels; without the special channels for individuals, the general scarcity would have been more evident.

It is not then simply that bureaucracies submit to the requirements of credit and property interests; it is that administrative action and official roles can be adjusted so that these requirements become functional to programme achievement, organisational survival and career advancement. However it is also true that official statements of interest and more importantly some aspects of practice appeared frequently to express a contrary logic. Even while BNH's 'social interest' programmes were in relative decline, their fundamental importance was continually reasserted. EMURB and Metro officials pursued 'friendly agreements' and area improvement in the 'general interest'. COHAB officials were in continuous search for new more rational, fair and predictable forms of assessment of need and new low income programmes. It is important not to imply a cynical interpretation of officials' motives; however, it is clear that such statements and practice offered no challenge to the main dynamic of programmes. Instead, they served the governmental interest in sustaining the mythical existence of mass welfare programmes and disguised the exclusive nature of distribution and expulsion.

The formal statements and procedures of policy assume that the administration acts upon society from outside, embracing the interests of all citizens and responding to identified needs with suitable packages, bringing services to the deprived, planning to chaos. In practice, certain interests (those referred to above) are included not simply in the specific benefit or advertised output of policy, but in the process of policy formation and implementation (a) which set the terms on which the distribution or intervention is to take place, and (b) through which other 'input benefits' (contracts, patronage, career development, credit and land) become available.

These are the interests which Cardoso (1975 p.206) refers to as being incorporated through 'bureaucratic rings'. In using that term, however, Cardoso is concerned to indicate that all interests, including the major beneficiaries of the regime, are disorganised and individualised by being drawn into a relationship with the state which depends (a) on their involvement in specific policies and (b) therefore on their acceptance of divisive administrative categories.

I would prefer to distinguish between the point at which admission is gained or avoided for particular administered benefits or penalties, and the more general admission of interests into account in the formation of policy: the first, on the whole, divides all interests into individual applicants, but the second includes certain interests as 'corporate members of the polity' (Rew 1977 p.22). Corporate members 'have legitimate demands on government and routine means of making claims at the highest levels' (Rew 1977 p.22). Because these interests (in my studies, above all large scale property and finance capital) are incorporated as major requirements on policies, the way is prepared for successful application on an individual basis for programme benefits sought by particular representatives (for example property owners and credit agencies) of the corporate membership. Administrative categories are themselves a product of a definition of reality imposed by these major requirements; the rules of the game are not neutral (Saunders 1979 p.62).

The experience of the mass of the population, however, is wholly in relation to the distribution of benefits or penalties and not in relation to policy formation. They do not set the terms of policy and therefore cannot assume a claim on government resources; they are incorporated in distributive procedures as 'individual members' (Rew 1977 p.23) dependent upon their capacity to conform with administrative categories. A collective attempt by 'individual members' to change the basis of distribution can only be made at the point of distribution (in COHAB, when allocations are made and, in the Metro case, when removal is negotiated) by which time it is too late - such action appears as disruptive to officials and probably as futile to applicants.[4] It challenges not only the outcome but also the individualised procedures of distribution. It is noteworthy that, where popular mobilisation has occurred in relation to urban policy, some evidence indicates that it is where government programmes have been concerned with areas rather than individuals (Rew 1977 p.25, Batley 1978b p.225, Palma and Sanfuentes 1977).

More typical of the Brazilian experience, even in the case of area related programmes, is the applicant's attempt on an individual basis to conform with administrative definitions in what has been described as 'a rational adaptation to what structural circumstances permit and encourage' (Portes 1976 p.108). This does not mean that individual applicants must always lose out: the needs and capacities of some may accord well enough with administrative definitions; others may be able to manipulate the rules to gain eligibility and priority treatment usually as part of an exchange relationship with appointed or elected officials who would permit special passes without disrupting overt procedures (Valladares 1978a and b on squatter removal; Wygand 1966 on water distribution; Leeds 1966 on political interventions in favelas; Leeds, Leeds and Morocco 1966; Leeds and Leeds 1970 on water and electricity distribution).

> 'Can we say that an applicant's encounters with the institution will always take place from an unequal position of powerlessness and ignorance of bureaucratic rules and procedures, when it is obvious that in some instances applicants are adept at manipulating the rules and procedures or are in a favoured position?'.(Schaffer and O'Keeffe 1978 p.4).

The COHAB, Metro and market studies demonstrated both possibilities, of favoured administrative categories and of manipulated access; but neither possibility suggested the assertion of 'applicant power'. Manipulated and chance inclusion are the other side of arbitrary failure. Devious routes of appeal for services, or for relief, offer the possibility of success precisely because the 'normal channels' offer no routine expectation of success. Unexpected and covert procedures are hierarchical in effect; they favour the more adept at dealing with the administrative connection; they favour the insertion of patronage; they therefore favour the already relatively privileged. By contrast, the condition of routine expectations, standard channels and known procedures puts the rules open to question and therefore invites organised attempts by applicants to change them.

THE NATURE OF ORGANISATIONAL ROUTINE - CONSTRAINING, CONSTRAINED AND IDEOLOGICAL

I conclude with a series of linked propositions about the nature of routine administrative practice. These emerge from the empirical work but are addressed to the wider question raised in chapter one about the significance of organisational analysis.

(a) The market penetrates allocation by public authorities; equally, administrative relations permeate the credit, housing and urban land markets, not only in redressing but primarily in strengthening their effects. These relations are not, of course, peculiar to states where

overt political action is suppressed, but the terms of the exchange
between administrators and the administered are modified where
independent avenues of organisation, mobilisation, appeal and redress
are closed.  Administrative contacts are anyway important, but the
power of assertion of administrative definitions becomes greater.  This
is not to put undue emphasis on any greater degree of openness in
organisation or on the independence of the poor in periods in Brazil
where overt political activity has been permitted.  Politicians in
these periods have been shown to thrive on scarcity:

> 'His greatest fear is not the presence of a hostile enemy,
> but administrative avenues sufficient to realise the aspirations
> of the masses'. (Medina 1964, cited in Leeds 1966).

The point is to indicate the crucial nature of the organisational
connection and therefore of the procedures through which it is
managed:-  the categories which are established for treatment, the
fit between categories and needs, and the capacity of applicants to
respond.  The point is then not only that procedures may tend to select
certain groups over others, but also that the rules of procedure are
themselves constructed out of certain assumptions, perceptions and
interests.  In other words, the rules both act to constrain distribution
and are the product of constraints.

(b) A first approximation at locating the policy forming constraints
might be that they are the product of interests included in the
organisational structure.  That the service acquires its own momentum
in response to the demands which can be expressed within it was
illustrated in the examination of the BNH's history of development.
It could equally be illustrated from a British case in which the
formation of a new urban poverty programme came to be based upon the
existing relations and division of responsibilities between the central
government departments charged with setting it up (Edwards and Batley
1978 p.66).  In neither case did the constraints or pressures forming
policy appear as external factors imposing themselves as obstacles upon
organisations.  They were internalised in the organisational structure,
continuously present as common understandings of what was possible and
proper practice.  To the extent that they are effective, 'external'
constraints lose their externality$_5$and are represented in the internal
routines of administrative action.$^5$  The constraints on practice appear
therefore not as obstacles to policy implementation but as the
'unconscious mobilisation of bias' (Lukes 1977a) in the process of
implementation.  They are therefore to be identified in established
patterns of administrative action, in 'mundane interaction' (Saunders
1979 p.61) and 'in uneventful routine' rather than in the 'conscious
and active exercise of will' (Westergaard and Resler 1976 p.144).  This
is not then a matter simply of technobureaucratic values or conspiracies
of officials.

(c)  The last paragraph suggests a two stage process in policy formation:
(i) the prior decision to set up organisational structures and policies,
(ii) the routine implementation of policies in which structured interests
assert themselves.  In practice, however, the 'prior decision' also
emerges out of an organised situation.  There are hierarchies of
organisational structure which ultimately delimit official action all
the way up the scale.  Rules of procedure do not only operate in the
specific and the local case.  There is no prior stage of free formulation
of policies, no neat beginning or point of initiation beyond

organisational constraints.[6] Action at all levels is socially
conditioned. Administrators do not only, as the managerialist thesis
suggests, exercise rules 'downwards' upon applicants; they operate
in a wider context which is itself organised, constrained and rule
bound. There are requirements on them from 'outside' and 'above'.
There are the limits on their action provided by their and their
organisation's survival. Because of this chain of constraints, it
is possible to use observation of locally applied rules as a channel
to the understanding of these wider limits and interests. All actors
are captive though within an ideology which favours some.

(d) If procedural rules are part of a chain of constraints, it makes
no sense to argue that they are rational constraints - open to the
exercise of choice and interpretation - as opposed to structural
constraints acting as deterministic and absolute limits (Saunders 1979
pp.57-60), interpreting Lukes 1977b). Choice is neither so free nor
so determined but always within a conditioning social context (Ranson,
Hinings and Greenwood 1979). All administrative operations are
conditioned by interests which are mobilised in administrative procedures as requirements on the particular organisation or actor. This
does not, however, imply an immutable and immobile determinism where
action is the end result of an unlimited hierarchy of structures. The
point is that while all action is socially conditioned, the organisational
structures and the procedural rules that govern bureaucratic action are
not constructed monolithically from the same source or at the same time.
They have different origins and represent different more or less
compatible interests and values; they therefore also have different
levels of resilience or mutability depending on the strength of the
interests which are represented in them. Officials and applicants
are faced with rules of procedure and with constraints on change whose
force and compatibility with each other may vary both in time and in
accordance with position in the administrative structure. Thus, the
routines of data collection may be observed strictly at the counter
in COHAB but discounted at higher levels where there was clearer
experience of the incompatibility between overt selection procedures
and the need to limit access. These variations are not the product
of free choice but of action constrained differently at either level.
Actors are variably exposed to a complex of different requirements.
The outcome (the procedural rules and policy effects) is therefore not
determined but is explicable in terms of the requirements, and hence
interests, which are effective in practice.

(e) Administrative routines are the product of and biased towards certain
interests, but they also appear as anonymous requirements on actors at
all levels. To the extent that all actors come to participate in a
definition of reality which favours some, these routines take on an
ideological character. Because they represent everyday practice, for
some they may also come to represent normal and proper practice; in
any case they are the condition of participation - those who do not
accept them are excluded from the organisational connection which
offers access. Thus, as Cardoso (1975 p.195) argues, the very practice
of dominance establishes its own legitimacy, by asserting the power
of the values which underlie the practice. In the Metro case, the
people of Bras might recognise their own loss but accept the thesis
of progress; in the case of COHAB, organisational procedures perform
the function of selecting and excluding while giving the impression

of inclusiveness. There is, then, more than the question of the distributive product of bureaucratic action but also the

'ideological structures used by bureaucracies which mediate the disjunctions between what they have to say — and what they also have to think — they do, and the actual results, the exchanges of their actions: the outcomes in effect'. (Schaffer and O'Keeffe 1978 p.3).

There are the queues, the evaluation procedures, the form filling, the documentary requirements, the assessments of need, the friendly agreements, the social interest programmes which suggest fairness, availability and bureaucratic rationality; there are the rehabilitative schemes, the language of malingering, special cases and recuperation, the exemplary evictions which attribute failure to applicants and to local administrators rather than to stated policies or higher organisations; there are the 'low profile' of the administration and the physical inexorability of demolition which suggest the inevitability and impersonality of the process occurring. Ideology is least importantly enunciated and most importantly present in mundane experience as the shared assumptions and meanings which make interaction possible.

NOTES

1. The same point is argued by Hindess (1978) and Saunders (1979 pp.180-189).

2. For similar conclusions see Schaffer and O'Keeffe (1975 p.34) and Lamb (1976).

3. This externality is what some studies of British urban policy suggest (Lambert et al 1978 pp.151-157, Saunders 1979 pp. 194-197).

4. Similar statements are made by Rew (1977 p.22), Dearlove (1973 p.58), Saunders (1979 pp.230-236).

5. '... that external causes are the condition of change and internal causes are the basis of change, and that external causes become operative through internal causes. In a suitable temperature an egg changes into a chicken, but no temperature can change a stone into a chicken, because each has a different basis'. (Mao Tse-tung 1937).

6. Pickvance (1976 p.204) seems to suggest the need to get at such a beginning point in policy formation. Saunders (1979 p.54) seems to adopt a similar view in citing Parry and Morris (1974) on the initiation and maintenance of routines.

# Glossary

| | |
|---|---|
| Favela | Shanty town |
| Favelado | Resident of shanty town |
| Cortico | Slum tenement building |
| APE | Savings and Loans Association |
| BNH | National Housing Bank |
| CEBRAP | Brazilian Centre of Analysis and Planning |
| CECAP | Housing company of the State of Sao Paulo |
| CHISAM | BNH agency for Favela removal in Rio de Janeiro |
| COHAB | Municipal or state housing company |
| CURA | Programme for the Accelerated Recuperation of Urban communities (urban renewal programme of BNH) |
| DIEESE | Inter-union Department of Statistics and Socio-economic Studies |
| EMPLASA | The Sao Paulo State Metropolitan Planning Company |
| EMURB | Municipal Urban Development Company |
| FIMACO | BNH programme to finance production and acquisition of building materials |
| FGTS | Social security fund for employees |
| GSP | Greater Sao Paulo |
| IBMEC | Brazilian Institute of the Capital Market |
| INOCOOP | Institute for the Guidance of Cooperatives |
| PLANASA | National Sanitation Plan |
| PLANHAP | National Plan for Popular Housing |
| PNAD | National Sample Survey of Households |
| RECON | BNH sub-programme to finance building materials acquisition. |

197

| | |
|---|---|
| SABESP | Sao Paulo State Sanitation Company |
| SAC | The Constant Amortization Scheme of mortgage repayment |
| SBPE | Brazilian System for Savings and Loans |
| SCI | Real Estate Credit Company |
| SFH | Housing Finance System |
| SM | Minimum monthly salary |
| UPC | Standard Capital Unit (a constant value for financial indexation) |

# Bibliography

Aguiar, N. Urbanizacao, Industrializacao e Mobilizacao Social no Brasil, in *Dados 11*, Instituto Universitario de Pesquisas do Rio de Janeiro, 1973.

Allen, B.K. The Administration of Discretion, *Case Conference*, June 1968, pp.43-48.

Almond, G. & Verba, S. *The Civic Culture*, Princeton University Press, 1963.

Ames, B. *Rhetoric and Reality in a Militarized Regime: Brazil since 1964*, Comparative Politics Series Vol.4, Sage Publications, California, 1973.

Anderson, N. *The Urban Community*, Routledge & Kegan Paul, London, 1960.

Apter, D. *The Politics of Modernisation*, University of Chicago Press, Chicago, 1965.

Associacao Brasileira de COHABs in CECAP, Reuniao de Conselho de Governo, *Documento Tecnico No.1*, contributions to consideration of the State Housing Plan 1975.

Azavedo, S. de, Politica de Habitacao Popular:  Balanco e Perspectiva, in *Dados 22*, 1979.

BNH (Banco Nacional da Habitacao), *BNH Para Milhoes*,  Banco Nacional da Habitacao, Rio de Janeiro, no date.

BNH *Report 1969*, Banco Nacional da Habitacao, Rio de Janeiro, 1969.

BNH  *O Sistema Brasileiro de Poupanca e Emprestimo no Plano Nacional de Habitacao*, Banco Nacional de Habitacao, Rio de Janeiro, 1973.

BNH  *PLANHAP: Objetivos e Normas de Execucao*, Banco Nacional da Habitacao, Rio de Janeiro, 1973b.

BNH  *Basic Legislation*, Banco Nacional da Habitacao, Rio de Janeiro, 1974.

BNH  *BNH Documenta*, Banco Nacional da Habitacao, Rio de Janeiro, 1974a.

BNH  *BNH - Solucao Brasileira de Problemas Brasileiros*, Secretaria de Divulgacao do BNH, Rio de Janeiro, 1974b.

BNH  *BNH 1974*, Banco Nacional da Habitacao, Rio de Janeiro, 1974c.

BNH  *Pesquisa de Comercializacao.do Mercado Habitacional Cidade de Sao Paulo*, quarterly reports for 1974 and 1975, Rio de Janeiro 1974 and 1975.

BNH  *Modificacoes no Sistema Financeiro da Habitacao*, Banco Nacional da Habitacao, Rio de Janeiro, 1975.

BNH  *Custos e Indices de Construcao*, Banco Nacional da Habitacao, Rio de Janeiro, 1976.

BNH  *BNH: Atuacao e Metas*, Banco Nacional da Habitacao, Rio de Janeiro, 1979.

BNH  *Relatorio de Atividades 1979*, Banco Nacional da Habitacao, Rio de Janeiro, 1980.

Barat, J. The financing of urban development in Brazil: the case of Sao Paulo metropolitan area, in *Third World Planning Review* 4(2), May 1982.

Batley, R.A. An Explanation of Non-Participation in Planning, *Policy & Politics*, Vol. 1, No.2, December 1972, and in Lambert and Weir (eds) *Cities in Modern Britain*, Fontana, Glasgow 1975.

Batley, R.A. Technocracy and Exclusion, *International Journal of Urban and Regional Research*, Vol.2, No.1, 1978a.

Batley, R.A. Urban Services and Public Contracts: Access and Distribution in Lima and Caracas, *PREALC Working Paper 165*, ILO, Santiago 1978b, also in a Spanish version *PREALC Investigaciones sobre Empleo No.20*, Oficina Internacional del Trabajo, Santiago, 1981.

Bell, D. Technocracy and Politics, *Survey 16*, 1971.

Berger, P. & Luckmann, T. *The Social Construction of Reality*, Penguin University Books, Harmondsworth, 1971.

Berlinck, M. *Marginalidade Social e Relacoes de Classes em Sao Paulo*, Editora Vozes, Sao Paulo, 1975.

Blau, P.M. *The Dynamics of Bureaucracy*, University of Chicago Press, 1955.

Bolaffi, G. Aspectos Socio-Economicos do Plano Nacional de Habitacao, *doctoral thesis*, University of Sao Paulo, 1972.

Bolaffi, G. *Habitacao e Urbanismo: O Problema e O Falso Problema*, XXVII Reuniao Anual da Sociedade Brasileira para O Progresso da Ciencia, Belo Horizonte, 11/7/75.

Bolaffi, G. Militarism in Brazilian Politics, in *IDS Bulletin*, Vol.9, No.1, July 1977.

Boletim Habi, *Estudo Sobre O Fenomeno Favela no Municipio de Sao Paulo*, Prefeitura de Sao Paulo, Caderno Especial 01, Outubro 1974.

Boletim Habi, *Diagnostico sobre o Fenomeno Cortico no Municipio de Sao Paulo*, Prefeitura de Sao Paulo, Ano 2 No.6 April 1975.

Bonduki, N. and Rolnik, R. Periferia da Grande Sao Paulo: reproducao do espaco como expediente de reproducao da forca de trabalho, in Maricato (ed) *A Producao Capitalista da Casa (e da Cidade) no Brasil Industrial*, Alfa-Omega, Sao Paulo 1979

Bull, D.G. *The Welfare of People in Clearance Areas*, mimeo, University of Manchester, 1967.

Burnham, J. *The Managerial Revolution: What is Happening in the World*, John Day Co. Inc., New York, 1941.

Camargo, C.P.R. de, et al, *Sao Paulo 1975 Crescimento e Pobreza*, Edicoes Loyola, Sao Paulo, 1976.

Cardoso, F.H. *O Modelo Politico Brasileiro*, Difusao Europeia do Livro, Sao Paulo, 1973.

Cardoso, F.H. *Autoritarismo e Democratizacao*, 2nd edn., Paz e Terra, Rio de Janeiro, 1975.

Cardoso, F.H. The Consumption of Dependency Theory in the United States, *Latin American Research Review*, 12 No.3, 1977.

Cardoso, F.H. On the Characterization of Authoritarian Regimes, in D. Collier (ed), *The New Authoritarianism in Latin America*, Princeton University Press, New Jersey 1979.

Cardoso, F.H. & Faletto, E., *Dependencia y desarrollo en America Latina*, Siglo XXI, 1969, and in English version, *Dependency and Development in Latin America*, University of California Press, 1979.

Castells, M. L'Urbanisation Dependente en Amerique Latine, *Espaces et Societes*, No.3, Juillet 1971.

Castells, M. *The Urban Question*, Edward Arnold, London 1977; originally published as La Question Urbaine, Francois Maspero, Paris, 1972.

Castells, M. *Luttes Urbaines*, Maspero, Paris, 1973.
Castells, M. Theoretical Propositions for an experimental study of urban social movements, in Pickvance, C. (ed) *Urban Sociology: critical essays*, Tavistock Publications, London, 1976.
Castells, M. *City, Class and Power*, Macmillan, London, 1978a.
Castells, M. Urban social movements and the struggle for democracy: the Citizens' Movement in Madrid, *International Journal of Urban and Regional Research*, Vol.2 No.1, 1978b.
Cawson, A. Pluralism, Corporatism and the Role of the State, in *Government and Opposition*, Vol.13, 1978.
CEBRAP, (Centro Brasileiro de Analise e Planejamento) *Recursos Humanos da Grande Sao Paulo*, Vol. 1 GEGRAN, Sao Paulo 1971.
CECAP (Caixa Estadual de Casas para O Povo), Sistema de Administracao do Plano Estadual de Habitacao, *Documento de Trabalho* No. 016/01-04, Sao Paulo 24-26 agosto 1975.
CECAP, *Pesquisa Mercadologica, Mercado Habitacional das Regioes Leste e Nordeste da Grande Sao Paulo*, Julho 1972.
CEPAL (Comission Economica para America Latina), *Estudio Economico de America Latina*, UN, New York, 1970.
CEPAL, The Economic Evolution of Latin America in 1981, *Notas sobre la economia y el desarollo de america latina*, No.355/356, January 1982.
Chinelli, F. Os Loteamentos de Periferia, in Valladares (ed) *Habitacao em Questao* Zahar, Rio de Janeiro, 1980.
CIDOC (Centro Internacional de Documentacion), *The Squatters Rights of Favelados*, Cuaderno No.2, Mexico 1969.
Clarence-Davies, J. *Neighbourhood Groups and Urban Renewal*, Columbia University Press, New York and London 1966.
Cleaves, P.S. *Bureaucratic Politics and Administration in Chile*, University of California Press, Berkeley and London 1974.
Cloward, R. & Piven, F. The Professional Bureaucracies: benefits systems as influence systems, in Cloward and Piven (eds) *The Politics of Turmoil*, Vintage, New York 1974.
Collier, D. *Squatters and Oligarchs: Public Policy and Modernisation in Peru*, John Hopkins University Press, Baltimore 1976.
Collier, D. (ed) *The New Authoritarianism in Latin America*, Princeton University Press, Princeton, 1979.
COMMUNITY DEVELOPMENT PROJECT, *Inter Project Report*, CDP Information and Intelligence Unit, February 1974.
COHAB (Companhia Metropolitana de Habitacao de Sao Paulo), *Carateristicas Socio-economicas da Populacao Cohabense (SP)* - trabalho a cargo da divisao socio-economica da COHAB - SP, Sao Paulo 1969.
COHAB, *Pesquisa COHAB: Nivel de Satisfacao em Carapicuiba*, COHAB 10/6/73.
COHAB, *Viabilidade Social de Intervencao no Jardim Mabel*, COHAB - SP, Sao Paulo, 19-20 Abril 1976.
Costa, M.A. *Estudos de Demografia Urbana*, Instituto de Planejamento Economico e Social, Instituto de Pesquisas, Monografia 18, Rio de Janeiro, 1975.
Costa, R.V. da *O Sistema Nacional de Habitacao e os Corretores* de Imoveis, Banco Nacional da Habitacao, Rio de Janeiro, 1972a.
Costa, R.V. da *Novas Atitudes e Novas Mentalidades*, Banco Nacional da Habitacao, Rio de Janeiro, 1972b.
Costa, R.V. da *Estrategia e Programa de desenvolvimento Urbano, a experiencia Brasileira*, Banco Nacional da Habitacao, Rio de Janeiro, 1973.
Cupertino, F. *A concentracao da Renda no Brasil*, Civilizacao Brasileira, Rio de Janeiro, 1976.

Dahl, R. *Who Governs? Democracy and Power in an American City,* Yale University Press, 1961.

Davies, J.G. *The Evangelistic Bureaucrat,* Tavistock, London, 1972.

Dean, W. *A Industralizacao de Sao Paulo,* DIFEL, Sao Paulo, 1971.

Dearlove, J. *The Politics of Policy in local government,* Cambridge University Press, 1973.

Dennis, N. *People and Planning,* Faber & Faber, London 1970.

Dennis, N. *Public Participation and Planners' Blight,* Faber & Faber, London 1972.

Deutscher, I. The Gatekeeper in Public Housing, in Deutscher, I. and Thompson, E.J. (eds) *Among the People: Encounters with the Poor,* Basic Books New York 1968.

Dias, G. (University of Brasilia) Seminar at Institute of Development Studies, University of Sussex, July 1977.

DIEESE (Departmento Intersindical de Estatistica e Estudos socio-economicos) *10 Anos de Politica Salarial,* DIEESE, Sao Paulo 1975.

Dillon, G.M. Policy and Dramaturgy: A critique of Current Conceptions of Policy-making, in *Policy and Politics,* 5, 1976.

D'Incao e Mello, M. *O Boia Fria: Acumulacao e Miseria ,* Editora Vozes, Petropolis, 1976.

Djilas, M. *The New Class, An Analysis of the Communist System,* New York, 1957.

Dunleavy, P. Protest and Quiescence in Urban Politics, *International Journal of Urban and Regional Research,* Vol. 1. No.2 June 1977.

Dunleavy, P. *Urban Political Analysis,* Macmillan, London, 1980.

Dye, R.D. & Souze e Silva C.E. de, A Perspective on the Brazilian State, in *Latin American Research Review,* Vol. XIV No.1 1979.

Edwards, J. & Batley, R. *The Politics of Positive Discrimination,* Tavistock Publications, London 1978.

Elliott, B. & McCrone, D., Property Relations in the City: The Fortunes of Landlords, *Centre for Environmental Studies Conference Paper 14.* London 1975.

EMPLASA (Empresa Metropolitana de Planejamento da Grande Sao Paulo), *Diretrizes da Politica Habitacional na Grande Sao Paulo,* Vol. 1 1975.

EMPLASA, *Colecao de Mapas da Grande Sao Paulo,* Sao Paulo, n.d.

EMURB (Empresa Municipal de Urbanizacao), *A Reurbanizacao de Santana e Jabaquara,* EMURB, Sao Paulo, 1973.

Engels, F. Letters to Joesph Bloch and to Conrad Schmidt, September and October 1890, in *On the Theory of Marxism,* Little Lenin Library, International Publishers, New York, 1948.

English, J., Madigan, R., & Norman, P., *Slum Clearance,* Croom Helm, London, 1976.

Fagence, M. *Citizen Participation in Planning,* Pergamon Press, Oxford, 1977.

Fundacao Getulio Vargas, *Conjuntura Economica,* Vol.30 No.2, Rio de Janeiro, Feb 1976.

Fundacao IBGE, *Censo Demografico Brasil, VIII Recenseamento Geral, Serie Nacional,* Vol. 1, 1970.

Fundacao IBGE, *Sinopse Preliminar do Censo Demografico,* VIII Recenseamento Geral 1970, Rio de Janeiro, 1971.

Fundacao IBGE, *Pesquisa Nacional por Amostra de Domicilio,* Rio de Janeiro, 1973

Fundacao IBGE, *Anuario Estatistico,* Rio de Janeiro, 1973a.

Fundacao IBGE, *Censo Demografico Sao Paulo,* VIII Recenseamento Geral 1970, Rio de Janeiro 1973b.

Fundacao IBGE, *Pesquisa Nacional por Amostra de Domicilio*,    Rio de
Janeiro, 1976.
Furtado, C. *Diagnosis of the Brazilian Crisis*, University of California
Press, 1965.
Furtado, C. *O Mito de Desenvolvimento Economico*, Paz e Terra, Rio de
Janeiro, 1974.
Gerth, H.H. & Mills, C.W., A Marx for the Managers, in *Ethics*, Vol. Lll
University of Chicago Press, 1941-42.
Giddens, A. *The Class Structure of the Advanced Societies*, Hutchinson
University Library, London, 1973.
Governo do Estado de Sao Paulo, *Regiao Metropolitana de Sao Paulo:
Diagnostico 75*, Sao Paulo, n.d.
Governo do Estado de Sao Paulo, *Conheca seu Municipio*, Sao Paulo, 1974.
Governo do Estado de Sao Paulo, *Sistema de Administracao do Plano
Estadual de Habitacao*, Documento de Trabalho No. 015/01-04, Sao Paulo,
agosto 1975.
Governo do Estado de Sao Paulo, *Politica Habitacional do Estado de Sao
Paulo*, Sao Paulo 1976.
Graham, L. *Civil Service Reform in Brazil: Principles Versus Practice*,
Institute of Latin American Studies, University of Texas Press, Austin,
1968.
Gray, F. The Management of Local Authority Housing, in *Housing and
Class in Britain*, Political Economy of Housing Workshop, London, June
1976.
Habermas, J. (ed) *Antworten auf Herbert Marcuse*, Frankfurt 1968.
Hall, A.S. *The Point of Entry: A Study of Client Reception in the
Social Services*, National Institute Social Services Library No.27,
Allen & Unwin, London 1974.
Hardoy, J.E. & Langdon, M.E., *Analisis Estadistico Preliminar de la
Urbanizacion de America Latina Entre 1850 and 1930*, mimeo, April 1977.
Harloe, M., Issacharoff, R., & Minns, R., *The Organisation of Housing,
Public and Private Enterprise in London*, Heinemann, London 1974.
Hatch, S. Estate agents as urban gatekeepers, paper presented to the
Urban Sociology Group, British Sociological Association, University
of Stirling, 1973.
Hidrobrasileira, S.A. *Municipio de Sao Paulo*, Hidrobrasileira S.A. 1975.
Hill, M.J. The Exercise of Discretion in the National Assistance Board,
*Public Administration*, 47, 1969.
Hindess, B. Class and Politics in Marxist Theory, in Littlejohn, Smart,
Wakeford and Yuval-Davis, *Power and the State*, Croom Helm, London 1978.
Hirschman, A.O. *Exit, Voice and Loyalty: responses to decline in firms,
organisations and states*, Harvard University Press, Cambridge 1970.
Hogan, D.J. Internal Migration, Access to Information and the Use of
Urban Resources in Sao Paulo, Brazil: A study of population
adaptation in a changing economy, *Ph.D. dissertation*, Cornell
University 1972.
Hungria, H.P. *Analise dos Projetos Cooperativos*, Banco Nacional da
Habitacao, Rio de Janeiro, 1975.
IBMEC (Instituto Brasileiro de Mercado de Capitais), *Sistema Financeiro
da Habitacao*, IBMEC, Benfica, 1974.
INSTITUTO GALLUP de OPINIAO PUBLICA, *O Mercado Habitacional na cidade
de Sao Paulo*, Gallup, Sao Paulo, Jan. 1971.
Inter American Development Bank, *Economic and Social Progress in Latin
America, 1980-81 report*, IADB, Washington, 1982.

IPT (Instituto de Pesquisa Tecnologica), FUPAM (Fundacao para a Pesquisa Ambiental), CNPq (Conselho Nacional de Pesquisa), Relatorio Final da 1$^a$ Fase da Pesquisa Voltada para Diretrizes Habitacionais, mimeo, Sao Paulo, 1979.

Jennings, H. *Societies in the Making*, Routledge & Kegan Paul, London 1962

Kaplan, H. *Urban Renewal Politics: Slum Clearance in New York* Columbia University Press, New York & London, 1963.

Kitching, G. Modes of Production and Kenyan Dependency, *Review of African Political Economy*, No. 8 Jan-April 1977.

Kowarick, L. *Capitalismo e Marginalidade na America Latina*, Paz e Terra, Rio de Janeiro, 1975.

Kowarick, L. *Estrategias de Planejamento social no Brasil*, Caderno No.2 Cadernos CEBRAP, Sao Paulo 1976.

Kramer, R.M. *Participation and the Poor*, Prentice Hall, 1969.

Lamarche, F. Property development and the economic foundation of the urban question, in Pickvance C. (ed) *Urban Sociology: critical essays* Tavistock Publications, London 1976.

Lamb, G. Marxism, Access and the State, *Development and Change*, Vol. No.2, April 1975.

Lamb, G. *Hierarchy and Access in the Trinidad Housing Authority*, Mimeo, Institute of Development Studies, University of Sussex, 1976.

Lamb, G. & Schaffer, B., *Institutional Development: A Critique and Alternative Approach*, IDS mimeo 1977.

Lambert, J. Housing Class and Community Action in a Redevelopment Area, in *Cities in Modern Britain*, Penguin 1975.

Lambert, J., Blackaby, B. & Paris, B., Neighbourhood Politics and Housing Opportunities, *Centre for Environmental Studies Conference Paper* 14, London, 1975.

Lambert, J., Paris, C., & Blackaby, B., *Housing Policy and the State, Allocation, Access and Control*, Macmillan, London 1978.

Langoni, C.G. *A Distribuicao de Renda e o Desenvolvimento Economico do Brasil*, Expressao e Cultura, Rio de Janeiro, 1973.

Leeds, A. Political, Economic and Social Effects of Producer and Consumer Orientations toward Housing in Brazil and Peru: A Systems Analysis, in *Latin American Urban Research*, Vol.3, Sage, Beverley Hills 1973.

Leeds, A. Housing Settlement Types, Arrangements for Living, Proletarianization and the Social Structure of the City, in Cornelius W. and Trueblood, F. (eds) *Latin American Urban Research*, Vol.4, Sage Publications, Beverley Hills and London, 1974.

Leeds, A., & Leeds, E., Brazil and the myth of urban rurality; urban experience, work and values in squatments of Rio de Janeiro and Lima, in A.J. Field (ed) *City and Country in the Third World*, Schenkman Publishing Co., Camb, Mass, 1970.

Leeds, A., Leeds, E., & Morocco, D., Political Administrative Power in Relation to Electricity in Rio Favelas. Paper presented to the American Association for the Advancement of Science, Washington DC. Dec. 1966.

Leeds, E. Interaction of National, State and Local Political Structures in the Favela. Paper prepared for 36th meeting, International Congress of Americanists, Mar del Plata, Mimeo, September 1966.

Leeds, E. Forms of squatment political organisation: the politics of control in Brazil, *MA Thesis*, University of Texas 1972.

Lees, R. & Smith, G. *Action Research in Community Development*, Routledge & Kegan Paul, London, 1975.

Lehmann, D. (ed) *Agrarian Reform and Agrarian Reformism: Studies of Peru, Chile, China and India*, Faber and Faber, London 1974.

Levenhagen, A.J.S. *Leis de Inquilinato Comentadas*, Editora Atlas S.A., Sao Paulo, 3rd Edition 1976.
Lojkine, J. Contributions to a Marxist theory of capitalist urbanisation,in Pickvance, C. (ed) *Urban Sociology: critical essays*, Tavistock Publications, London 1976.
Lopes, J.B. *Desenvolvimento e Mudanca Social*, Nacional, Sao Paulo, 1968.
Lukes, S. Political Ritual and Social Integration, in S. Lukes, *Essays in Social Theory*, Macmillan, London 1977a.
Lukes, S. Power and Structure, in S. Lukes, *Essays in Social Theory*, Macmillan, London 1977b.
Lynes, A. The Secret Rules, *Poverty*,No.4, 1967.
Mao Tse-Tung, On Contradiction, cited in A.G. Frank, *Dependent Accumulation and Underdevelopment*, Macmillan, London 1978.
Marcuse, H. *One Dimensional Man*,Sphere Books, London 1972.
Maricato, E. (ed) *A Producao Capitalista da Casa (e da Cidade) no Brasil Industrial*, Alfa-Omega, Sao Paulo 1979.
Marris, P. & Rein, M. *Dilemmas of Social Reform*, Routledge & Kegan Paul, London 1971.
Marx, K. The Eighteenth Brumaire of Louis Bonaparte, in Fernbach D (ed) *Surveys from Exile*, Political Writings Vol.2,Penguin, Harmondsworth 1973 pp.143-249.
Medina, C.A. de, *A Favela e O Demagogo*, Rio de Janeiro, 1964.
METRO (Companhia do Metropolitano de Sao Paulo), *Estudo Exploratorio e Programa de Intervencao Social nas Areas Desapropriadas*, Metro, Sao Paulo, 1976, Mimeo.
Ministerio da Agricultura, *Sinopse do Recenseamento realizado en $1^o$ de Setembro de 1920*, Rio de Janeiro, 1924.
Ministerio de Interior, *O Sistema Brasileiro de Poupanca e Emprestimo*, Banco Nacional de Habitacao, Rio de Janeiro, 1974.
Ministerio do Interior, *Interior*, Ano 11 numero 8 fevereiro 1976.
Ministerio do Trabalho e Previdencia Social e o Ministerio Extraordinario para o Planejamento e Coordenacao Economica, *Exposicao de Motivos*, No.62, 20 de Maio 1964.
Ministerio do Trabalho e Previdencia Social, *Mercado do Trabalho*, 4, 3 Oct. 1968.
Morse, R. *Formacao Historica de Sao Paulo*, Difusao Europeia do Livro, Sao Paulo 1970.
Niner, P. Local Authority Housing Policy and Practice, *Occasional Paper* 31, Centre for Urban and Regional Studies, Birmingham 1975.
Norman, P. *Managerialism - A review of Recent Work*, Centre for Environmental Studies Conference Paper 14, London 1975.
O'Donnell, G. *Modernisation and Bureaucratic-Authoritarianism*, Politics of Modernisation Series No.9, Institute of International Studies, University of California, 1973.
O'Donnell, G. Reflections on the Patterns of Change in the Bureaucratic-Authoritarian State, in *Latin American Research Review*, Vol. XIII No.1 1978.
O'Donnell, G. Tension in the Bureaucratic-Authoritarian State and the Question of Democracy, in D. Collier (ed), *The New Authoritarianism in Latin America*, Princeton University Press, New Jersey, 1979.
Offe, C. Political Authority and Class Structures, in P. Connerton (ed) *Critical Sociology*, Penguin 1976.
Oliveira, F. A Economia Brasileira: Critica A Razao Dualista, *Selecoes CEBRAP*, 2a Edicao, CEBRAP, 1976.
Otero, O.G., & Amaral, L.C.G. (eds) *Brazil Development 4, Urban Development Housing*, Telepress Servicos de Imprensa Ltda, Sao Paulo, 1973.

Pahl, R. *Whose City?* Longman, London 1970;   2nd edition, Penguin Harmondsworth, 1975.

Pahl, R.   *The Sociology of Urban and Regional Development as a Problem in Political Economy,* 8th World Congress of Sociology, Toronto, August, 1974.

Pahl, R. Collective Consumption and the State in capitalist and state socialist societies, in R. Scase (ed), *Industrial Society: Class, cleavage and control,* Tavistock Publications, London 1977.

Palma, E. & Sanfuentes, A., *Politicas estatales en un contexto de movilizacion social:  Analisis parcial de algunos casos en Chile,* Universidad de Chile, Santiago 1977.

Parisse, L. *Favelas do Rio de Janeiro, Evolucao-Sentido,* Caderno CENPHA 5, Centro Nacional de Pesquisas Habitacionais, Rio de Janeiro, 1969.

Parker, R.A. Social Administration and Scarcity – The Problem of Rationing, *Social Work,* Vol.24, No.2 9-14 April, 1967.

Parry, G. & Morris, P. When is a decision not a decision? in I. Crewe, *British political sociology year book vol.1: Elites in western democracy,* Croom Helm, London 1974.

Peattie, L. The Concept of Marginality as Applied to Squatter Settlements, in Trueblood & Rabinovitch (eds), *Latin American Urban Research,* Vol. 4, Sage Publications, 1974.

Pereira, L.C.B. O Novo Modelo Brasileiro de Desenvolvimento, in *Dados,* 11, Instituto Universitario de Pesquisas do Rio de Janeiro,1973, 122-145.

Perez, Perdomo, R. & Nikken, P., *Derecho y Propiedad de la vivienda en los barrios de Caracas,* Universidad Central de Venezuela, Caracas, 1977.

Perez-Diaz, V.M.  *State, Bureaucracy and Civil Society,* MacMillan London 1978.

Perlman, J. *The Myth of Marginality, Urban Poverty and Politics,* in Rio de Janeiro, University of California Press, 1976.

PNAD, (Pesquisa Nacional por Amostra de Domicilios), $4^o$ *trimestre 1971-1972, Regioes Metropolitanas, Rio de Janeiro e Sao Paulo,* IBGE, Rio de Janeiro.

Pickvance, C. (ed) *Urban Sociology: Critical Essays,* Tavistock Publications, London 1976.

Pickvance, C. Marxist Approaches to the Study of Urban Politics, *International Journal of Urban and Regional Research,* Vol. 1 No.2,1977.

PLANASA (Planejamento e Assessoria Administrativa) *Area CURA – Bras/ Bresser, Estudo de Viabilidade Economico – Financeira, Relatorio Parcial I,* Mimeo, 1976.

Polsby, N.  *Community Power and Political Theory,* Yale University Press, New Haven and London, 1963.

Portes, A. Em busca da integracao, a politica de remocao de favelas no Rio de Janeiro, *MA Thesis,* National Museum, Rio de Janeiro, 1973.

Portes, A. The Politics of Urban Poverty, in A. Portes and J. Walton, *Urban Latin America,* University of Texas Press, Austin 1976.

Prefeitura do Municipio de Sao Paulo, *Sistema Municipal de Habitacao, Proposta de Criacao,* SEBES, Sao Paulo mimeo 1972.

Prefeitura do Municipio de Sao Paulo, *Serie: Indicadores Sociais No.2,* SEBES, Sao Paulo, mimeo 1973.

Ranson, S., Hinings, B. & Greenwood, R., The Structuring of Organisational Structures, *Administrative Science Quarterly,* Dec. 1979.

Ray, T.F. *The Politics of the Barrios of Venezuela,* University of California Press, Los Angeles 1969.

Rees, A.M. Access to the Personal Health and Welfare Services, *Social and Economic Administration*, Vol. 6, No.1 34-43, January 1972.

Rew, A. Accumulating Applicants: The State and Shanty Town Property, Paper to Burg Wartenstein Symposium No.73. Shanty Towns in Developing Nations, Wenner-Gren Foundation for Anthropological Research, July 1-10, 1977.

Rex, J. & Moore, R. *Race, Community and Conflict*, Oxford University Press, London 1967.

Rex, J. *Race, Colonialism and the City*, Routledge & Kegan Paul, London, 1973.

Rodrigues, J.A. *Sindicato e Desenvolvimento no Brasil*, Difusao Europeia do Livro, Sao Paulo, 1968.

Roett, R. (ed) *Brazil in the Seventies*, American Enterprise Institute for Public Policy Research, Washington, 1976.

Rose, S.M. *The Betrayal of the Poor*, Schenkman Publishing Co., Cambridge Mass. 1972.

Rossi, P. & Dentler, R. *The Politics of Urban Renewal*, Free Press of Glencoe, Illinois 1961.

Royal Commission on Local Government in England Vol. 1, *Report of the Commission*, Cmnd 4040, HMSO, London 1969.

Sande, L. *Beneficio Fiscal para a Habitacao*, Banco Nacional da Habitacao, Rio de Janeiro, 1975.

Santos, T. dos The Crisis of Development Theory and the Problem of Dependence in Latin America, in H. Bernstein (ed) *Underdevelopment and Development in the Third World Today*, Penguin Harmondsworth 1978.

Saunders, P. They Make the Rules, in *Policy and Politics*, Vol.4 No.1 September, 1975.

Saunders, P. *Urban Politics, A Sociological Interpretation*, Hutchinson, London 1979.

Schaffer, B.B. *The Administrative Factor*, Frank Cass, London 1973.

Schaffer, B.B. Regional Development and Institutions of Favour, in Seers, Schaffer and Kiljunen (eds) *Underdeveloped Europe: Studies in Core-Periphery Relations*, Harvester Press, Hassocks, Sussex. 1979.

Schaffer, B.B. & Huang, Wen-hsien, Distribution and the Theory of Access, in *Development and Change*, Vol. 6 No.2, April, 1975.

Schaffer, B.B. & Lamb, G. *Can Equity be Organised?* Gower, Farnborough 1981.

Schaffer, B.B. & O'Keeffe, E., *People and Agencies*, Institute of Public Administration National Monograph Series No.4, Brisbane 1978.

Schulman, M. *Pronunciamento no Senado Federal*, Comissao de Legislacao Social, Brasilia, 16 Set. 1975.

Schulman, M. *Seminario do Mercado Habitacional*, Sao Paulo, 23 October 1975.

Seebohm Report, *Report of the Committee on Local Authority and Allied Personal Social Services*, Cmnd 3703, HMSO, London 1968.

Secretaria de Bem Estar Social (SEBES), Estudo referente as familias residentes nos conjuntos residenciais de Ype, Tatuape, Guarulhos, e Mal Mascarenhas de Morais, que estao en situacao de inadimplencia contratual com a COHAB/SP, Prefeitura de Sao Paulo, Sao Paulo, 9 September - 2 December, 1973.

Selznick, P. *TVA and The Grass Roots*, University of California Press, 1949.

Serran, J.R. Perspectivas do Plano Nacional da Habitacao, *Revista Civilizacao Brasileira*, Rio de Janeiro, Vol.1, No.8, Jul 1966.

Simonsen, M. *Brasil 2001*, APEC Editora SA, Rio de Janeiro, 1975.

Simonsen, M. & Campos, R., *A Nova Economia Brasileira*, Livaria Jose Olympio Editora, Rio de Janeiro, 1974.

Singer, P. *O Milagre Brasileiro: Causas e Consequencias,* CEBRAP, Sao
Paulo, 1972.
Singer, P. *Economia Politica da Urbanizacao,* Editora Brasiliense, Sao
Paulo, 1975.
Singer, P. *A Crise do 'Milagre',* Paz e Terra, Sao Paulo, 1976.
Skeffington Report, Committee on Public Participation and Planning,
*People and Planning,* HMSO, London 1969.
Skidmore, T.E. *Politics in Brazil 1930-1964, An Experiment in
Democracy,* Oxford University Press, London, Oxford, New York, 1969.
Souza, B.N. Guimaraes de, O BNH e A Politica do Governo, *MA Thesis,*
Universidade de Minas Gerais, Belo Horizonte, 1974.
Stewart, J.D. *Management in Local Government,* Charles Knight and Co.
Ltd., London 1971.
Sunkel, O. La Universidad Latino-americana ante el avance cientifico y
tecnico: Algunas Reflexiones, in *Estudios Internacionales,* Vol. III,
No.4, 1970.
Sunkel, O. External Economic Relations and the Process of Development:
Suggestions for an Alternative Framework, *Discussion Paper No.51,*
Institute of Development Studies, University of Sussex, 1974.
Tapia-Videla, J.I. The Endless Search for the Chile that Never Was: A
Critical Reaction to Three North American Views, *Latin American
Research Review,* Vol. XIV No.3, 1973: 280-293.
Taschner S. Pasternak, Favelas de Municipio de Sao Paulo: Resultadas de
Pesquisa, in Blay, E.A. (ed) *A Luta pelo Espaco,* Vozes, Petropolis
1978.
Tavares, M.C. *Da Substituicao de Importacao ao Capitalismo Financeiro,*
Zahar, Rio de Janeiro, 1972.
Torres, Maria C.T.M., *O Bairro do Bras,* Prefeitura Municipal, Sao Paulo
1969.
Touraine, A. *La Societe post-industrielle,* Paris 1969.
Trindade, M. *Habitacao e Desenvolvmento,* Editora Vozes Ltda Petropolis
1971.
Trindade, M., *O Sistema Brasileiro de Poupanca e Emprestimo no Plano
Nacional da Habitacao,* Banco Nacional da Habitacao, Rio de Janeiro,
1973.
Turner, J. Uncontrolled Urban Settlements: Problems and Policies, in
*International Social Development Review,* No.1, UN, New York, 1968.
Turner, J. Barriers and Channels for Housing Development in Modernising
Countries, in Mangin, W. (ed) *Peasants in Cities,* Mifflin, Houghton,
1970.
Ungerson, C. Moving Home: A Study of the Redevelopment Process in Two
London Boroughs, *Occasional Papers in Social Administration,* No.44,
Bell 1971.
Valladares, L. Operation de Relogement et Reponse Sociale, *doctoral
thesis,* Universite de Toulouse-le-Mirail, 1974.
Valladares, L. Working the System, squatter response to resettlement in
Rio de Janeiro, *International Journal of Urban and Regional Research,*
Vol. 2 No.1 1978a.
Valladares, L. *Passe-se uma Casa,* Zahar Editores, Rio de Janeiro 1978b.
Valladares, L. and Figueiredo A., Housing in Brazil: an Introduction
to Recent Literature, mimeo 1982.
Vereker, C. & Mays, J. *Urban Redevelopment and Social Change: a Study
of Social Conditions in Central Liverpool,* 1966-56. Liverpool
University Press, 1961.

Warren, R.L. Community Change: Some Lessons from the Recent Past, Paper presented as the first Louis and Gillian Goldstein Memorial Lecture, School of Social Work, University of Connecticut, 10 April 1973.

Wells, J. Distribution of Earnings, Wealth and the Structure of Demand during the 1960's, *World Development*, Vol.2, No.1 January 1974.

Westergaard, J. & Resler, H. *Class in a Capitalist Society*, Penguin, Harmondsworth, 1976.

Williams, P. The role of institutions in the inner London housing market: the case of Islington, in *Transactions of the Institute of British Geographers*, NSI, January, 1976.

Williams, P. Urban Managerialism: a concept of relevance? in *Area*,Vol.10 No.3 1978.

Willmott, P. & Young, M., *Family and Kinship in East London*, Penguin, Harmondsworth, 1957.

Winkler, J. The Corporate economy: theory and administration, in R. Scase (ed) *Industrial Society: class, cleavage and control*, Tavistock Publications, London 1977.

World Bank, *World Development Report,1980*, Oxford University Press, 1980.

World Bank, *World Development Report, 1982*, Oxford University Press, 1982.

Wygand, J. Water Networks: Their technology and sociology in Rio Favelas, Paper prepared for 36th meeting International Congress of Americanists, Mar del Plata, Mimeo, September 1966.

Yap, L. Internal Migration and Economic Development in Brazil, *Ph.D. Dissertation* , Harvard University, 1972.

NEWSPAPERS AND PERIODICALS CITED

Conjuntura Economica

Folha de Sao Paulo

Latin American Regional Reports, Brazil

O Estado de Sao Paulo

Opiniao

Veja

# Author index

# Subject index